Enjoy these titles from Susan Carpenter Noble

Cowgirls Don't Quit

The Free Horse

Dear Toots

For Sandy!

Dear Toots

Half a War-torn World Apart
1941-'45

Grant H. Carpenter
as told to
Susan Carpenter Noble

Best wishes!

Susan Carpenter Noble

Published by: Book Services
www.BookServices.us

Dedication

Dear Toots is dedicated to Carp (Grant Hess Carpenter, Jr), Judy Carpenter, and, of course, "Toots" (Margaret L. Carpenter)

Acknowledgments

I'm grateful to so many people for their help with this project. Thank you:

- Peggy Carpenter King for discovering these letters and making sure I knew about them;

- My brothers, Bob and Rich Carpenter, for unfailing encouragement;

- My husband, Glen Noble, for his amazing patience and support;

- Rick Noble, for teaching me how awful it is to send a child off to war and how joyful it is when they return;

- Janet Noble, for sharing her never-quit attitude and for her uplifting confidence in this project;

- Robin Carlin, Stacy Stramel, Twila Cook, and Shari Parkhill Charnock for reading early drafts of the novel and offering feedback and encouragement;

- Michael Feinberg and Betsy Hoyt for their belief in the importance of preserving history; for Michael's brilliant layout and cover design; and for Betsy's eye for editorial detail.

Contents

Foreword

In early 2008, my sister Peggy went to visit our folks. She noticed Dad reading some papers and then throwing them into the trash. She asked what he was up to.

"Just reading some old letters I found," he told her and handed her one. She was stunned to realize they were letters he'd written to his mother while he was serving in the U.S. Army during World War II. She quickly rescued the letters he'd thrown out and asked him not to pitch any more of them.

When I arrived a few days later, she showed me the letters. Once they were put in order, they told a fascinating story. I began typing them into the computer and asking Dad questions about the backstory. He may have been 90-years-old at the time, but he was still sharp and his answers came fast and sure.

This book is a compilation of those letters and his memories. I edited out extraneous bits of the letter, things like, "Sorry to hear about John," or "That's good news about Sally," because there is no mention of what the news is or even who these people are. Those sentences hit the cutting room floor. Then, on occasion, I added a few words to clarify someone's identity. For example, when Carp refers to "Gil," I included "*my fraternity brother*, Gil…" Obviously, his mother would've known who Gil was, but those few "extras" should help the reader keep people sorted out without changing the story that's being told. Other than those minor changes, you are reading the letters as Marg/Toots would have read them.

Before the war, Carp's mother had been nicknamed "Toots" by one of her friends. That had shocked and/or amused Carp when he first heard it, since it was an abbreviation for Tootsie. And, while Tootsie could be an innocuous synonym for "dear" or "sweetheart," it could also mean a "woman of questionable morals" – not something that fit his mother, which is why he was amused.

Carp and Marg always had a very honest relationship. They could – and did – discuss anything, as you will see.

In reading the letters the first time myself, I was struck by the amount of humor in them. But I completely understood: Five years before seeing these letters, I, like Marg, was working for a newspaper while my son went off to war in Iraq. It was March, 2003. I was barely holding it together. Letters from my son were sporadic. He wrote when he could, but between his being "a little busy" and the difficulty in mailing letters, it would sometimes be several weeks without hearing from him. Every day, as I reached toward my mailbox, my hands would be shaking.

When a letter would come, I would rip it open and start reading as fast as I could, hungry for every word. Soon, unexpectedly, I would be laughing. That kid wrote some very funny letters. Even then, I understood why. He was trying to ease his parents' minds.

I see that in Carp's letters too, the humor aimed at taking the edge off of a mother's fears.

So, settle in for a trip through history with a man who may soon seem like an old friend.

Chapter 1

1941

I tossed my suitcase into the trunk of my brand new 1941 blue Ford convertible, kissed my two favorite women goodbye, and drove away. For how long? I had no way of knowing.

Glancing in the rearview mirror, I caught one last glimpse of my mother, smiling bravely through her tears. Beside her, my girlfriend flashed a dazzling smile. I found myself hoping she was fighting back a few tears, too, which made me feel like a bit of a bastard.

I had a long drive ahead of me to consider that.

As a little boy, I had frequently been called a bastard. I wasn't one. My parents had been married briefly. But trouble broke out in Europe, and the lure of adventure (combined with an eye for other women) was just too much for my father to resist. Off he went to fly Navy airplanes during The Great War, World War I, leaving my mother with a newborn.

With the realization that he would never be faithful to her, Mother did something nearly unheard of in 1918. She divorced him.

Except for people gossiping about my parentage, or perceived lack thereof, it was a great childhood. Mother, Marg Carpenter, doted on me and worked hard to earn a living for us. Her sisters helped keep a watchful eye on me, and I had uncles and my grandfather for male role models. Grandfather Charles Lose was the principal of the Lock Haven Normal School (Teachers College) in Pennsylvania.

After Father abandoned us, Mother and I moved in with Grandfather in the Principal's House.

1

We were only there a few years though. Grandfather was blinded in an automobile accident, forcing him to resign from his position. He moved the family back to his hometown of Montoursville, Pennsylvania.

Mother quit her bookkeeping job to serve as Grandfather's housekeeper, cook, guide, secretary, and assistant. In those days, Grandfather traveled the state, giving lectures on his two favorite topics: teaching and fly fishing. In 1928 he was elected to the state legislature where he served for six years. In 1931, he published a book, *The Vanishing Trout*.

Money was tight—it was for everyone during the Depression—but we got by.

In fact, I thought life was pretty terrific. I spent my youth hiking, running, reading voraciously, working on Boy Scout merit badges, going to parades and dances, and enjoying small-town life. Grandfather shared with me his love of the outdoors, and I whiled away many happy hours down by the Loyalsock Creek, swimming and fixing up old canoes to test in the water. Mother and Grandfather even let me take over one room in the house to build my own kayak – a twelve-footer, built in a 10'x10' room. I guess engineering was in my blood.

In fact, my uncles were all engineers, either mechanical or civil. Each pushed me to make school a priority. But football was my real passion and because of that, so was food. A lot of effort went into eating because Mother wouldn't let me play football until I had built my 6'2" frame up to a whopping 150 pounds.

Mother was always there for me: my biggest fan, my disciplinarian, my confidante, my best friend. We could, and did, talk about anything. She had a quick wit and was great fun to spar with verbally.

In my late teens, my father stepped back into my life. He and his third wife had a summer home in the mountain resort of Laporte, Pennsylvania. He invited my half-brother, Don, (from his second failed marriage) and me to come spend the summer with him. With the Depression continuing, I couldn't find a summer job anyway, so I went, and finally got acquainted with him.

After graduating from high school, I packed my bags and headed off to Penn State to study Mechanical Engineering. I joined "Triangle," the engineering fraternity, was a member of the cross-country track team and was competitive on our nationally-ranked (Top Ten) rifle team.

I also joined R.O.T.C., the Reserve Officer Training Corps. It was 1936. Things were stirring up in Europe once more and I had the idea that, if trouble broke out again, being an officer would be a lot more interesting—and less scary—than being an infantryman.

Once I'd finished at Penn State in 1939, I talked with one of my uncles, who worked for the Pennsylvania Railroad in *the* dream job. He mentioned that the P.R.R. had an opening, so I applied and was thrilled to be hired.

Arriving in Philadelphia, I reported for my first day of work and was fired within hours. Turned out the P.R.R. required new employees to pass a physical. Their doc gave me an eye exam and promptly showed me the door.

I slunk back home, discouraged, but soon heard about an engineering job for Jones & Laughlin Wire Rope. My need for glasses didn't bother them a bit and they put me straight to work.

Sadly, in 1940, Grandfather died. Along with dealing with the grief of losing her father, my mother was suddenly out of work. But with her usual resolve to make things happen, she marched into the office of the *Grit* Publishing Company in the neighboring city of Williamsport and landed a job in the editorial department. (The *Grit* was a Sunday newspaper that printed a local edition, along with an edition that went all over the East Coast and Midwest, to three-quarters of a million subscribers.)

With both of us working, Mother and I were able to afford to rent half of a nice little duplex.

By now I'd been at the Jones & Laughlin job for over a year and had come to the happy realization that, quite by accident, I actually had managed to land in my dream job. And with a steady paycheck, I had been able to buy my dream car. Now for that dream girl…

Labor Day weekend, 1940, my friend Baldy talked me into going with him to the New York World's Fair. While there, he claimed to know a gal from home (well, Williamsport anyway) who was working at the Fair. We found her hostessing at the Chase & Sanborn Pavilion. Judy Marshall. What a looker—5'10", willowy brunette, with gorgeous eyes, the prettiest mouth, and long, long legs. I found out she'd been working as a model in New York City before the Fair. I could sure believe that.

We went out on a group date, and I talked to her enough to wish she hadn't moved so far from home. But after that terrific weekend, I had to get back to work.

Six months later, I heard Judy was back in Williamsport. I put on my most charming voice, dialed her family's number, and started with, "This is Grant Carpenter. You probably don't remember me, but..."

She cut me off in mid-sentence. She not only remembered me, she described me. Wow! I had sure made an impression with this gal. (Okay, so later I learned she had a 'mental file' of *any* man she'd ever met who was over six feet tall.)

I asked her out on a double date that night, March 23, 1941, and she accepted. In fact, she accepted every date I invited her on, every single evening for the next five weeks.

Then I got my own invitation. This one was from Uncle Sam. I was to leave my perfect girl, leave my perfect job, and report for active duty to the Army's Ft. Belvoir, Virginia, the beginning of May 1941.

At least I got to take the car along.

Judy & Carp March 1941

Envelope bears a three-cent stamp and is addressed to:

GH Carpenter 2nd Lt. CE
5th Instructors Course
Engineer School Cantonment
Ft. Belvoir, Va.

Mrs. Margaret L. Carpenter
Editorial Dept.
Grit Publishing Co.
Williamsport, Pa.

Ft. Belvoir, Va.
May 6, 1941

Dearest Mother,

One good breakfast under our belts, an hour's instruction and we're waiting to go over to the post theater for more instruction, and it's only quarter of eight. Time for you to go to work and I've been up for two hours – shame on you.

This camp, or course, has 240 men from 2nd Lieutenants to Majors in it, and we've got about 25 of these small Army texts to study. Think kindly of your poor boy – the amount of work I'll be doing, I mean.

So long, Pal.
Love to you and Aunt Pee.

Carp

Aunt Pee on the left

Aunt Pee was the nickname I used for my spinster aunt, Phoebe, who had moved into the duplex with Mother.

Ft. Belvoir, Va.
May 8, 1941

Dearest Toots,

I'm going to drive up Saturday afternoon. I'll pick Judy up as I come through Williamsport between 6:00 and 7:00 and we'll come down and get you and go somewhere for some food.

Can you lend me a five to get back to camp? I hope.

Love,

Carpy

Ft. Belvoir, Va.
May 13, 1941

Dear Mother,

My letter writing proclivities were nipped in the bud yesterday by my second typhoid shot, which made me sick as a pup for awhile.

It's a wonder I don't put on a lot of weight – the way I eat here. I guess we work a little too hard to put on weight fast.

Tomorrow we go on the rifle range for a little firing. My arm is a little sore from the shot but otherwise I ought to still be able to shoot.

It was awful nice to get home. I think I'll do it again this week.

Write soon, Love,

Carp

Ft. Belvoir
May 14, 1941

Dearest Maw,

I kinda skimped a little on that letter yesterday, but they were keeping me busier than hell. The mapping problem was interesting. They took us out in trucks and then dropped us off two at a time along a mile-and-one-half of back road. We then had to figure out exactly where we were on the map we had, and figure the direction to our common destination, a road junction about a mile away across the woods. We laid out our course and followed it by compass and came out within thirty yards of the spot, which was doing pretty good, we thought.

This morning we had rifle marksmanship and your son was moderately successful. I have to get quite a bit of practice before I get at all good, so I just had to be satisfied with shooting about even with the best of 'em.

I probably won't be home quite as early this Saturday as I was last Saturday so don't start worrying if I'm late.

From midnight tonight to tomorrow noon, I'm O.D. - Officer of the Day. Boy what a life. I'll be seein' yuh.

Love,

Carpy

I didn't have a lot of spare time at Ft. Belvoir, but what I had I used organizing my thoughts about Judy. And in the practical fashion of an engineer, I made lists. One list was what I liked about her, the other, what I didn't like. The negative list had only two items: She liked New York City too much, and I wasn't about to live in New York City. The second concern was that she looked expensive. But the list of what I liked was VERY long. In fact, I had a hard time figuring out where to stop it; it just kept growing.

That list won.

Ft. Belvoir, Va.
May 19, 1941

Dearest Mother,

We have that Saturday morning off after Memorial Day. I just wrote Judy and suggested that we be married in Williamsport Saturday morning. It's possible to get a license and be married the same day if the judge grants permission. Our case certainly justifies such a request and I thought that you could get it from the judge. He might even be willing to perform the ceremony. However don't say anything about this unless Judy mentions it first. She may not want to be married in Williamsport. I told her to talk to you about it if she wanted to do it that way.

Whatever we do, the fewer people around the better I'll feel. Just our immediate families and I mean only a few. But that's up to Judy.

Aunt Pee said she might be able to lend me a little money. Will you ask her if she could lend me $20 to be paid back, half the first of July and half the first of August. If you know that she can't do it, don't bother her about it. I'll make out. (Would Aunt Edie do it?)

They offered 26 posts in Hawaii to members of this course today. Dependents could be taken along too, but it's for two years duty. I can't see anything that would take me away from my job that long except an act of Congress – so I didn't volunteer. I guess I ain't patriotic.

I learned a trick today. I take two pictures – aerial photographs taken about one second apart from a plane flying at about 10,000 feet – hold them up side by side at arm's length in front of me and look in back of them. First you see three pictures and by focusing closely on the middle one you can get stereoscopic vision and everything stands out in relief. It enables you to study strange territory as it actually is.

Write and tell me the news, especially if Judy tells you anything.

Love,

Carpy

Ft. Belvoir, Va
May 23, 1941

Dearest Mother,

As usual Judy shows up as the brains of the outfit. She vetoed my idea with very logical reasoning, and for the best as it turned out. Tonight I received word that within the next few days I'll be ordered to Fort Jackson, near Columbia, South Carolina with the 38th Combat Engineer Regiment. That is approximately 700 miles from Williamsport. From what I can find out it's a pretty fair place to live.

That raise you got is just swell. I think you're marvelous. It should make you feel pretty darn good because it proves that you're valuable to the Grit. It'll make you awful independent though. I'll bet you hardly speak to people now.

Yesterday we built a trestle bridge across a deep little ravine back of the post. It took us about six hours to build a 90 foot bridge capable of carrying 15 tons (the next to the biggest tank) and it worked too. One boy had slight sunstroke and the rest of us darn near did.

Man it was blistering – and so humid you could hardly stand it to move. The heat broke with a heavy thundershower just before we completed the job and we finished in a driving rain. All of us soaked to the skin.

Love,

Carpy

Fort Jackson, South Carolina
May 27, 1941

Dear Toots,

I got here about 2:30 today and I'm telling you I'm tired of driving. 700 miles is a real jaunt.

It's a hot darn place – all sand and pine trees. There is a lake right on the post and a couple of hundred more within twenty miles. At night as soon as the sun goes down it cools off fast and you sleep under a blanket. –That'll be okay by me.

I have a room to myself but I'm going to have to fix it up with hooks and nails to hang things on. It's a lot nicer than Belvoir.

This is only a note 'cause I don't have much time. More later.

Love,

Carpy

Ft. Jackson, S.C.
May 29, 1941

Dearest Mother,

Well a week ago I was planning on heading for home and being almost to Harrisburg by this time, but such is the Army. Maybe next week I'll be in California. I don't think I will be though because this seems to be our permanent assignment and probably our permanent post except for maneuvers. There is a rumor around that maneuvers for sometime late this summer may consist of moving the 1st Army (of which we are part) across the continent and back as rapidly as it can be done. That is, in our own transportation, which consists of 1½ ton trucks, 1/2 ton pickups, and combat cars. It's only a rumor, but it would be practical experience and a whale of a lot of fun. If you see anything about this in your newspapers, let me know, will you?

Judy is having her tonsils out Saturday. Keep an eye on her for me will you, please? I wrote to Judy's Aunt Grace and asked her to wire me as soon as Judy is thru it okay, so will you verify it by a letter? I just can't help but worry a little. I'm a dope, but I like the girl.

Yesterday the boys moved in and we got them divided into companies and into their proper areas. I was appointed or assigned to the 2nd Platoon of Co A. Captain Gilbert is my commanding officer and a Major Dunaway is our Battalion leader. Both men are good officers and the Major is especially so. Captain Gilbert has had very little experience, but I think he's going to be a good man to work with. I've caught the assignment as Mess officer, which is mostly a job of supervising and inspecting the mess (kitchen) and mess personnel, in addition to my platoon command. Now that we're getting organized, we spend all morning and most of the afternoon studying and assigning the differently talented men to different platoons. I have one of the best platoon sergeants. I'm beginning to enjoy life again. Yesterday I was pretty well disgusted with the whole set-up.

This is an enormous camp. The reserve must be twenty miles long by ten miles wide. The post is about two miles long by a mile wide and is plumb chuck full of barracks. Some 2100 men moved out of here the day before 1000 of our men moved in, yet three-quarters of the personnel of the camp don't know that a change occurred.

I haven't located any good swimming holes yet, but they say that there are a couple of good places here on the post and two or three off. I'm company OD (Officer of the Day) tomorrow and will have to stay in the Regimental Area all day, but Saturday and Sunday I'll see something of the country.

Columbia looks like a nice city to me. It's about the size of Harrisburg, but it's a H--- of a lot nicer. The movies are a little behind Williamsport, but so am I, so we just about jibe.

I hope Babson knows what he's talking about. I still like my job at the Wire Rope plant better than this. Why don't you "nine out of ten women" do something to clamp down on the 'boss?' Roosevelt's speech Tuesday night sounded like a declaration of war to me. I don't see how the Germans could take it any other way.

You're darn right that Judy's people are swell. I'm glad that they like you and that you like them. It's a help.

Taps is just sounding at the different Regiments all over the post. That's an odd and rather awe-inspiring sound coming through the dark.

Love,

Carp

Ft. Jackson, S.C.
June 3, 1941

Dearest Mother,

Well I'm getting myself organized and adjusted here. I've invested in a cheap card table and chair to take care of my studying and letter writing and I've got a couple of racks that I'm going to put up for clothes hangers when I get a little time. Over the weekend we didn't have too much to do. Just enough to keep us here part of each day. That's the Army for you. Sunday afternoon a gang of us drove down to Augusta, Georgia and bummed around the town for awhile, then went to a movie. Now I can brag that I've been as far South as Gawja. The Georgia peaches were not too much in evidence.

Yesterday morning we started a regular training schedule. Part of it was a five-mile hike in this blasted sand. I didn't mind it while we were hiking, but last night I was worn to a frazzle and my legs really ached. I think I slept about nine hours last night, which is three more than I've been averaging. I've been feeling swell since I got here. The heat gripes me a lot, but as soon as you settle down you cool off and that makes you feel good.

Judy has been feeling like the devil with those tonsils. I'll be glad when they're out safe and sound. Just little things she says tells me how she feels. Keep an eye on her for me, please. She said that after arrangements were made for the operation, her boss wanted her to change it and work through the end of the week. She's going ahead with it anyway even if they fire her.

I didn't see the pictures of you, but the ones of Judy were swell. It doesn't give me much of a break to be photographed with her. Good thing she doesn't love me for my manly beauty. The one of her standing spraddle-legged is my favorite too.

You and Phoebe are getting to be regular gad-abouts.

They are nice to you in that office, but that's as it should be. You're a nice girl and my favorite.

Love,

Carpy

Fort Jackson, S.C.
June 5, 1941

Dearest Mother,

I hope I'm still here next winter. That'll help to make up for the heat this summer. It's as hot around here right now as it is all summer at home and the natives say that this is cool weather. Oh boy.

Gee but your account of that picnic made me homesick for the old Loyalsock Creek. What I wouldn't give for a picnic at the Cove. Mmmmmh.

I'm awful glad that your financial arrangements are working out. I think I'm going to get straightened out in time. Not as quickly as I would if I'd stayed at the mill, but I'm going to make out pretty good too. My only complaint is that the blasted Army doesn't pay for the work you do. I'm putting in more hours than I did at the mill – and I _enjoyed_ that work. Seriously though I'm getting in the swing of things and enjoying this too.

I've been made battalion instructor for rifle marksmanship and am to concentrate on that for the next couple of weeks. That'll be fun for me.

I need a few things, my love. Can you send me a small box with some sewing equipment in it? Needles, brown or black thread and some assorted buttons, mostly tan. Huh!

This afternoon I had my platoon out on scouting and patrolling and while I was sitting on the ground waiting for them to sneak up on me, some little ants got into my trousers and started biting. I had to take 'em off and shake 'em inside out to get rid of the little bastards. – How they can bite.

The boys and I really enjoy extended order drill and scouting and patrolling. This platoon of mine is a darn good bunch. They're willing to do anything and work hard at it too. Keeping a jump ahead of them is a full time job.

For supper last night we had cold ham, macaroni salad, cheese, crackers, pretzels and ale. I drank two (count 'em) bottles of ale and was feeling fine when I came out of the mess hall. My eyes wouldn't quite focus but it was a grand sensation. I don't much care for ale, but maybe I'll learn.

Gotta go for chow now. Lots of love.

Your affectionate son,

Carpy

Fort Jackson, S.C.
June 9, 1941

Dearest Mother,

Time is so balled up for me that I'm not sure when I wrote to you last. If I start repeating myself, just holler.

I got a telegram from Grace today and sent one to Judy tonight. I certainly hope the poor kid is feeling better soon. She's really had a siege of this.

Your clipping about letting men with specialized abilities out of the Army interested me, but I'm afraid that applies to enlisted only. I'm in this for quite awhile, I guess.

Baldy is a nice guy and would probably keep his offer, however, I really don't want anybody but Judy and myself and a couple of disinterested spectators at my wedding. I don't know why, but that's always appealed to me as being a nice way to get married. Maybe it's because the wedding ceremony itself has never meant much to me. It's what the two people say to themselves and privately to each other that counts, not what they say for publication. I've told Judy that it's up to her and she apparently feels as I do.

I think I told you that we took out five blind dates Friday night. They were technicians from the hospital. I had a fairly good time, but never again. Sunday afternoon I played bridge with my buddy Kit and two of them, but those two episodes are the first and last of my dating. In the first place, the gals just don't stack up with Judy. Any of these girls compared with Judy are just ridiculous. No kidding, they'd shoot me if they knew some of the things that run through my mind as to their brains, conversational ability, damn foolishness status, and beauty as against Judy's. Hell's bells, they just don't rate, and another thing is that I don't feel right about it. Judy and I didn't tie any strings on each other, but she's got strings on me without tying them. Another thing is that I've got to save every penny I can so that when Judy and I get a break we can take advantage of it. So I'm a bachelor and glad of it, temporarily.

It sounds as if the desk is neat. Now you can sprawl as ungracefully as you wish. Gosh you must be an important personage up there at the <u>Grit</u>. Does the owner of the paper ask you for advice yet?

Taps just sounded so I'll finish in the morning. G'night.

Gosh I sounded mournful last night. I guess it was because I didn't get a letter from Judy yesterday, but today I got two already this morning. She's an awfully nice girl.

It's so hot it's funny. You can't walk a hundred yards without sweating so that your clothes stick to you. I haven't been in swimming yet.

Yesterday morning I started training my boys in rifle marksmanship and I have until next Tuesday to get them ready to go on the range Wednesday. If possible I'm going to arrange to have them travel back and forth in trucks and eat at their home mess halls. If they can't, it'll mean a lot more work for me, damn it.

You and Phoebe are having fun bumming around aren't you? That car, and her being able to drive it, makes a difference.

Well, Apple Dumpling, that's all for today.

Lots o' love,

Carp

Ft. Jackson, So. Carolina
June 16, 1941

Dearest Mother,

Gosh did you begin to think that you were an orphan? I've been paving the road to H---, again. If you start to get worried about me you can always call Judy and inquire after my doings. You see if I don't write to her I may lose her, but you were born with me and you're stuck.

I've done a good bit since last Wednesday. Mostly I've been working with my rifle marksmanship crew. They're beginning to shape up pretty well. Wednesday morning we start out on the range. Cross your fingers for me and maybe I'll qualify them all. Anyway I'm hoping. One of 'em is so dumb, though, that I've assigned a good man to the job of coaching him with express orders to keep an eye on him so that he doesn't pull a boner and shoot someone. This Army has everything from men with Master's Degrees to boys like this one who's so dumb that you can ask him a question and then sit back and watch it trickle through his mind. No kidding. There are both kinds in my platoon alone.

Have you heard this tune "Let's Get Away From It All"? Every time I hear it, I think of Judy. Speaking of the brat again, I've hinted to her that I'd like her to come down over the 4th. It's impossible for me to make it home, but she could get good bus connections here. If she does come down I'll revive my old idea. You once said that you could borrow $50.00 in a pinch. If I could pay you $25.00 the first of August and the rest the first of September could it be done? If it can't be done, say so pronto. I know you and you'd move H--- itself for your brat of a boy, but I don't want to ball up your finances as badly as mine.

Saturday I played nine holes of lousy golf with Kit. There's a course just off the edge of the post that the men from the post have practically taken over. It's cheap and not too bad a course. It was the first time in two years for me and about the same for Kit. We both stunk.

What does Aunt Pee want me to get her for her birthday? If she's hinted anything, say so, please. She said she had something in mind for me. If it's something you think I'd like, okay it. Otherwise all I want are white shirts. The same goes for you, my Pet.

Tell Flossie that I'm regimental Rifle Instructor and that's bigger than a battalion, in fact it's two battalions – and a battalion is three companies, or more than a thousand men.

Sunday we went swimming at a State Park near here. It's a really nice beach kinda like home only not quite as nice clear water. However, it's the best I've seen in So. Carolina.

I'm developing into a baseball player, or I'm trying to. We've got another game with the 128th Field Artillery coming up. They're a good crew of lads. Quite a number of them are boys from the ranks, that is, national guardsmen, who have worked up to a commission. Eleven were made Second Lieutenants in the last two weeks. I get along better with them than I do the regular Army officers.

Gosh, but I miss Judy. The gals down here couldn't make one of her if they combined 50 of the best of them. They just are lacking all the way around. I've only seen a couple of them since I hit this state that are worth whistling at.

I'm O.D. (Officer of the Day) today and tonight which means that I've got to get up sometime between midnight and six AM and check the guard. I also carry sidearms, a .45, and am supposed to uphold the peace in the area. Already I've inspected them twice, which leaves me only that last one to go. You ought to see me traipsing around with this heavy artillery on my hip. I look like Billy the Kid.

It seems as if it's been more than three weeks since I last saw Montoursville. Has the town missed me yet? They really ought to, to be flattering. Keep me posted on the guys that I know. Some of the towns are sending their local paper free to draftees. See if the <u>Sun Gazette</u> wants to favor me in this manner. I'd even read it if they did.

Well Sweetie Pie I need a bit of sleep. Good night all.

Lots of love,

Carp

Ft. Jackson, So. Carolina
June 18, 1941

Dearest Mother,

Hi Pal, you can forget about me borrowing the fifty, or trying to. Judy can't come down so I won't need it. I'm glad that I won't have to borrow it and damn sorry she can't come down. Anyway I thank you.

I just got in off the range and am entertaining a splitting head-ache. The blasting of those rifles all day kinda got me. It was fun, though, and you know me, I like to run things so I just enjoyed every minute of it, including the responsibility. I never before realized how much there was for the range officer to look after. Damn, it's a job. My two non-comms are good, thankfully, and the boys will work with me so I don't come out too bad. It's only 2:30 and I've put in more than my eight hours today and Wednesday is supposed to be a half-holiday. Such is the Army. I got up at 4:00 AM. That's early.

In a few minutes I'm going down to the QM supply and get myself a couple of big towels, Turkish bath for 24 cents and some undershirts for 18 cents per each.

Tell me, did Barney get the job or did Howard talk him out of it? Children shouldn't allow their parents to boss them that much. –I didn't and she never tried.

Did you send me the <u>Grit</u> again? I enjoyed it very much. It's fun to keep track of what's going on in Williamsport and vicinity.

Write when you have time, please. You're an awfully good girl about writing and I haven't been such a good boy, but I keep trying. So long, Pal.

Lots of love,

Carp

Ft. Jackson, S.C.
June 25, 1941

Dearest Mother,

The birthday presents are priceless. Aunt Pee's idea is just the best thing ever. You are a couple of swell peoples.

I'm going to throw a birthday party for the entire bunch of us here in the barracks after supper tonight. That stuff is too good for me to make a pig of myself and there's enough for the whole gang so I'm sharing it. We'll have soft drinks and beer to go with it. And we'll have a swell time of it. Thank Aunt Pee and all of you who had a hand in it.

Judy sent me the cutest card yesterday. It was all about the fact that I ain't perfect, nor a saint, and not a good example and I got lots of faults and I am not angelic, but I should stay just as I am 'cause she likes me a lot. It was so true to me that I'll have to save it. The brat sent me a letter today from which I gather that she's sending me a camera for my birthday. You know my old one went bad. She's the damnedest person I know, but she is awfully nice. I've got just the swellest family and she's part of it.

Boy am I lucky. I'll break in one of the new shirts at the Hop Friday night. They're perfect and so are you. Mmmmmh I am practically speechless. But not typewriterless.

As usual it has been raining cats and dogs for the last hour or so. Up until 3:30 it had only sprinkled a little so I didn't get soaked today, which is unusual. If this isn't the nearest thing to a rainy season that I ever saw. The boys all call it our California dew.

Last night Kit and I saw Bill Powell and Myrna Loy in "Love Crazy." I think that you saw it and said that it was good. I almost laughed myself sick and I could just imagine you getting some of the cracks which I got, but which most of the crowd missed. We got the nicest kind of minds.

Lots and lots of love,

Carpy

P.S. And a great big kiss for my mother.

Ft. Jackson, S.C.
July 1, 1941

Dear Maw,

This will have to be strictly a note. I didn't realize how little time I'd have this morning. At one o'clock we're moving out for our first overnight bivouac. It'll be a nine-mile hike with full pack. Thankfully, being an officer cuts that pack down a bit. Mine weighs about 20 pounds and the men's must weigh 40 pounds. Tomorrow noon my feet won't even speak to me.

Kit and I are sticking to camp for the 4th except for little wayside excursions and picnics. I've got a date with the same girl I took to the dance. She's a nice kid and she knows about Judy so I'm not chiseling, or am I?

This is a great gang of guys we've got here. At least I think so. It took us about a month to get to know each other because the whole crowd with only a couple of exceptions doesn't warm up until they're pretty sure of the other guy. There are a couple of bastards naturally, but really it's a good bunch.

Judy gave me the nicest camera and boy am I using it. Aunt Edie sent me five bucks and I bought a new pair of slacks, very nice.

I gotta scram now. I'll have more time later in the week.

Lots of love,

Carpy

P.S. I love you

Wednesday noon, July 2, 1941

I couldn't find an envelope yesterday and was practically late for formation so I decided to finish this today.

The hike was a killer. It was 10.4 miles at a temperature of about 92 degrees. We lost seven boys out of the company on the way out, but this morning they were all ready but one to walk back with us and we all made it back in.

My mess sergeant misjudged the water situation very badly and we hit camp without any water in our canteens and no water there. The trucks had just left for the post to get more. It was an hour and a half before they got back and we almost had mutiny on our hands for awhile. I had to stand over the water can and ration it out a half a cup at a time to keep the men from killing themselves. One hundred and thirty men used up four twenty-four gallon cans of water in an hour after the truck arrived. And they weren't wasting it either.

I lost a little more than two pounds in the twenty-four hours we were out. My uniform was soaking wet when we made camp yesterday and when we got back today I stripped and laid my shirt down on a newspaper. It soaked through four pages of the paper. I managed to wring a half a cupful of water out of my underwear too. As soon as I got in, I hit for the shower and then drank a half-pint of milk, two glasses of lemonade, and uncountable quantities of water. I'm slowly becoming undehydrated again. –I think they're gettin' us ready for Africa.

Have a good one over the 4th. I'd like to get home but it's out of the question. I'll be thinking of you and a picnic along the Loyalsock. Walk out to the edge of the stream and spit in it once for me, will you?

Remember my first trip to New York a year ago on the fourth? I've been thinking of that the last couple of days, and also my second trip over Labor Day, when I met Judy.

Lots of love,

Carpy

Ft. Jackson, S. C.
July 8, 1941

Dearest Mother,

Happy birthday, Mother. I wish I could give you a nice big kiss with the greeting, but anyway I'll think one to you. I hope you have as nice a birthday as I did. That will be hard to do though. The enclosed portion of last month's salary is my idea of a gift. I couldn't think of a suitable present, so maybe you can get yourself a little something with this. Be sure and tell me what it is.

I had a swell weekend. Friday Kit and I went out and spent the entire day at a State Park near the post. I got a beautiful sunburn which is turning to a tan. We had a lot of fun just swimming and lying around. Friday evening, we took the Ford out for a drive. It was a beautiful moonlight night and with the top down it was perfect. Saturday we bummed around camp all day.

Kit was OD, but I took over for him in the evening and made his inspections and stuff and he took his girl into town on a party. She's just a swell kid. Sunday morning we got up early and the three of us drove to Savannah and on down to Savannah Beach. We went surf bathing for about an hour and a half and then drove up to an old fort that is located in the mouth of the Savannah River. Fort Pulaski. We looked all over it and explored its inner regions. Then we drove home. We covered about 390 miles and got home at midnight just about dead tired but very happy. We took some pictures on the trip and I'm enclosing mine. Don't they look kinda southernish?

Gosh I covered that weekend in a paragraph didn't I? But the pictures tell more of the story. We had the top down most of the day. It was inclined to be a little showerish, but we only had to put the top up twice. Judy would have loved it. I mean the trip.

Judy neglected me very badly the past week. I had one letter in ten days then I started neglecting her, now it's a hell of a mess. I guess I'll look up some of these little southern babes. Only I don't want to because I'm crazy about Judy. Don't you say anything to her and I'll write lots of letters and get fixed up ok, I hope.

Yesterday we hauled logs all day and today we went out in the field and built anti-mechanized defenses such as the big tank blocks and traps and stuff. We had dinner in the field and worked most of the day. I challenged my boys to a foot race across a field and the only one who beat me was a boy who had a 30-yard start. This life is really putting me in the pink of condition. I've put back on a few pounds but I'm still under my weight at the start, and I doubt if I'll get that back during this weather.

We haven't had the intense heat you've had. It's been fairly nice except for the storms. It rains hard at least every other day and showers on the days it doesn't rain hard. It is a warm climate though and when that old sun comes down on you it's hot.

I sent Jake, the chief splicer at the mill, a picture of me and my gang using one of the winch assemblies which he and the rest of the crew at J & L Wire Rope Mill made that last month I was there. They are on Diamond T Trucks and are sure handy. That's what I call a coincidence. To have a dozen trucks equipped with them in the regiment. All brand new trucks and new wire ropes.

Tonight we're trying to rig up a kind of a party in a hurry. Just for the hell of it.

Thanks a lot for spitting in the creek for me.

Please don't stew at me when I don't write as often as I should. I can look after myself and I'm busy and no fooling. I do love you.

The <u>Grit</u> arrived today, but I haven't had time to read it. I like to go all through it and read carefully everything about Williamsport and vicinity.

Have a happy birthday. I can't remember which one it is, but I could figure it out. No! I am not a nasty brat because I'm not going to figure it.

Love,
Carp

Ft. Jackson, S.C.
July 13, 1941

Hi Toots,

Now I'm being neglected. I haven't yet heard how you liked the snapshot collection I sent you. Did you have a happy birthday? I hope so very much. I have just a feeling that you painted the town slightly pink. Is there anything to that feeling?

We had a hectic week last week and another one ahead of us. Friday morning we hiked out about 10 miles again and worked from 1:00 until 5:30 putting in the bridge foundations and trestles of a ten-ton bridge. After that day's work, Kit and I came back into town got cleaned up and went dancing. At 12:30 we got back to camp and hit the hay. At 3:30 they sounded "To Arms" and we got up, broke camp and started hiking back. We met our mess truck on the way in and had breakfast. By 8:30 we were back in camp and dead tired. I slept the remainder of the morning and half the afternoon. It was fun though, and other than the tiredness I was okay. Not exhausted as I was after the first march. Apparently we're going to have one bivouac a week from now on, to toughen us up and get ready for maneuvers. I'll be so tough that you won't know me.

I wish you wouldn't worry about me. When I don't write it's because I'm too busy working and having a good time. As I've said before, the crowd here is great. It's like a big, good fraternity with all of us working at the same thing. I'm not any pepped up soldier boy and I do my share of griping, but as long as it's got to be done, this is the way to do it.

So long, Toots. You'll hear from me.

Lots of love,

Carp

Ft. Jackson, S.C.
July 18, 1941

Dearest Mother,

Nowadays I seem always to be owing you letters, but that's nice because that means you write to me nice and often.

So you don't believe that this is only a pleasure jaunt? Why lady that's treason. You surely don't think that they want to get permission to send us out of the country so that they can use us to fight do you? That's going to be done purely to show us some more of the world and how the other side lives, or maybe how they fight.

We had another scorcher of a rain yesterday. It tore out roads and washed our company street down between the barracks again. Some guy decided to wade across the gutter down by the 102nd. It was about 20 feet wide and much deeper than he knew because he stepped in over his head and two guys pulled him out a hundred yards down the road just before he could get into a three-foot culvert. Even the culvert is gone this morning. Remember the storms we get every once in awhile that fill up the streets? Well we've had storms like that down here on an average of one every two days for the past twenty days. It's terrific. You get so used to them that you go right on working or doing whatever you were doing, provided you can keep your feet.

The other day we decided to build a bridge across a little stream near here. The stream's about five feet wide and three or four feet deep. We figured on two spans and an 18-inch clearance to allow for small floods. Yesterday we worked on it again and decided to make four spans and allow another 18 inches, as it kept on raining we raised it to five spans and another 12 inches. The creek is now six feet deep in the bed and has spread back 30 feet on one side and 80 feet on the other. It's neat.

We were supposed to go out on an overnight bivouac tonight but it was canceled so that we could prepare for a week's bivouac next week. At least that's the rumor. If it's true I won't be writing you much, if any, but don't worry about me because a week's bivouac is nothing to an ex Boy Scout, especially with the bedding rolls the Army supplies. They're really neat. They are a brand new heavy, waterproof sleeping bag with a mattress and bed made up with sheet, pillow and blankets inside. The roll has pouches for your extra clothes, mess kit, toilet articles and anything you want. It's rolled up and carried in the back of your truck and one of the strikers pitches your tent and fixes up your sleeping quarters each day. With the exception of insect life, we're more comfortable in the field than in the barracks.

The 102nd is away and their band didn't play this morning. That's my alarm clock and as a result I didn't wake up until quarter of seven. Now I'm eating a breakfast of Ritz and peanut butter and root beer. Not good for you, but satisfying.

I saw the swellest movie last night. Don't miss it on any account. It's Madeleine Carroll and Fred MacMurray in "One Night in Lisbon" and it's priceless. I laughed the whole time I was in the show. No kidding it's just your kind and my kind of a show. Her reaction to one of the kids in the picture was worth the price of admission alone.

I gotta go to work now. We're hauling out big timbers again. The only job I'll be fit for when I get out of here will be handling a labor crew.

The docs taped my back up for fair the day before yesterday and it's really good now. I worked all yesterday without noticing it and it's good today so I'm going to leave the tape on a few days and be okay. I still can't figure for sure how I wrenched it but I'm damn sure it was the government's fault, i.e. while on duty. It itches like hell. I hope I'm not allergic.

Will you sneak around and find out when Judy's birthday arrives? I think it's the 28th of Aug. or Oct. but I'm not sure. If you can find out whether she has that camera that she wanted yet or not it would be a help. Thanks, Pal.

Write 'cause I like to hear from you. The Grit is kinda like a letter from you too, now.

Lots of love,
Carp

Fort Jackson, S.C.
July 26, 1941

Dearest Maw,

I was on a court martial Wednesday and Thursday. We tried two cases and it was very interesting to me. However, the next time I want to be a defense counsel. It would be so easy to get most of these cases off because the Trial Judge Advocates aren't after convictions and don't press their cases hard enough. I flared up at a civilian cop once and the president of the court had to close court 'til I got my temper back. You see, all members of the court are allowed to cross-examine any witness and this witness was obviously embroidering on his story. I crossed him up with a couple of questions and then got mad because he thought we were dumb enough to let him get away with it.

We were supposed to go on bivouac Wednesday, then for sure Saturday. Now it's for sure Monday, I hope. What with the Court and this bivouac being called off and on, we haven't known from one day to the next what we'd be doing.

I got a nice little compliment today and I have to tell you. The boys from one of the platoons, not mine, approached me as to the possibility of there being a trading of officers. I'm afraid possibly that's because I give my men a break whenever I can. However I still get more work done than the other platoon leaders, so maybe it isn't a bad idea.

What a lousy military man I am. I'm taking a substitute O.D. for a guy tonight. A friend of his is in town and I had nothing special so he's going to take one for me some weekend.

I walked into my guardhouse on an inspection. The Sergeant of the Guard was taking a little nap. Two boys shook him like the very devil and finally he sat up. I started talking to him and he just keeled over and went back to sleep. I couldn't help it, but just walked out laughing. Never did I see a guy so sound asleep.

I put in for five days leave starting Thursday. I don't think I'll get it but if I do I'll wire Judy. Call her and tell her to call you if she gets a wire. Don't count on it though because there's only about one chance in a hundred of my getting it. But I would like to see you.

So long now.

Lots of love,
Carp

I got that leave! Kit and I drove up to the beach in New Jersey, and Judy took the bus down to meet us. It was fantastic to see her again. There was no doubt about it: I was going to have to figure out a way to marry that girl.

> Myrtle Beach
> Tuesday night, August 20, 1941
>
> Hello Mother,
>
> I'm in the corner drug store enjoying a milkshake after seeing Don Ameche in "Kiss the Boys Goodbye." The show wasn't too good but it had lots of laughs.
>
> We stayed over an extra day to finish up our work on the park. We've been clearing brush and making a parking space for the State Park in return for the privilege of camping here. We're about three miles out of the town of Myrtle Beach, but we've sent convoys in every evening and half the afternoons. The boys say this is the best time they've had since getting in the Army.
>
> I've been too busy to do more than swim a little. I was O.D. one night and acted as provost marshal's assistant two other nights. That's a good job. The chief thing is to keep the boys out of trouble. It's really remarkable how effective those little gold bars are. Two cops were having a hell of a time trying to break up a fight between two boys of the 128th Field Artillery. I just stepped up, tapped 'em on the shoulder and they quit scrapping and started straightening up their uniforms and getting presentable. It's a wonderful feeling of importance that it gives you.
>
> We go back to camp tomorrow – out to Broad River Thursday – back to camp Saturday, and out to Chester State Park Monday for a week of reconnaissance in that area. I won't be able to write often so I'll alternate between you and Judy. If you two keep in contact you'll know where and how I am.
>
> Judy and I are okay and I hope to gosh we stay that-a-way. I'm so afraid of losing her through some misunderstanding that the distance we're apart prevents straightening out. Keep your fingers crossed for me.
>
> My driver just showed up for me. So long now.
>
> > Your affectionate son,
> > *Carp*

Ft. Jackson, S.C.
August 30, 1941

Hello Toots,

   I got a nice long letter from you today and I'll start right off by answering your questions.

   1. You are still my favorite mother and always will be. I like you.

   2. Kit gets a new set of boils every time we get a tetanus shot. He's now getting over his latest set. They weren't as bad as the first.

   Annabelle's tale about Kitty and Judy tickled me. Judy is too darned smart for a little dumb bunny like Kitty. Sometimes I think she's too smart for me. But even if she is, I'm crazy about her. I wish to hell that she now would answer to the same name that you do. I'd feel a lot safer if she did.

   Kit has a diamond and wedding ring that he paid $135.00 for and would sell to me for $75.00 provided a good jeweler valued it at more than that. What would you think of my getting that? Superstition is the only thing that bothers me, and when you stop to think of it, half the diamonds you buy aren't new. Give me some good advice, will you?

   I've been O. D. three out of the last four days. Twice legitimately and one turn I took on for a guy who had a chance to go home to see his girl. Just between the two of us, I'm getting a callus on my ass from carrying a gun.

   Tomorrow Kit and I may drive down to Myrtle Beach for the day and come back Monday. If we do, we'll take sleeping bags and sleep in the car if it rains and on the beach if it's clear. I'm getting so used to sleeping out of doors that I feel like a Boy Scout. The life is good for me except that I miss Judy so much. Can two of us live on $183.00 per month and pay $50.00 per month for a car and insurance? I'm willing to live in a couple of rooms if I have her. We've both done it before and it wouldn't hurt us till I get my 1st Lieutenant grade. That will mean at least $60.00 more and I should get it at least by the first of May. I know she hates it there without me and I'd be a hell of a sight happier here if she were around.

   What do you think of Russia telling Japan where to head in at? Do you think it will do any good?

   Our regiment is now equipped with 113 of the required 115 trucks. The 12th Engineers and the 105th, both of which were organized here at Jackson long before us, are not more than 50% equipped to date. I'm afraid that if we make a good showing in maneuvers they'll move us out of here. That won't be too bad unless they put us on Foreign Service. Of course, that's only my idea. But if it works out that way I'm going to be bitched.

Tuesday we go out for four more days at Chester, I think. Anyway it'll be four more days on reconnaissance and I hope it's Chester. The boys had a good time there and it's the most comfortable camping spot we've had yet.

That's all for now.

Lots of love,

Carp

Ft. Jackson, S.C.
September 4, 1941

Dearest Mother,

I think you're right about the ring and I'm going to follow your suggestion. I was a little superstitious myself about the other and I wanted to be either reassured or confirmed. —I never was confirmed was I? Does that make me a bastard?

We got back from Chester today looking like a pack of drowned rats. It rained by the buckets last night and most of the boys hadn't ditched their tents. The result was a river through most of their tents. Not more than a half dozen men in the company stayed dry. I got rather damp while closing the flaps of our tent and Segall almost drowned from it raining in on him before he woke up.

The town of Chester threw a nice little dance for us Tuesday night again, and last night I got a request from a lady of the town to recommend four nice boys for invitation to a private dance someone was throwing. The boys I sent reported this morning that they had a grand time. They also had a community sing for us last night in the clubroom they have fixed up for the soldiers in the city hall. You just can't imagine how nice they are to us.

What makes you think that commissions as First Lieutenants will come through sooner than next May? Is it a hunch or something you read? Personally I don't expect it unless war is declared. Then they'll probably jump us. I told you that I'm now doing the work of two First Lieutenants. i.e. Mess officer, Supply officer, company council recorder, and platoon commander. In addition to those duties I've been put in charge of coordinating the work of the three platoons on this reconnaissance. I think that it is something of a compliment for me to be doing twice as much work as Segall, but still damn it, I'm doing the work and he's getting the pay. I ain't a patriot that way.

I'm looking for that box. But if Aunt Pee isn't feeling well enough and it's too much work, wait 'til later. Give Pee lots of love and tell her I hope she's feeling much better.

That's all for now.

Love,

Carp

Ft. Jackson, S.C.
September 6, 1941

Dear Mother,

Here are some very explicit (I hope) instructions I wish you would carry out.

I've made arrangements with Kit to buy that diamond because I do want Judy to have a diamond and I think the first ring I get her will probably mean more than any other that I ever do give her. However I want it reset. That should certainly ruin any Jinx that it might have because the ring itself would be new and I don't think Jinxes can stick to stones.

Kit is having it mailed to you and I would like you to take it to Ralph at his jewelry store, and then you and Ralph and Ralph's wife, and Pee pick out a white gold setting for it and ring to match. I want a very plain setting and something very similar to the design of the setting it now is in. The price range should be from $35.00 to $50.00. I'm enclosing a check for 20 bucks and will divide the rest into two payments the first of November and the first of December, or as soon as I get paid.

If you don't like the committee I picked to pick the ring, you can pick a number of different styles and have Judy go in with you and decide on one of them. Either method will please me. I trust your judgment completely. It's a hell of a sight better than mine.

I'm going to write Judy a letter and send it to you and I'd like to have the letter and ring delivered to her on the 18th, for her birthday.

I'm particularly anxious to have Ralph set the stone and also appraise it while he's at it, because I think he's darn good on diamonds. If he suggests platinum or something like that, listen to his reasons and use your own judgment.

If I've missed anything important and there is time, write me. If not, decide for yourself for me. As I've said before and again repeat, your brain is something hard to beat.

The one thing I've missed is how to present it to her in person and I can't figure any way to do that. So this way will have to suffice. I'll appreciate it a lot.

I go back out in the field on Monday until Wednesday. Then out again Wednesday 'til Saturday, I think, I hope not, though. We go out the 15th for keeps. That's the present word.

Love to you and Pee.

Carp

I know this is asking a lot, but I count on you.

Ft. Jackson, S.C.
September 15, 1941

Dearest Mother,

This is the last letter you'll get from Jackson for awhile. The regiment moved out this morning and I'm in charge of the clean-up detail and move out tomorrow. My address for the next ten weeks will be: Lt. G.H. Carpenter, Co A, 38th Engr Regt, APO 301 Ft. Jackson, S.C.

The APO is Army Post Office 301. Our base camp for maneuvers is up near Chester, S.C. I'll be at Jackson the week of Oct. 26 as commander of the guard detachment but the rest of the time I'll be in the field.

I got your letter about the ring this morning and I'm damn glad it got there and that YOU are taking care of it. It should please Judy, at least I think and hope it will. I'm wishing that she or Grace would announce our engagement but unless they think of it I won't suggest it. But you know me, I want it shouted from the house tops.

It's a good thing that Pee is feeling better. Asthma and hay fever are two of the damnedest things, but I'll take the hay fever any day in preference. Give her my love and tell her I think of her every day, and only nasty thoughts every other day. I do hope she gets over this quick, though.

About the ring. Of course it's to be in a box from Ralph's and as for the wedding ring, talk it over with Judy and decide which one of you ought to keep it. If I do I'll lose it and then we couldn't be married. I'm enclosing the letter for her. Gee but I'm tickled that it's worked out so she gets a diamond for her birthday.

Boy have I been busy for the past week. Getting ready to move out has included so many things such as getting woolen uniforms, and packing everything that is to go and everything that is to stay. Our orders read that everything we leave behind must be packed ready for shipment in case we don't return to Jackson. That order just adds to the rumors.

I was on two court martials last week. One was the case of the boy that went to sleep on guard. Remember? I was worrying about it. Well he got a month at hard labor and then had it suspended to go on maneuvers, which tickles me plenty.

Last Friday I had a demolitions class. My supplies consisted of a hundred sticks of 40% dynamite and caps and fuse. We went out to the site of the bridge which we built a couple of months ago and proceeded to try out different methods of placing charges to see which was quickest and gave the best results. We really blew that bridge to hell and gone with very little fuss and I picked up a lot of stray information on the use of dynamite. Think of it, some day I may be able to use some of this dope on civilian work that I do. I hope so anyway. Funny but all the formulae on calculating charges doesn't mean a thing until you've actually tried different charges and seen the results. Now I have a pretty good idea of what dynamite will do.

We got our first casualty today. One of the motorcyclists leading the convoy crashed head-on into one of these damned drivers who insist on making their right hand turns from the left side of the road. The boy never regained consciousness. While he was lying in the road, all the driver could say was, "Look at my car. Who's going to pay for my car?"

It's getting late and I have to get up early. I'll write as soon as I get settled. Lots of love to you and Pee.

Your affectionate son,

Carp

Base Camp, S. C.
September 20, 1941

Dearest Mother,

You probably know that I called Judy Thursday night. She sounded excited and pleased as the very devil. Thanks a lot pal you are my lifesaver. Will you write and tell me all the details about giving it to her and any facts you think I should know. Whatever story you told her is okay by me, even the truth. It was a funny way to give a girl an engagement ring, but next to giving it to her myself, I can think of no one I'd rather have subbing for me 'cause I know I can trust you to look after my best interests. Did you get a nice big kiss for it? Someone should and it may be some time before I can collect. Anyway when I do get it I'll give you one too.

This base camp was a pretty comfortable place when we moved in but they're doing their best to make it uncomfortable. First they took out the wooden floors from the tents and then our cots so we're sleeping right next to mother earth; and me, I don't particularly care for the idea for the next ten weeks. Some general who is sleeping in a hotel while on maneuvers probably thought of it. A couple of weeks at a time is okay, but even during war time we wouldn't likely hit a ten week stretch of this sort of crap and this is supposed to be a base camp with some few comforts.

I'm bitched at the guys who run this Army. Since Wednesday morning I've been putting in electric lights and plumbing for Corps Headquarters. It took us a day to hook up all their tents. Then chief of staff comes in and decides that the tents should be lined vertically with the road instead of parallel to the edge of the field and this throws one end out nine feet (one end of a 100 foot row) so they had to move all tents and we had to rewire the whole bunch. All the time they keep hurrying us to get everything ready. Hells Bells it seems to me that the higher up you go in this Army the dumber they get. It puzzles me greatly trying to decide why they apparently must always do things or have things done the hard way. Imagine Jones and Laughlin wasting a day's work from a full crew over something as silly as that.

Another thing that happens all the time is that you look over a job, make an estimate, and send in a requisition. One superior cuts a quarter off the requisition and another adds a quarter more work to the job and then everybody up the line sends down hell when the job isn't completed on time. There sure is room for some efficiency in this business. Maneuvers certainly should show up a lot of it, at least to us down here in the rank and file, but will the men who could improve it see the need? I'm just bitched and I've got to blow off steam to you.

These jobs have taught me a couple of things. For one I've discovered about six good electricians in the company and also a couple of good plumbers. I think that in the regiment you could find a man to do any sort of work you have in mind.

I just got your letters written Wednesday and Thursday nights and also one from Judy written Thursday night. She certainly was pleased and tickled. You were very diplomatic and the best emissary I could have had. She hadn't the least idea that she was getting it and I guess it was a very good complete surprise. Just reading about it from both of you made me glow all over. Thanks a million.

She apparently thinks I picked it out when we were in Ralph's together that time and I'll just let her go on thinking that. The idea of getting the wedding ring later is okay. She can bring it down with her. Will you have Ralph give you a bill for me so I'll know what I owe him? He understands that it will be in two payments on the first of November and December.

I'm glad that Phoebe is getting better even if it is slowly. Give her my love please. I hope she's as glad about Judy as you and I are. And I think she will be. Sorry, but I can't think of anything else to talk about. Isn't Judy just the swellest, sweetest girl in the world? I'm so tickled and proud.

That's all for now. I won a buck playing bridge while waiting for the mail to be sorted. Ain't I good?

Lots of love,

Carp

Base Camp, S.C.
September 25, 1941

Hello Maw,

Well, Judy has been wearing my ring (her ring) (who the hell's ring is it?) for a week now and I'm very proud. Gee, but I'm a lucky guy.

That was a lucky break about that Hospitalization insurance for Phoebe. Tell her I'm awfully glad she's back home again and I hope she keeps getting better right along.

I had a long letter from Baldy telling all about the gang. It seems that George and Dutch are about due for it, the Army I mean. He's all set on Jo and figures that when I get back we can have a good foursome for bridge. I hope he's right but somehow I don't figure the old gang will ever get together again regularly the way we did. When this is over we'll probably be spread all over the map. If I were single I'd head for Europe after this and try to get a job rebuilding. Maybe Judy would be willing to go along.

She's a darb isn't she? I had a letter from her the other day telling about a party at Kitty's the night after she got her ring. Apparently she and Kitty get along swell and that's good because I think that just because Kitty and I don't agree is no reason why Judy shouldn't enjoy knowing her. Kitty is interesting and fun if you don't let her get her claws into you and Judy seems to be able to take care of herself.

We've gotten ahead of our work for awhile and have had two days with only a few jobs to do so we put in the time on camp. The tent pegs are now lined up well enough to suit any General.

Lady, there's an awful lot of room for improvement in the top of this Army. Captain Gilbert and Lt. Putney with a driver were coming back to camp from a job the other day and passed some General's car. They went up to about 42 mph. The General pulled up, waved them over and gave the Capt. hell for exceeding the 40-mile limit. Can you imagine that he'd notice a thing like that? It'll be murder to send us against the Germans with men like that commanding us. Can't you picture it? "Bombs bursting! Shrapnel flying! A machine gun chatters on the left. And there is the 38th straightening up tent pegs at 30 to the minute."

Call Judy and see if she wants to announce our engagement in this week's <u>Grit</u>, if you have time.

Kit and I went into Rock Hill last night and saw "Lady Be Good." That's got the best lot of good songs I've heard in years. If you get a chance, go see it, it's good.

That's all for now. So long.

Lots of love to my family,

Carp

P.S. I'm gonna be too broke to send a ten this month. Can you make out okay? I'm paying for my wool uniforms and other stuff for the next few months and it's a little hard on that check.

Base Camp, S.C.
Oct. 1, 1941

Dear Mother,

I just got in from my first 48 hours of maneuvers. We moved into concealed Bivouac Monday noon and fought the "Reds" until this morning. The 9th Div. and the 30th Div. and Corps troops were against the Red 8th Div. supported by two other Divisions.

Company A's chief job was preparing some eight bridges for demolition in case the enemy got pressing us too hard. Monday afternoon I had four details out on bridges along a twenty-mile front so I hopped on a motorcycle and started out checking the jobs and trying to find the C.P. (command post) of the 102nd

Cavalry so that we could coordinate our work. I started out about 4:30 and still hadn't found them at 9:00 so I came back in, got some chow for myself and for the details and started out again.

I covered eighty miles of backcountry road on that motorbike, a lot of it with only blackout lights. Once, I got down inside the enemy lines and ran into a friendly scout who warned me and we both got the hell out of there. I had a lot of fun and we brought back some useful information even if I couldn't find the 102nd. I finally hit the hay about 2:30.

Tuesday morning my details went out on some more bridges but I had to stay in camp in command of the company while the captain made a recon. In the afternoon I made another trip around the bridge loop and talked to men of the different outfits. The situation was pretty much at a stalemate last night and didn't change a great deal during the night, so they called a halt this morning. We'll have at least a day in base camp and maybe until Monday, I hope. I get the impression of how difficult it is to keep abreast of the situation. Even the regimental head-quarters didn't know as much as I knew after my recon. So I informed them.

I got a hasty card from my old fraternity brother Gil on Monday. He's with the 803rd now. I think I told you about that and also that he was planning on being married to a girl from Massachusetts who went to Penn State. Anyway the card was mailed on a westbound train and he said to write him care of the Los Angeles Embarkation point. He doesn't know where he's going, but he says the girl will wait – He hopes. I'm going to write him right away. That outfit is attached to the Air Corps and could be going most anywhere. Hawaii, Philippines, or Alaska.

Judy says her Aunt Grace is giving a party for her Thursday night to announce her engagement. You make the Grit print it, and a picture too.

Gee but I feel good. The umpire who's checking our part of the maneuvers just broke out a bottle of Seagram's 7 Crown and I had about 4 fingers. Maybe when dinner comes I'll come down to earth.

Next on the program is a bath. I haven't been out of this uniform since Monday and I'm beginning to smell... myself. Kinda like a goat, anyone who gets downwind of me moves.

You ought to see your little boy roaming around with a gun on one hip, a canteen and gas mask on the other, a pack on my back and a tin hat on the back of my head. What with the two days growth of beard and the dust of two counties I look tough.

Give my love to Aunt Phoebe. I hope she's beginning to pick up by now. How's your hay fever? Is the fog still bothering Aunt Pee? I can't imagine what the weather is like at home. Down here it's like the weather the last of August. Plenty hot days but the nights cool off until it's cold enough in the morning to make you sneeze.

Did I tell you about the time last week when Kit and I stopped in at Winthrop College to see one of Kit's prospects? Winthrop is a girls' school of about 1300. I waited out front until Kit and his girl motioned to me from the lounge and then parked the car and went in. I had to go between a couple of buildings into a quadrangle and up on a terrace to make it. The first whistle didn't faze me, but as I came up on the terrace a crowd of about twenty girls were at the other end of the quad and about half of them whistled. It sounded like a basketball game at Penn State between halves when a girl walks in. No kidding, it was swell. Boy did I enjoy it.

That's about all for now.

I don't mean to ignore you when I don't write very often, but I do write when I get a chance, which isn't often. Anyway you're my favorite mother, by far, and I love you muchly.

So long now. Love to my family and the neighbors. I'd sure like to see you all.

Carp

Chester, S.C.
Oct. 4, 1941

Dearest Mother,

You sounded so darned excited when I spoke to you last night. I'm glad. I know she's the best girl in the world and I'm so glad you think so too. But then we both have good taste.

I'll bet you knocked 'em cold in your new dress.

They changed officers around in the regiment and I have a new company commander. He's a West Pointer, which I don't like, but he's the best officer of the W.P. boys we have and I think we'll get along O.K. I'm not very much worried if we don't though.

Did you see the nice write-ups that <u>Life</u> and <u>Time</u> magazines gave the engineers for their work in the Louisiana Maneuvers? Just goes to show that people are recognizing a good arm of the service.

I'm looking forward to the picture of Judy and the announcement.

Love and lots of kisses,

Carp

Bivouac, S.C.
Oct. 9, 1941

Dearest Mother,

We moved into bivouac Monday afternoon and my platoon went on the "alert." Our first job was to make a culvert crossing into the woods where we're bivouacked, and then to camouflage it so it wouldn't look like a new job from the air. We did this by planting a few bushes on the crossing and sprinkling dust over the new cut. Our bivouac is in about five acres of scrub oak and pine just off a backcountry road. All trucks, tents, and personnel are under cover against aerial observation. They're really concealed too. Tuesday night a red scout car, trying to escape from a couple of blue cars drove into our entrance road and was captured by a sentry before they realized what a bad place to hide they'd picked out.

All day Tuesday I was acting company commander and Tuesday night I was back on "alert" with another platoon. That's the trouble with being the only Lieutenant with the company.

Wednesday at noon they called an armistice until today noon and we spent the afternoon getting showers and clean clothes. Last night I took a convoy into Chester until midnight and had more darn drunks on my hands. One driver said he'd had only one glass of beer so I let him drive. About three miles out of town he ran off the road and almost hit a post so I pulled up along side of him and made him stop and then drove it the rest of the way in. I'll never again let a guy drive when I know he's had even one drink.

I saw the notice in the <u>Grit</u> and Judy sent me the ones from the <u>Sun</u>. I'm so damn proud and happy about everything that it's like a permanent jag. Some fun.

Give lots of love to Aunt Pee and tell her I keep hoping she's lots better each day.

Lots of love to you,
Carp

Mitford, S.C.
October 15, '41

Dearest Mother,

Gee but it's good that Aunt Pee is really getting better. Tell her that I'm laughing at the idea of her going on a diet whether she wants to or not. If the diet is so good, maybe she won't have to go down to Johns Hopkins. I hope so.

I've written some funny letters to Judy. If some of the letters we write to each other were published it would create a riot or something. Neither of us has any more shame or disgrace about us than you. And that's going some.

I can just see you puffing up with pride when you introduce Judy as your future daughter-in-law.

When you get a chance to do some real writing, tell me what things to look for so I can read them and swell up with pride. I'm awful glad and proud about this new chance you've got and I'll bet anything you make good. Can't you just hear me? My mother? Oh she's a feature writer for a big newspaper. —Hot dog.

Kit got a card from Judy last week telling him to take me out on some of his dates because she was afraid I was sitting around camp too much. That's a real girl for you. So Kit and I went on a spree together and went to see Deanna Durbin's latest picture. But I can't go running around, I'm saving my money to get married.

We've been playing bridge whenever four bridge players can get together, which is only weekends. I don't know whether my bridge is improving or otherwise but at least it's getting practiced. Maybe Baldy and Jo and Judy and I will eventually make a four-some. Who knows!

Our problem this week has been to defend the point where route U.S. #22 crosses Big Wateree Creek. We did this by putting in a 'minefield' across the road on the far side, 'blowing out the bridge', and sending patrols up and downstream from the bridge. So far we haven't developed any action. The Reds showed up once to kinda feel us out, but immediately withdrew.

It's hot during the day but gets plenty cool at night. Monday night I tried to sleep with my clothes on, just lying on top of my bedroll with a blanket pulled over me and darn near froze to death. Last night I got smart and crawled inside and got a good night's rest. The advantage of being a Lieutenant is that I just spread out my bedroll in the back of the pick-up truck and sleep there. It ain't too bad.

Did I tell you how much I enjoy your letters? Well I do. Muchly.

Lots and lots of love to you and Phoebe.

Your affectionate son,
Carp

Base Camp, S.C.
October 19, 1941

Dearest Mother,

Gee Maw, I didn't know you were so keen on me as you said in that last letter. I thought we were just platonic and here you say you love me. Well, confidentially, I love you too, but I'm engaged to another woman so I guess we'll just have to go on being friends. Your competition is extra good so don't be discouraged.

Your writing business is hard work, I know, because we had to do a lot of it at Penn State, or do you remember that you sent me to State? To me, the hardest part was always the first sentence of the first paragraph. If you can get started it will roll out fine and after you're finished and while you're still going strong you can go back and improve the start. –That's advice from an expert.

To straighten you out on this maneuvers proposition: I am under Gen. Drum in the First Army, but way under him. An Army is made up of two or more Corps. The First Army is made up of the 1st, 2nd, and I think the 8th Corps. A Corps is made up of two or more divisions plus attached troops called corps troops. The first Corps (called I Corps) consists of the 8th, 9th, and 30th Divisions plus a regiment of Cavalry, a regiment of Engineers (the 38th), and some attached medical units and air corps units. So you see we're called Corps Troops and come under Maj. General Thompson, and then under Lieut. Gen. Drum. –See?

Next week the I Corps is against the II Corps plus attached troops. We (I Corps) are the Reds for a change. The Reds are usually the smaller force fighting on the defensive, but in free maneuvers such as these they may take the offensive if it seems the best defense. We move up to Cheraw, S.C. tomorrow for the next few phases of these maneuvers.

If your friend Major Brass was a sergeant major that's a pretty fair job. It pays better than $200 cash per month plus living quarters, uniforms and grub. That's top non-comm job in the Army. –I wouldn't get a retired major if I were you. These regular Army men are too much stuffed shirts. And besides when the Army retires them they aren't good for much. –Sooooooooo.

Some of the funniest things come up in this Army. The boys' latest expression is "666 good for colds, chills, fevers and AWOL."

The reason is that our Captain has started a punishment scheme for AWOL's. Every man that goes over the hill has to dig a 6 ft X 6 ft X 6 ft hole in the ground. It's a good stiff punishment – (He calls it extra engineer instruction) – and it's getting results.

Confidentially, Pal – Judy and I are going to have to watch finances pretty close when we do get married. What do you think that'll do? Judy isn't very used to it. Will it break us up? I don't think so but I want some reassurance. I know I can get along on damn little if I can have her with me, and I hope and think she feels the same. What do you think?

I love you,

Carp

Near Kershaw, S.C.
October 27, 1941

Dearest Mother,

I've been kinda neglectful of you this last week, but I didn't mean to be. I figured you'd read Aunt Pee's letter and get some news of me that way.

Phoebe wrote me a nice letter. She says she's feeling better and better all the time and that's good news. She says you're more interested in your job every day and that's good news. I now refer to you as, my Mother – The ~~Ass~~ (oops) Ace Reporter.

We completed last week's maneuvers Thursday and spent the day moving down here. Friday we put up tents and fixed this as our base camp for the next couple of weeks. I fiddled around camp taking care of some company business on Saturday and then yesterday, believe it or not, I drove 110 miles into Jackson and back for the sole pleasure of getting a good hot shower and a clean electric shave. I never thought to see the day when I'd drive one hundred miles for a bath.

Kit has now gotten his can in a sling for fair. Against two specific orders forbidding the wearing of civilian clothes or driving personal cars in the area, he arrived in camp Friday night driving my car and wearing civvies and drove up in front of the Colonel.

Saturday the Colonel drove down to Jackson to see Kit and removed him from his job as maneuvers umpire and restricted him to the regimental area for an indefinite length of time. How Kit could have been so dumb as to drive right up in front of them is what gets me. I guess it was just that 'don't give a damn attitude' of his, much like mine only I control mine a little better.

Those two new Lieutenants are taking a load off me. For instance I'd be out on a job right now, but one of them is doing it.

Did I tell you that I now have my bunk cut to fit my pick-up truck and yesterday my driver built a shelf over the forward half of the body to keep my footlocker and his barracks bag and other stuff on? All together it makes wonderful sleeping quarters for one shavetail (G.I. – Government Issue).

You've heard me use the word SNAFU (pronounced snaffoo). We picked it up from the 102nd Calvary. Just the other day, I learned the derivation of it. SNAFUAU - Situation Normal All F----- Up As Usual.

A couple of other phrases we use: "Tough shit" - meaning too bad buddy, just grin and bear it. "This shit must cease" - meaning what it says.

Those might make an interesting article for your paper. But I'm against writing it. Some people aren't as broad-minded as you and I.

Tomorrow is Tuesday and the way I look forward to Tuesdays! Boy oh boy. On Tuesdays I get a nice long letter from my Maw and also the <u>Grit</u> with all the local news and news about how my Penn State is making out. It's a remarkable newspaper and I'm one of its biggest fans.

All my love to you and Pee.

Your affectionate son,

Carp

October 29, 1941

Hello Toots,

Damned if I didn't get screwed yesterday. Not only didn't my <u>Grit</u> arrive, but no letter either. Both got here this morning, but the bum operation of the message center ruined yesterday for me.

I admired your articles very much, but I must admit that your articles are too much the newspaper woman. I expected individuality but your articles sound like they'd been written by any good reporter who's been in the game for thirty or forty years. I guess I'll have to wait for that first novel before my mother's style of writing makes an impression on the literary world.

I always wanted a rich uncle. I wish my rich Uncle Sammy would hurry up and promote me.

That's awful tough about Connie. Tell her I'll worry about her if it'll do any good.

We built an airport yesterday for the 103rd OBS. Squadron. They required two 100' X 1000' runways, so we built drags and hooked on to our trucks and made nice clear smooth runways. Then we improvised a wind sock for them by putting up two poles and tying a piece of white cloth on a weighted string between them in such a way that it wouldn't foul. The Colonel congratulated us on our job. The Air Corps Colonel, I mean, not ours.

I'm getting awfully tired of these maneuvers. Being Corps troops we don't get enough action to suit me.

Lots of love to you and Phoebe.

Carp

Ft. Jackson, S.C.
November 1, 1941

Hiyuh Toots,

Cheers, thrills and what have you! Only a month until December. Oh boy. Can you believe it?

Yesterday, Kit and I drove around all afternoon with the top down. It was beautiful shirt-sleeve weather. No kidding, it was swell. I had on slacks and my Penn State numeral sweater, no shirt or undershirt and I was too warm.

We came into town Thursday afternoon and had showers, a good meal with our feet under a table and took in a movie. Yesterday we bummed around town and saw two more shows, then I found out that I'm to be here at the post as O.D. for next week, so I'll have a nice lazy week with a hot shower every day and plenty of sleep.

Last night by accident I walked into the show of the year, I think. It was Humphrey Bogart and Mary Astor in "The Maltese Falcon." It was unusual, exciting, astounding and darn good besides. It was a detective picture, not a scary mystery but a well-done story. If you get a chance, see it, please, I know you'll like it.

Think of it, after this week in here at the post, I'll have only three more weeks of maneuvers, Hot Dog. That damn "foreign service" rumor is back again. The 102nd is being prepared to move some-where very soon, that's straight goods, and the rumor says that we'll be next because we're the next best equipped of the Corps Regiments. Roosevelt has certainly declared war for us, hasn't he? And the worst of it is that most of us in the Army aren't mad at anybody. What a situation.

I won't get any mail all this week so if I don't answer questions you'll know why. And remember, you're my favorite mother.

Tonight I'm going to see "Smilin' Thru" and tomorrow I'll see "A Yank in the R.A.F." and all this week I'm going to movies whenever I can. You can see what a hick the Army is making out of me. But hell, I ain't got nobody to dance with. Wait 'til Judy comes down here. I'm going to wear her out just talking, dancing and necking (spooning, to you.)

Kit says if they send us abroad and if they allow us to take wives along, which is doubtful, he's going to get married so he'll have something to do besides drink and play bridge. I don't know what he means.

Give my love to Pee. I keep my fingers crossed for her to keep improving fast.

Love to all,

Carp

November 5, 1941

Dearest Mother,

Judy is on a fence now. Everybody has been so nice to her about the Bridal showers and everything that she is beginning to think it might be nice to be married at home there. That sounds like an all right idea to me, provided it's really what she wants. I know you can't pump her, but you might try again. I've told her that it's her wedding and the one thing I think she must decide for herself. Anything she wants will be okay by me. She knows that too. One thing I do know is that all the honeymoon she's going to get for awhile will be a leisurely trip down here. I'd like to spend one night in Washington and one in Richmond or Raleigh, but the budget doesn't go for any gallivantin'.

I haven't had any mail since Saturday and I'd sure like to hear from you and get my <u>Grit</u> but I guess I just wait 'til tomorrow or Friday afternoon if someone remembers to bring it in.

I'm eating at the station complement and enjoying darn good meals and lots of it. My weight is about 165 just like usual. What a guy. I couldn't get fat if I tried.

So long, Sweet. Love to you and Pee.

Carp

November 7, 1941

Hiyah Toots,

Gosh I feel fresh tonight. I'm sore though, no mail yet. If somebody doesn't bring me a few letters pretty soon I'm gonna send a bloodhound out looking for it. A big, nasty bloodhound looking for a nice soldier to bite.

Of all the good luck… A hillbilly program started and I turned the dial idly to see what I could find and picked up a voice saying "and now we hear them sing 'Fight on, State,'" and sure enough I did. I heard the entire half-hour program that they put on – including cheers, songs, the introduction of this year's House Party Queen and everything. Oh man, it was swell because I hadn't even remembered that it was House Party weekend and I didn't know that we could get KDKA even faintly down here. I'm all excited and fuzzy around the edges. It was so damned easy to remember being back in the Rec Hall taking part in the program, and seeing the freshmen down on the floor with the Nittany Lion running around heckling them. Oh man but it was a thrill to pick that up so unexpectedly. Boy, I'd like to see that Syracuse game tomorrow. It should be one H--- of a good game. State hasn't lost a House-Party game since before my freshman year. Here's hoping they keep that slate clean tomorrow. I'll never forget the year the underdog State team licked Syracuse 33-3 and made one prognosticator apologize over the air.

Something like that really puts the edge on that homesick feeling. Boy but I'd like to be stepping at the Triangle House Party tonight instead of sitting alone in a barn of a barracks.

The maneuvers problem ended yesterday morning but none of the boys have gotten in yet. Must be another critique tonight. Oh well, I'm probably not the only guy with a touch of the itch tonight and I won't be the last.

I saw a swell movie last night. Margaret Sullivan and Charles Boyer in "Appointment for Love". It was a swell comedy, beautifully done. You'll like it if you get a chance to see it.

It's turned cool and I ain't looking forward to going back in the field.

Lots of love to you and Peep.

Your affectionate son,

Carp

November 12, 1941

Dearest Mother,

If this writing is even worse than usual it's caused by the fact that I'm wearing a pair of woolen gloves.

I got back to base camp Monday morning, and in the afternoon and evening we went to a critique at Monroe. It was <u>cold</u>. When we got back to camp at 11:00 that night the temperature was 28 degrees. I put my long handles on to go to bed and I don't intend to take 'em off, except to take a shower, if I get a chance to take a shower.

This morning there was heavy frost on all the tents. I know that it isn't cold compared to up home, but you people aren't sleeping out in it and, Lady, we are. Both mornings that I've been in camp we've found ice in the lister bags (canvas bag of water with a spigot) and we didn't put it there.

Yesterday I was on another court and today we've got another case coming up. The lack of evidence in these cases is remarkable. The Army could use some trained MP's. One of the cases we tried would have been an open and shut case if they'd known anything about fingerprinting.

Are you going to do some of my Christmas shopping for me? It'll have to be as economical as usual if not more so. I don't know what to get Judy for Christmas and I also don't know if I'm supposed to get her a wedding gift. Am I? I'll have enough dough to pay my share of the wedding. That'll be about $25.00, I think and I'll have enough to buy my presents and get home for Christmas, but I sure wish I could borrow about $50.00 for a couple of months to get us down here and settled. Do you know any member of our family who could make such a loan? Our tentative plan now is for me to get ten days leave if possible starting about the 20th of December and we'd be married at home the last of December. I'll have all my debts down here, uniform, etc. paid by then so we'll start off even, anywho.

Last week they had all of us sign a paper as to whether or not we'd be willing to take an extra year of Foreign Service. Most of us answered NO but a few answered HELL NO!

Tell 'em to be sure and match that ring properly and to keep it under their hats.

Speaking of nice silver for Judy, is that set of China around that Aunt Pee, Aunt Edie, and you gave to me? Is there enough of it that we could dig out 6 or 8 of each and take with us? I've got my eye on a nice little bungalow about 5 miles from the post that rents furnished for $35.00. Two other 38th officers live right near by. We may be able to get it, I hope.

I wish I knew what is going to happen to the 38th.

That fudge sure tasted good. You are a Pal to send it to me.

Tell Flossie I send her lots of love, and you too.

Tell Connie I feel for her – but I can't reach her. That must be something to have all your teeth pulled. Wooie.

Only 2-1/2 more weeks of maneuvers. 18 days to be exact.

At the critique Monday one of the generals in his speech said we should try to learn all we can in maneuvers because it will help save lives next spring. –Oh.

Lots of love to you and Phoebe,

Carp

Sunday night
Nov. 16, 1941

Hi Toots,

I started to write to both you and Judy last night, but at 6:30 we moved out to concealed Bivouac near the PeeDee River. The PeeDee is the 'international boundary' for this problem. At 7:30 this morning when the problem started, we were concealed in the woods on the river at the site where I Corps wanted a reinforcement pontoon bridge capable of carrying 25 ton loads. By eight o'clock, the infantry had secured a bridgehead on the far side for us and we started work.

Headquarters had allowed us until 2:00 p.m. to finish, but at 12:20 the first truck rolled across. –4 hours and 20 minutes to span 290 feet with the re-enforced bridge. The Division engineer had said the night before that it would take well-trained troops four hours. We were delayed 15 minutes waiting for material to arrive so we were only 5 minutes behind well-trained troops. Everybody from the General on down was well pleased.

Shortly after we started work, the Red bombers attacked us. Then the Blue pursuits drove them away and the anti-aircraft around us helped. This kept up off and on all morning and all up and down the river we could hear firing. It was the most real of the maneuvers to date.

A Blue pursuit squadron had a field about a half-mile from our bivouac and they've been taking off and landing all day long. Man how those little babies do travel.

----- We move out NOW -----

Monday noon

We were ordered out to protect I Corps Headquarters last night and from there I was sent back to move our base camp up nearer the front. I just got in from that trip and I think I have to move out pretty soon with my platoon to go on guard again.

I saw a newspaper account of the Blue engineers (that's us) repairing bridges that were bombed out and replacing them with pontoon bridges, all theoretical. I wish that reporter had been doing some theoretical work with me yesterday. He'd have been too damn tired to write.

This is a busted up letter. It's now 3:30. When I finished chow I got sucked into a bridge game with Kit and it ended a few minutes ago. We got word that the 30th Division is folding up and we're to be ready to move on a minute's notice to take part in the battle of PeeDee. I don't know how we're to protect I Corps Headquarters and support the 30th Division too.

Judy is practicing driving with her sister's car. I hope she gets real expert before she starts driving the Ford.

My Alma Mammy is doing pretty well this year. Five wins against two losses so far. I'm hoping we get in in time to see the So. Carolina game but we probably won't.

Tomorrow comes the <u>Grit</u>. Goody, goodie, ditto. The way our mail avoids us I may not get it 'til next Sunday.

The General got captured by the 84th Recon Bn. They must have had a room in the same hotel.

Lots of love to you and my family,

Carp

November 22, 1941

Hiya, Pal,

I've neglected my mailing list something awful this past week. We've been busier than the proverbial cat. And I mean busy. The first phase of this problem ended yesterday noon. But instead of getting a rest we had an inspection of all vehicles by the Corps automotive engineer in the early afternoon and in the evening we took down the pontoon bridge that we built earlier in the week. And I mean that bridge came down. The Captain put me in charge and we took it apart and put it up on the bank in 2 hours and 10 minutes – half of that in the dark too.

The captain of the pontoon company (the outfit that carries the bridge around and takes care of it) said that the job we did putting it up last Sunday was a damn fine job.

The vehicle inspection yesterday was a beaut. The inspector knew his stuff and we all learned a few tricks. My chief job is motor officer. And I got a new motor sergeant out of yesterday's inspection and things are going to be different. I'm going to have the best-serviced trucks in the regiment or know why.

I went to H & S (Headquarters & Service) Company for some parts this morning and he said I couldn't have 'em. I said I could and if I didn't get 'em by this afternoon, I would notify Corps headquarters. They arrived this afternoon.

I've been waiting to get H & S since the time the H & S Company Captain gave me hell for saying he didn't know how to run the Company. I still think that <u>and</u> I'm going to prove it to him. More damn fun.

We (the blues) won the war this week. Maybe you noticed. After we built the bridge we protected I Corps HQ for 36 hours. I did all my sleeping one night with a telephone lying by my ear. Then we moved over to protect the Route 1 Bridge across the Pee Dee River. We protected that with clubs to make sure that no one would sneak up on it in the dark and place charges to blow it up. This war was really interesting. We had over 1000 parachute troops against us and were always being attacked by bombers and attack planes. The tanks got within a mile of us but we didn't get any actual contact with them.

I don't think you have to worry about giving Judy an expensive wedding present. Some of that silver should tickle her especially as it is related to her – or rather her kids (I hope.) And if she's marrying me for my money, which she ain't, she's sure going to get a screwing. She knows the facts and if she's as much in love with me as I am with her, she's willing to take a chance; and if she isn't, now is the time for her to change her mind.

Maybe you think I'm not looking forward to the 20th of December. It may not be exactly the 20th but it'll be thereabouts and I'm looking forward to the end of this week and the end of maneuvers. Three blankety-blank months in the field. Phooey.

I sure appreciate your getting that dough for me.

Tomorrow is the Army's Thanksgiving Day. Tomorrow morning at 4:00 a.m. we move out of this bivouac to a new one fifty miles away and in the afternoon we get our turkey and stuff.

That's all for now. Lots and lots of love to you, Sweet.

Carp

Nov. 27, 1941

Hi Sweet,

I've damn near forgotten how to write. This morning I wrote to Judy, the first letter I've written since last Saturday when I wrote to you.

After I wrote you last Sat. I went into town and had a bath and a meal at the hotel, then the top kick and I started bumming around town and we ran into a dance at the armory. I danced with a school teacher (hell of a nice kid, if I weren't engaged I'd go after her) who introduced me to her mother. The mother invited me to Sunday dinner. It seems that Mrs. G. picks up a couple of soldiers at each dance and has them come to her place for the weekend. The daughter teaches about 150 miles away near Greenville, S.C. and Mr. & Mrs. G. have the big house all to themselves, except when she's home on vacation. Anyway, after getting the convoy off at 4:00 AM and up country about 50 miles I hopped in my truck and went back for dinner. Turkey and all the trimmings at a table with nice people, our kind, to talk to. It was swell. I really enjoyed myself and boy I did need that. This being out in the woods is getting monotonous. Should be over tonight. Oh boy! We still don't know when we go in.

Monday we moved again and started reconnoitering all the roads on the south flank with an eye to blocking them with mines or demolitions. Tuesday we moved again and started mining and blocking all the roads in an area of 80 square miles. By Wednesday noon the company was spread from hell to high water all over our sector. Last night B Company took over from us and we had to collect the company and move down near Cheraw again. This afternoon we advanced another 15 miles south of Cheraw. All together we've been busier than two cats the whole week. Problem is supposed to end tonight and then back to Ft. Jackson, but maybe tomorrow.

Aunt Pee doesn't seem to be improving near as fast as I hoped she would (and I guess as she hopes too). Is she taking good care of herself? That diet the Doc prescribed sounded to me like it did the most good. I sure hope she's feeling in the pink by Christmas.

Judy said her stomach was upset on the trip to New York. She thinks that she'll buy a bottle of 4 Roses and keep a straw in it 'til after the wedding. Can't you see the write-up: "It was a lovely wedding, except for the incident when the slightly pie-eyed bride and groom tripped upon leaving the church and refused to leave the gutter claiming that they were home and intended to stay there."

You seem to be doing okay on your reporting. "Front Page Marg" they call her.

Tell Aunt Pee that I'll be damn glad to see her newspaper clipping of the maneuvers so I can know what has happened. They are on such a big scale that the only things I know about are the happenings in my own little sector.

My latest worry is this: Do you suppose I ought to buy Christmas presents for my new in-laws? They won't be my in-laws until after Christmas so I don't think so.

What are you doing about my Christmas shopping?

I'll do better on my letters after I get off maneuvers. Here's looking forward to the 20th.

Lots of love to you all,

Carp

P.S. I just happened to remember you've been working for the <u>Grit</u> for more than a year now. Congratulations, Pal.

December 3, 1941

Dear Toots,

All over and we've been back at the post almost 48 hours. Two nights in a bed, well anyway a bunk and not much more comfortable than my woods bunk.

We had Monday afternoon and yesterday off, and binged around Monday and slept yesterday. Today we started work cleaning up equipment, both personal and company. The trucks are my big problem. That's my one and only chief job now, well, that is, in addition to commanding second platoon, I'm the motor officer. There are a lot of tricks to maintenance that I've got to learn.

Gee but Aunt Phoebe is having the damnedest time. Is it the location of the job that makes trouble or is it the nervous strain of working for an investment advisor?

Judy tickles me. She is a swell girl and I darn well know it.

I did miss up on my writing during the past two weeks but I just was too damn busy. She didn't get sore about it either, even if you did want to divorce me. Aren't you ashamed of yourself?

I've been studying how to get my 1st Lt., but have at last decided that it can't be done until May. I wish you were a better prophet, but Army Regulations are against you.

We haven't learned the exact dates for our leave but I think my guess of the 20th to 30th will be close. Maybe you think I'm not looking forward to getting home. Oh boy.

I'm enclosing a check for $5.00 with which I wish you'll get my winter coat and suit out of hock, my tux pressed and a clean shirt available.

Thanks, Pal.

Lots of love to all my family,

Carp

On December 7, 1941, the Japanese attacked Pearl Harbor, Hawaii.

December 8, 1941

Hello Toots,

It certainly started with a bang, didn't it? If the Japs didn't make a tactical error I'm a blind pig. I think that if they'd just gone ahead and attacked Singapore, which seems to be their chief objective, and not bothered us we'd have maintained our indifference and let 'em get away with it, but no, they had to kick us in the seat of our red, white and blue pants. However if the Philippines are their objective, then it wouldn't make much difference to us because we consider them as still our possession. And they did have the element of surprise in their favor.

The present attitude of the boys seems to be "Give us our Christmas furloughs and then we'll come back and fight anyone, anywhere and Japs two at a time." So far, our leaves have not been canceled. I'm still hoping to see you a week from tonight. Barring an attempted invasion, I think it's probable that I will.

I'm going to leave the decision as to what we do pretty much up to Judy. She's level-headed and pretty wise. I want to marry her very much, but I'm not selfish enough to want to marry her for a month and then be shipped off and leave her married, but not working at it for a period of possibly three years or longer. But we can make final plans later, I hope.

I can do my shopping when I get home, what little I'm going to do. I've already ordered a nice manicure set for Judy. She's probably got one, but I do like her with those beautiful hands fixed up nice so I think she'll always have use for it.

Dearest Sweetie-Pie, the pajama idea is swell. I'm in hellish shape for them and I mean that. As to the dressing robe or lounging robe, I think that's going too far. You ain't no millionairess, sister, even if you would like to be one for your spoiled brat's sake. I love you.

Gosh, but I wish there was something I could do for Aunt Phoebe. It seems funny that they can't find out what's giving her such violent attacks and either remove the cause or treat for it. What happened to the diet that seemed to be doing so much good?

The radio has been having a field day this evening playing old war songs and favorites of '17 to '20. The 102nd Cavalry played

"Over There" this morning at Reveille. People do like to dramatize things, don't they?

Well, Sweet, I've got to go mail this.

Love,

Carp

Dec. 13, 1941

Hello Toots,

Have I been bitched and have I been bitching this last week. We've made and changed plans every day until yesterday. Now it seems that we're absolutely certain of what we're going to do. I wired Judy today and she's probably told you that I expect ten days leave starting the 19th. We'll leave here at midnight Thursday and be home sometime Friday night depending on the condition of the roads. I'll have to be back in Jackson by midnight of the 29th.

I have a plan that I talked over with Al this morning. It is that he get married the 1st of January instead of February as planned and that he and Vivian and Judy and I live together. Rentals are awfully high in this town, but for $60.00 - 70.00 we can get a nice furnished apartment or house at a cost of only 30.00 - 35.00 each. The two girls will have someone to talk to and pal around with. Al and Vivian are nice people and we should be able to get along quite well – together, at least until we're made 1st Lieutenants in May. It's the only way I can see to make both ends meet. Oh hell! Al just walked in and told me that Vivian vetoed the idea. What the hell, maybe it wasn't such a good idea, but I still think it was. I don't quite see how we're going to make both ends meet so maybe I should just call the whole thing off. Anyway when I get home we can talk it over. What I can't see is what there is in it for Judy now. At the most we can only count on 4 or 5 months before I get shipped to Foreign Service, so maybe she ought to start looking for some nice guy with flat feet, and a 4F rating.

Friday the Major inspected us and Saturday the Colonel looked us over and tomorrow Gen'l Thompson of I Corps is going to give us a going over. It ought to be some fun.

Anyway, I'll see you about Friday night, I hope.

Lots and lots of love,

Carp

I did, in fact, make it home on leave. Judy and I were married Christmas Day. It was a small wedding with just family and a few close friends. My pal Baldy stood up with me as Best Man and Judy's sister Evie served as Maid of Honor.

Carp, Judy, Evie, & Baldy

A few days later, Judy and I headed south to set up house-keeping in South Carolina.

Chapter 2

Training

Jan. 2, 1942

Dearest Mother,

Boy have we been having a hectic time. SNAFUAU. When we got in, we learned that the 2nd BN was being sent on maneuvers which was a relief, but then on Wednesday I was attached to the 2nd BN as Supply Officer for the maneuvers. So on Wednesday the 7th I leave for two weeks work out in the field.

Judy is going to stay with Emma while Joe is in the hospital and I'm gone, which is a lucky break.

We had a hell of a time finding an apartment and finally stumbled on one by luck. It's a new, clean little place, nicely furnished and real neat. We can move in on the 15th. It consists of a neat modern kitchen and dining room combined, and combination living and bedroom and a bath. Darn small and very nice. Both of us are tickled with it.

We expected to have New Year's Day off, but at 3:00 p.m. on Wednesday a TWX (orders) from Washington came through making Thursday a day of duty for everyone. We didn't do much work, but we did have to be here.

Kit has also been assigned to the 2nd BN for these maneuvers so we'll be fighting this war together too.

Gee but I did have a nice leave, Mother, and got myself a nice wife too. Judy is thriving on the life and I think she'll enjoy being down here even more after she gets better acquainted.

The trip down was fun and very easy. Taking it in two trips makes it a snap. We got into Columbia 9:30 Monday evening and had time for a date afterward. We drank the champagne at midnight to bring in the New Year a few days early. And boy it was good.

Half the boys are still on leave, so except for preparations for this maneuver, things are pretty quiet. Co. A is building a bridge for the 128th Field Artillery so they can get in and out of their area quickly in case of an air raid.

I'd like to be in on that but no luck. Anyway I'll learn more at this new job. It reminds me of my work for Pete at the wire rope plant. It consists of keeping after all sorts of more or less important details and seeing that the supply problem is being handled properly and quickly. The responsibility is the main thing.

Give my love to Pee and tell her to let me know when she goes to Huntsville.

Lots of love to you, Sweet,
Your son,

Carp

January 5, 1942

Dearest Mother,

Saturday morning I learned that the maneuvers had been called off for us, so I was ordered back to Co. A. That was swell. This morning I walked in and discovered that I'm now assigned to H & S Co. (Headquarters and Services Co.) That is almost the lousiest assignment you can get in the regiment. I haven't as yet learned what my exact duties will be so I'll tell you more about that later. H & S is responsible for regimental supply, for vehicle maintenance, for heavy equipment work such as shovels, bulldozers and scrapers, and for issuing all equipment to the line companies.

I'm glad to hear that Phoebe is going to go to Johns Hopkins. There's a good chance that they may be able to find out something about her and give her some real relief before she goes to Alabama. Give her my love and a big kiss for me.

The dance proposition fell thru so we just went on a binge New Year's Eve, however we're planning a dance in a couple of weeks and it will probably be formal.

Friday night we saw "Dumbo." It was swell. Saturday we took in one of the U.S.O. stage shows. They consist of 6 or 8 good vaudeville acts and I mean good. Two of the acts we saw were ones I've seen in the movies so you know they're good. Judy still seems to be having a good time. We don't scrap much either.

We're trying to get into our apartment ahead of the 15th now that I'm staying here. We've got a nice room, but we'd like a place of our own.

I just found out that the three officers in H & S Co. who outrank me are away so I will be acting C.O. for awhile. What a nice job that will be.

Yesterday Kit took Judy and me for a ride in B Co's half-track and this morning I took A Co's out and gave it a work out. They're quite some trucks and they don't ride at all bad across country.

That's all for now. Lots of love to you and my family,

Carp

H & S Co. 38th Engineers
January 9, 1942

Dearest Mother,

I've just spent the morning going over the company fund of H & S Co. in preparation for taking this over. The company I mean. It's a lousy job, but I've got to admit that it is kinda fun and I'm enjoying myself. The trouble with H & S is that all the men in it have definite and special jobs to do and when something out of the way comes up you can't find anyone to do it.

I've been wanting to write Pee a note but didn't know where to write so you tell her I've been wishing for her. But tell her I still won't let her cry on my shoulder. I like to cheer her on, not dry her off.

Judy hasn't threatened to divorce me yet so I guess we're getting along okay.

Lots of love to my family,

Carp

P.S. Can I call you the enquiring reporter?

H & S Co. 38th Engrs
Jan. 12, 1942

Dearest Mother,

I'm glad Pee got off to Johns Hopkins. Maybe they'll be able to help her. I sure hope.

This job is interesting and different. My hardest work so far has been organizing my work and that of two other officers. Van Hoy, the regular (a West Pointer) whom I displaced as C.O., tickles me. He treats me very much as the "boss man" and even "Sirs" me officially, and asked my permission to be away over the weekend.

What are you going to do about my clothes, and personal effects such as skis, skates, etc.? If you have to store 'em after you move out of the duplex, I can foot the bill – I sure hope I get that 1st Lt. soon.

It's really swell how your friends come to your aid isn't it? I think it also shows that you are a nice person to have such nice friends. Be a good girl and go out as often as you can. Don't hang around that house too much.

We move into 104 Sims Ave. Apt 3-A on Thursday and that'll be home for awhile, we hope. Saturday we ordered a set of every day silver and a toaster and today and tomorrow we're getting some china and some cooking utensils and stuff. I'm having fun and I think Judy is.

Kit is falling and falling hard for a darn nice kid down here. Remember my speaking of Mary, whom I'd gone dancing with just before Christmas? – Well he's been dating her ever since. Judy and I both approve so we're working on 'em both. He says he's going to propose to her if neither of the two gals he took out over Christmas turn up pregnant this month. We're hoping for him and for us too.

Lots of love to you all from we all,

Carp

H & S Co. 38ᵗʰ Engrs
Jan 17, 1942

Dearest Mother,

We're now at home at Apt 3A and having more darn fun. Judy is a good cook and I don't mean maybe. She turns out good meals with a minimum of fuss and seems to know exactly what she's doing at all times. I'm very proud of her.

Mechanically speaking though, she needs me. Yesterday afternoon she went to the store and then couldn't unlock the door when she got home, so she sat in the car until I got here. I took the lock apart and oiled it up so now it works okay. You remember me, I'm mama's little handyman around the house.

Last night Kit and Mary were out and we played bridge and ate crackers and peanut butter and drank high balls all evening. Judy got a giggling jag on and wouldn't let me go to sleep, but this morning I promptly forgave her because of the nice breakfast she got me. It's more darn fun having this place of our own even if it is awfully small. It's nice and clean and Judy keeps it as neat as a pin. In the evening I get into my robe and slippers and sit down in the big chair with my newspaper and am "lord of the manor" in great style.

Tonight we're going to a formal dance at our new officer's club as a farewell party to the Colonel. I'll bet Judy will be really neat and I'll be so proud of her.

This job is the damnedest thing. It's been keeping me busy as hell the last few days just taking care of all sorts of small administrative matters. I'm learning though, and that's what is important.

Send Phoebe my love and let me know how she's getting along please.

Lots of love to you - all,

Carp

Judy, the "good cook" confessed years later that she didn't know a thing about cooking when we got married. So each afternoon she walked down to the Butcher Shop, pointed to a cut of meat and said to the Butcher, "If you'll tell me what that is and how to cook it, I'll buy it."

Wednesday night
January 28, 1942

Dearest Mother,

I've been awful bad on letters this past week, but honestly I've been so darn busy I haven't had time to spit. This commander is a slave driver. I get here at 8:00 in the morning and go home for dinner (sometimes) and run classes in the evening 'til 7:30. Every night this week I've been here until after 7:30. And at night I'm tired. Kit and Mary were out to the house last night to play bridge and I fell asleep on the couch and slept all evening.

Sunday we drove down to Mary's home near Myrtle Beach. On the way we passed innumerable little sloughs with the "peepers" in 'em peeping away at a great rate. January 25th too. Today it's colder – about down to freezing. It's always damp here when it's cold and the cold does penetrate, but I still have to admit that the winter climate has been kinda nice.

Judy is a swell cook and I mean it. She is always fixing things up, new and different.

I've got to beat it and teach a class in rifle marksmanship, now.

Lots of love,

Carp

Sunday afternoon
February 2, 1942

Dearest Mother,

We just finished our first dinner at which we had guests. Kit is stretched out on the couch. Mary and Judy are doing the dishes and I'm writing.

For dinner Judy had French-fried scallops, creamed potatoes, stewed corn, peach salad, celery, and vanilla pudding with chocolate drops in it. It was swell, no kidding. Last night Kit took the four of us to Ships Ahoy for dinner to celebrate Mary's birthday and then we went out to the club and danced and fooled around the evening. We had a swell time. I'm teaching Judy to shoot pool.

Last week was the longest one I've spent since I got in the Army. I had a class every night and was O.D. two successive days, which meant that I spent 48 hours at the post. And once or twice a week I have to stand both reveille and retreat, which are at 7:00 a.m. and 5:15 p.m. respectively. That's a ten-hour day right there, and then a class in the evening on top of that makes a full day.

This letter was interrupted to play Hearts. Mary won. By the way, Mary and Kit got a marriage license yesterday. Maybe he's serious. It seems so.

We were going to the movie "Louisiana Purchase" tonight but somehow the schedule was balled up and it won't be at the post until later in the week. So we rode around awhile and then parked in front of the house and necked until a neighbor tried to turn the radio off thinking that we'd forgotten it. Then we got out, shot off three Roman candles, chased Kit home and came in to go to bed. –Yeah, we're crazy but we have fun.

Tomorrow we go on the rifle range. I'll get my first chance to fire the Garand Rifle.

Love from both of us,
Your kids,
Carp & Judy

Columbia, S.C.
Feb. 12, 1942

Dearest Mother,

Kit was busy this afternoon, so I took the regimental basketball team up to the Field House to practice, and I (your unintelligent son) practiced with them. I'm so stiff and sore I can hardly move and expect to be a complete wreck tomorrow.

We've been busy preparing to move. We don't and won't know exactly where until after we sail, but from the preparations we think it will be a rather barren island somewhere near the equator. We think that the only communication will be by short-wave radio. If that is so, I'll try to send word how I am, but don't worry if you don't hear. I will write if I can send letters, you can be sure of that. Preparations also seem to verify the information that as soon as we complete the job, we'll leave it. I hope so.

Judy isn't sure just what she'll do, but I think she's coming home first off. She will keep in touch with you. I think we leave around the 1st and she'll be home then.

Judy just got in from a tea party the gals had with the Major's wife today. Should I give her hell for not having supper ready? –I guess not.

The new Colonel & Mrs. will be at home to the Officers & Ladies of the regiment on Sunday afternoon. It's a darn shame we have to go for a ride that afternoon or we'd go to it. –After the screwing he gave us on promotions I wouldn't touch him with a ten-foot pole. They decided that only two 2nd lieutenants would be promoted and then they picked two of the lowest ranking 2nds (men with only three months service) and jumped them over our heads. Am I mad! I think I'll probably be a 2nd Lt. for another six months now. And no real reason for it either.

We're still having a swell time. No offspring this month.

Judy says hello and to send you some love, but not all because I must keep some.

I wrote Flossie – a lousy letter because I couldn't say what I feel. But she's my pet.

Lots of love, Honey,

Carp

Monday night
Feb. 23, 1942

Hello Toots Honey,

I've been an awful rat about writing, but honest I've been busier than hell. We're going into this thing pretty well stripped down and we've been turning in property right and left. Last week I had to turn in our half-tracks, our pontoon bridges, and our extra trucks. Now I've been made supply officer for H & S Co. – A lot of promotions came through but Kit and I are still 2nd Lts. Two boys who were 2nd Lts. with us when we came down here in May are now Captains, so maybe your little boy isn't as good as he thinks he is. And Kit and three other lieutenants are being transferred to the 12th Engineers and not going with us.

Judy is coming home this weekend and ought to be in by Monday or Tuesday and she thinks she'll be able to get her old job back. She'll be staying at home and will probably be seeing you pretty frequently. I'm giving her your power-of-attorney for me and want her to get the car in both of our names. So when you see my little battered blue Ford around town you can pretend it's me.

We ship from a southern port sometime after Saturday. I'll write as often as I can to both Mrs. Carpenters, and honest, I won't be quite as bad as I have been, but mail will probably be erratic.

I'm wearing a nifty new wristwatch – issued by the government and tomorrow I'll have my two new pairs of glasses at gov. expense. So I'm beginning to make out in this man's Army.

Judy and I have been having just the most perfect time. She can cook TOO, and even if she couldn't "Oh boy, what a wife!" I'm gonna miss having her in my bedroll. With her working and me sending home my base pay, she figures to be able to pay off most of my debts and get me in pretty fair financial state. It's the kind of wife to have. She's fed us damn well on $15.00 for 23 days this month.

Lots of love to you,

Carp

South Carolina
March 3, 1942

Dearest Mother,

Boy, one more hectic week is behind. We pulled out of Jackson this morning and are now at the Overseas Departure and Replacement Depot outside of Charleston, S.C.

Judy was going to leave sometime this afternoon or tomorrow and expected to take about three days for the trip. She was pretty well fixed for tires so she ought to make it pretty much O.K.

Talk about surprises. Capt. Wilcox walked up to me this afternoon and informed me that he was part of the Medical Detachment going with us. I think having my family doctor going along with us is stretching the long arm of coincidence a bit.

I've started missing Judy already, and worrying a little. Thankfully she's a reliable little wench and pretty damn good at looking after herself. Gee, but we did have a swell nine weeks of mussing around. I'm a lucky guy to have such a swell wife. That's a pretty big trip for an inexperienced driver, but she's darn good and getting more confident the more she drives. She gets such a big kick out of that little Ford that it makes me feel good to think of her driving it around home.

That's all for now.
Lots of love to you, Mother.

Your affectionate son,

Carp

Addressed to:

Miss Phoebe Lose
Huntsville, Alabama
c/o W.C. Flack

March 3, 1942

Dear Aunt Pee,

You wouldn't guess in a million years whom I ran into this afternoon and who asked about you. He's with the attached Medical Hospital Unit that is going with us. Capt. W.W. Wilcox. I don't think I've ever been more surprised than I was when I ran into him.

Mother's reports on your progress at Johns Hopkins were very encouraging. I sure do hope you're really getting better, and that the climate there in Alabam' is right for you. I know the environment can't help but be good.

Every once in awhile Mother writes me of something that Uncle Bill has been doing in his work and I swell up with pride. That work he's doing is damned important. If more people in this country would begin to realize that to date we've lost every round of this war and that we can't start to win until we have the equipment to attack and not just defend. In a way, I'm pleased about this move of ours because it's a chance to get in and start really working toward winning.

But I've started to miss Judy already. She's an awfully nice wife and I don't mean maybe. When this war is over, I'll have to take her around to meet the family.

Lots of love,

Carp

March 8, 1942

Dearest Mother,

I wrote you a letter Tuesday night when we hit this place (Overseas Discharge and Replacement Depot), but learned last night that they usually don't send letters out from here until after the detachment has left. So if you get this first you'll know when the other arrives that we're on our way, but if you've already gotten the other, it don't mean nuttin partickular.

We've been indulging in physical exercise, close order drill, games, and hikes since we arrived in order to keep the boys happy and me tired, and boy it has worked. I've averaged 10 hours sleep a night, except for Fri. night when I went into town and called Judy. She's something, isn't she? Imagine driving 700 miles in two days with the little experience that she'd had. I was so proud of her I damn near busted.

After we leave here my mail will all be censored so if it seems kinda impersonal you'll understand why.

The more I learn about this trip the more pleased I am about it. We're going on a real job and no kidding.

You'll get a form post card after we arrive and it's quite a trip so don't worry.

Ask Judy to show you the two cartoons one of my boys made of H & S Co. taking a hike.

No mail for over a week now, so I can't answer anything. Don't forget to write me at APO 877 c/o Post Master, New York, N.Y. (Lt. GHC - H & S - 38th Engrs). They will delete the outfit number before sending it on a boat, but they have to have it to start it right.

Lots of love,

Your affectionate son,

Carp

Dear Toots

Chapter 3

Ascension Island

On the front of this envelope and all subsequent envelopes is an ink stamp stating that it was "Passed by U S Army Examiner".

At sea - March 25, 1942

U.S. ARMY POSTAL SERVICE
APR
02
1942
A. P. O.

PASSED BY
U 01234 S
ARMY EXAMINER

Dearest Mother,

These restrictions on what you may or may not write have us a little befuddled. I re-wrote my letter to Judy three times, finishing it today. If you both get letters about the same time then they both were okay. If neither one gets through... Well, I tried. Mail service is going to be pretty lousy I'm afraid, but one thing you can be certain and that is that I'll be thinking about home and you and Judy plenty.

We have an important job to do and we're going to do it. But I think that some of us are going to be a little homesick and me especially for the little old Loyalsock Creek. Only one swim in her last summer and probably none this summer ain't so good.

The size of this ocean tends to get me down, but lately I've been sleeping on deck at night and those familiar groups of stars help a lot. They are a little misplaced, but essentially they're okay.

Enclosed is a check for $10.00. Five of which is for you and five is to take you and Judy on a little binge some night. I had intended it for Easter corsages for both of you, but I guess this letter will get home too late. Take in a good movie on that binge because that's something I'm afraid I won't be seeing very much and certainly not new ones.

I haven't forgotten the $50.00 I borrowed. You can count on it in June. If you get in a spot for dough, see Judy because she's handling most of the Carpenter finances now. That (the fifty) may or may not come in two installments beginning in May. Depends on how we get paid.

Whenever you write, will you give me news of the family? Uncle Tod's and Uncle Jim's gangs too. Remember to write on one side only because of censoring and tell Judy this too. The censors will be in New York and will be absolutely impersonal from that end.

> Lots and lots of love to you, Dearest.
>
> Your affectionate son,
>
> *Carpy*

After nearly a four-week voyage (with a stop in Brazil along the way) we arrived at our destination—Ascension Island, a seven-mile-wide island in the southern Atlantic between South America and Africa. Our orders were to build a top secret air base, including a runway, fuel farm, radar station, sleeping quarters, and a mess hall, for the purpose of refueling fighter planes being flown across the Atlantic to Africa & Europe.

Before our 1,700+ men arrived, the island was inhabited by about 30 British citizens and 50 natives from another island several hundred miles away. The residents ran communications for the British.

The island was mostly lava fields, although at the highest point (elevation about 2,700 feet) there was a two-acre bamboo rainforest. Just below that, elevation-wise, was approximately 400 acres of green farmland, which tapered into the volcanic rock.

In one spot there was a huge crater, over a mile wide and with walls 30-80 feet high. The crater was filled with white sand and had a little oasis in the middle of it.

NEW YORK WORLD TELEGRAM

Girl Finds Paradise On So. Atlantic Isle

Just back from a 12,000-mile whirlwind airplane tour, Ann Jacobs, 25 Fifth Ave., tall, trim and 24, bubbled with excitement today recounting her experiences as the first woman correspondent to reach Ascension Island and the only woman on the island during her five days there.

Traveling in an Army Transport Command C-46, Miss Jacobs, never out of the country before, also made stops at Puerto Rico, Trinidad, British Guiana, Brazil, Haiti, Jamaica and Cuba.

Ascension Island lies in the middle of the South Atlantic. It is a 35-square-mile area of lava waste, topped with one mountain abounding in vegetation. Owned by Great Britain, it is used by the ATC as a refueling base.

About it, members of the ATC quip:

"If we miss Ascension
My wife gets a pension."

"Ascension is the island once considered too lonely even for Napoleon in exile," says Miss Jacobs. "Except for the absence of women, today it is a paradise. Grass, trees and flowers adorn the mountain. Cattle, sheep and horses roam it, grazing. Trade winds cool the island's shores. Fish fight to get on a line. And, unlike the Garden of Eden, Ascension has no snakes.

"The morale of our men is astonishingly high. The food, all brought in, is good. New movies are shown daily. The boys take part in sports, play baseball at Ebbets Field, Yankee Stadium and Shibe Park. They all talk of coming home when it's all over. But they often vote against rotation within their theater."

Within four of the seven weeks on tour Miss Jacobs encountered the four seasons of the year.

Miss Jacobs, a graduate of Sweet Briar College, Va., is an associate editor of Young America, a national weekly for youth. She will write a series of articles on ATC's operations.

Ann Jacobs

World-Telegram Photo by Palumbo.

Article written after Ascension was declassified

Along one edge of the island was a beach that looked to be covered by a strip of sand 70-80 feet wide. But it wasn't sand. It was finely-ground seashells. We slept on that beach for the first month before moving up and building a base near the site where we were building the airfield.

The island didn't have an adequate fresh water supply when we arrived. For drinking water, we had to install pumps to suck up ocean water, boil it, collect the steam, and cool it.

We nicknamed our new home "The Rock."

Destination - April 8, 1942

Dearest Mother,

Letters from me are going to be pretty infrequent for awhile because of the difficulty writing them and mailing them. We're still in our temporary camp on the beach and my footlocker and barracks bag are stored up at headquarters, so I'm living out of a musette bag. My shirt is so dirty that when I take it off it stands on the beach and waves at the ships going by. A bath is again a luxury and I shave every 2 or 3 days if the idea strikes me.

Easter Sunday struck me funny. We're about a couple of hours or so ahead of you on time so about the time that people at home were going to church, I was starting out on a surveying cruise to lay out a preliminary center line for the project I have. Instead of new Easter clothes, I had on a very dirty uniform, a .45 on one hip, a canteen on the other, and a pair of binoculars over my shoulder. My sun helmet is practically standard equipment with me nowadays because you get a headache going without one, but I can go without a shirt most of the day and I'm really brown. We'd have made a marvelous contrast strolling down little old Broad Street.

It's been over a month since I've had a letter from either you or Judy now and I practically have lost the feeling that there is such a place as home, except that I dream of getting back to it all the time. To get a cold drink of good, clear water or even better yet a milk shake and to have a chair to sit down in, boy oh boy! Don't get me wrong though, it's rugged here but actually not a bad life after the first few days. The days are full. I get up at 6:00, on the job by 7:00, work 'til noon and an hour for lunch in the field, work 'til 5:00, come in and get a short swim to clean up and eat at 6:00. It gets dark about 7:00 so we sit around and bat the breeze until about 9:00 or occasionally (like this) come up here to headquarters where there's a light and write a letter. And at 9:00 I retire for the night.

The last two days we've had a crew of three men to help us and we've been doing the preparatory blasting on our project. I'm getting to be a fairly experienced powder man, having now used dynamite, blasting gelatin, nitro-starch, and TNT with time fuse, instantaneous fuse, and electrical hook-up and I've performed all operations from drilling the holes to capping the shots and setting them off. Maybe I can get a job when I get home, who knows.

The waters around here are lousy with game fish. Sunday morning Doc Keseric and Doc Wilcox were out for an hour and a half and got better than 350 pounds of real good fish. Three fish made up that weight, and were they good eating.

This is a dumb letter because I'm awfully sleepy. I'll try to do better later. Lots of love to you, Mother.

Your affectionate son,

Carpy

P.S. Enclosed is $15.00 to put toward the $50.00 I owe.

After we'd been on the island a few weeks, we got word that our supply ship had been torpedoed and we would not be re-supplied for a while. We sent some of our guys out fishing. For the next few days, our 1700+ guys ate fish.

Fortunately a few days later, our supply ship DID show up. They'd been torpedoed, but hadn't been hit. So they'd turned off their communication systems and had laid low for a while, until they could get safely to us.

The Booby Bird Is Not So Dumb

By the Associated Press.

WASHINGTON, Dec. 29, 1945.—And now the hazards of war include booby birds.

On a tiny ascension island in the South Atlantic, the army built an airport and made it one of the most strategic points of the world through the funneling into Africa of 5000 planes.

But in building the field, the War Department disclosed yesterday, birds of the tern and booby families insisted on nesting at the foot of the runway, making plane take-offs dangerous.

The army imported cats which promptly took care of the terns. But the boobies—which are so-called because of their apparent stupidity—were smart enough to catch the cats and carry them off.

Finally the army imported a bird expert who advised stealing the eggs of the booby and covering the nesting places with chicken wire, which proved effective.

April 23, 1942

Dearest Mother,

There are so many questions I'd like to know the answers that I don't know where to start. Some of the answers are probably in the mail between here and home, but Lord only knows where. First I'd like to know that both you and Judy are well and doing okay and then I'd like to know how Phoebe is and how your job is going and what you did about the house, and a lot of things. Someday soon I'll find out, I hope.

Me, I'm doing swell, working moderately hard, fairly long hours, and eating lots and sleeping enough. No booze, no women, some song. The climate is marvelous and everything leads to a good life. I should be in damn fine shape when we move from here. My project (I can't describe it at all) is moving along very satisfactorily. I've got plenty to keep me busy and interested for awhile yet. That's the one thing I fear on duty of this sort, boredom. It could really get you down.

I'm now company censor and have to read all the mail going out of H & S Co. If my letters seem kinda stilted, it's because I'm so used to reading, "Dear Mom, I'm fine, censor won't let me write more, G'bye. Your son," end quote. Actually it is pretty hard to write, especially the kind of letters I always wrote to you describing everything I've been doing. We don't dare talk about our work and our amusements are not many. We read a little, listen to the Victrolas playing the records the U.S.O gave us, see a movie once and sometimes twice a week and that's about all. I get up at 5:00 a.m. now and work 'til 5:00 p.m. often. It's dark around 7:00, so I hit the hay pretty early. My hours and shifts have been changing some but will settle down pretty soon.

I think about home quite a bit, especially in the evenings, but I'm not homesick in the real sense. I just want to do this job as soon as possible and get back to normal.

We don't dare lose, so we'll work like hell to win!

So long, Mother.

Lots of love,

Carp

Plans for the runway required that it be 6000 feet long and 200 feet wide. There wasn't a level spot anywhere on the island that was big enough to accommodate it. The best possible location was anything but level and passed right between two extinct volcanoes.

We set to work, digging tunnels and then placing explosives to blow out the excess rock. We hauled away the rock with wheelbarrows or with trucks when trucks could access the area.

In one section, we dug thirty tunnels (by hand and with compressed air tools) under the lava field and placed approximately one ton of blasting powder in each tunnel. We set them off all at once and the blast threw rock almost to where we'd withdrawn, a mile and a half away.

After the dust settled, we moved in with bulldozers to start removing the rock. Suddenly one of the men came running over to me and asked me to come look at something. It turned out that one of the tunnels hadn't blown. I pulled the guys back a quarter of a mile or so, set a cap and retreated to where I thought we'd be safe. When that tunnel blew, it rained down rock as far back as we were, sending us all diving for cover under trucks or anything else we could find. Fortunately, no one was hurt.

On the next shift, they found a second tunnel that hadn't gone during the initial explosion, and had to blow that one up as well. They had learned from our mistake and got the job done without anyone having to dodge flying rocks.

Even with all that blasting, it was impossible to make the runway completely level. We ended up with about 200 feet elevation gain over the first part of the runway, then a loss of 300 feet, after which it leveled out.

In the area between the two volcanoes, we had to blast quite a bit of rock out of the way, leaving the runway with a 40-foot wall of rock on one side and about 80 feet on the other.

One volcano was much larger than the other. Once the runway had been completed and put into use, we discovered that the pilots tended to steer away from the larger volcano, putting them in danger of clipping the smaller one. We solved that problem by painting an arrow down the center of the runway to keep them on track.

May 12, 1942
Overseas

Dearest Mother,

Your itinerant correspondent is back again. I'd be ashamed of myself for not writing oftener if it weren't for the fact that there is nothing to write and no way to send it if I did write. I have in my case now a letter to Judy written two weeks ago and still no mail out. However there is a chance of some going out in the next week or so and that's why I'm getting these in.

It has been more than two months now since we've received any mail so I haven't the slightest idea how things are going at home, and I don't dare let myself worry about it because there's damn little I could do. I certainly do hope that you got everything straightened out okay.

I still can't tell you where I am or what we're doing, but being a newspaper woman, you may know by now. I rather expect to celebrate my birthday here, however. Remember the box that you sent me last year? Boy, what I wouldn't give for one like it this year. That is not a hint, though, because it would not be feasible to even attempt to send anything like that to me with mail service as lousy as it is.

The enclosed money order for $50.00 is to clean up that loan you made me at Christmas. With the $15.00 I sent before, it will pay the interest and leave you a dollar for a new hat. I really ought to be there to help you pick out the hat, though, because our combined taste is so good.

DISTRICT MEN ON ASCENSION

Two Montoursville Officers Once Stationed on Lonely Island

ONE NOW ON FURLOUGH

Lt.-Col. W. W. Wilcox to Be Reassigned—Lt. G. H. Carpenter at New Post

Unknown to most of the world until a few days ago, Ascension Island is a very real place to two Montoursville men, Lt.-Col. W. W. Wilcox, of the army medical corps, and Lt. Grant H. Carpenter, of the army engineers.

The rocky little isle in the South Atlantic Ocean, disclosed by the War Department to be a vital link in the route supplying airplanes to the armed forces in Africa and described by a Reader's Digest correspondent as "the loneliest spot in the world," was "home" for more than 21 months to Lt.-Col. Wilcox, while Lt. Carpenter was on the island for about six months.

Lt.-Col. Wilcox, former Montoursville physician, is now spending a leave with his wife and two children at his home, 531 Broad Street, pending reassignment to a new station. Lt. Carpenter, husband of Mrs. Judy Carpenter, of 721 Market Street, this city, already has been reassigned to another post.

Secrecy Necessary

The two were among the first to land on Ascension, which is located roughly about half way between South America and Africa, in March, 1942, when the army decided to build a landing field there. Utmost secrecy veiled the movement and none of the men there was permitted to say where he was stationed until late last month.

Lt.-Col. Wilcox, a major when the troops arrived on Ascension, was a member of the hospital staff there until January, 1943, when he was made commanding officer of the hospital and surgeon of the armed forces on the island and promoted to his present rank.

Construction of Wideawake Field on the island was begun the day that Lt. Carpenter and other engineers moved in and began working day and night on the pile of volcanic rock, cinders, dirt, and one oasis of vegetation on a mountainside, according to an Associated Press dispatch from Washington. The work was completed in three months amid the greatest secrecy, the dispatch said, and only the most essen-

Continued on Page 2, Column 5, This Section

January, 1946

TWO DISTRICT MEN ON ASCENSION ISLE

Continued from Page 1, This Section

tial shipping was permitted near the island so attention would not be called to the project.

Serves as Plane Funnel

Since that time, the Associated Press reported, Ascension, which measures only five miles by seven, has served as a funnel for shipping 5,000 planes to Africa.

Writing in the New York World-Telegram, Peter Edson said that "selection of the island as a refueling base for the Air Transport Command came after the generals running the ATC wished that they had such a half-way base, then looked at a map to see that Ascension Island was right where they wanted it. With auxiliary fuel tanks, fighter planes could make the South Atlantic crossing in two hops, easily.

"But the island was a British possession. That meant making a deal with the British, which proved far easier than the next obstacle encountered—the fact that the island was volcanic, with 2,800-foot Green Mountain rising in its middle, and extremely triangular lava rock terrain cut by deep gorges, and no place level or big enough for an airport.

Landing Strip Finished

"That did not stop the engineers who were given the job of building a field in 90 days. Eighty-seven days later a minor peak that loomed up in the middle of the runway which the engineers mapped out had been removed. And in its place was a beautiful, 7,000-foot, hard-surfaced landing strip that has accommodated hundreds of American planes on their way to the fronts."

In a story in the January issue of the Reader's Digest, John Gunther declares that "Ascension is the loneliest and most isolated place I have ever seen on earth, or water. Before the war, not more than one ship a year stopped there. The nearest land is St. Helena, about 800 miles away, where Napoleon was 'detained' by the British until his death in 1821. Except for that, there is nothing but the vastness, the inconceivable emptiness, of the Atlantic. The British first picked Ascension for Napoleon's exile, but then reconsidered. Ascension was, they thought, too lonely."

Only community on the island, Gunther continued, is Georgetown, where live about 75 British subjects. Since the Americans arrived, however, the writer said, "the whole island is swarming with crowded activity. Several thousand American troops comprise its lively, vigorous garrison.

LT.-COL. W. W. WILCOX

LT. GRANT H. CARPENTER

81

I'm anxious to hear your comments on the current situation. We pick up some news by radio but it's mostly brief summaries and very little analysis. I'd like to know what the boys like Kaltenborn and Swing are saying. Is it as good as the summaries sound, or are we hearing a lot of propaganda?

Remember me telling you that my Fraternity brother, Gil, was headed to the South Pacific? Well since the fall of Bataan, I've been worrying about Gil's people. I want to write to them, and yet, not knowing any more than I do, I can't write for fear of saying just exactly the wrong thing. This year in the Army plus a couple of months of overseas duty have me at the point where I don't know a thing about either my family or my friends.

That's all for this time. Maybe I'll get back in the letter writing groove when I've got some to answer. By the way, the reason for the complete $50.00 this month is that I hit a lucky streak at poker the other night.

So long now.

Lots and lots of love,

Carp

Hans Von Kaltenborn was an American radio newscaster whose news analysis was highly regarded throughout WWII. Raymond Graham Swing was another well-known American newscaster.

Western Union   JULY 8, 1942

MARGARET CARPENTER
722 MARKET ST SOUTH WILLIAMSPORT (PENN)
HAPPY BIRTHDAY TOOTS EVERYTHING OKAY HERE MY
LOVE TO YOU AND JUDY
GRANT CARPENTER

Ascension Island did not have an easy place for ships to dock because of the shallowness of the water. Ships had to anchor about three-quarters of a mile offshore. As a result, once we got the tanks built and installed for the fuel farm, we had to build a long pipeline and float it out to sea far enough for ships to hook into.

Our supply ships couldn't get close to the island either, so we used a 30-foot boat to unload them and to ferry the supplies to shore. That was dangerous work. One day one of our guys fell off the little boat and would've been crushed between the two if a couple of his fellow shipmates hadn't reached down and snatched him out of harm's way just before the ships bumped together.

July 15, 1942

Dearest Mother,

I'm kinda behind on my letters to you, but I haven't forgotten how to write. It's just that I've been working long hours and didn't expect to be able to mail any for awhile yet. I got an unexpected chance to send some out the other day, but only had a short one to Judy finished so I'll try and get a little more news in this.

We got two batches of mail in the past week containing almost all of our mail since Mar 10th thru to June 10. I've been a happy lad reading all that I got. The newsy ones from you are just tops and of course Judy's are perfect. I'm a lucky guy and I know it. No <u>Grits</u> in this last batch of mail though, or not as yet.

I won't answer all questions in this letter, but will work on it a little at a time.

The news of Aunt Pee is encouraging. I hope she does get back to work. Aren't Aunt Edie and Uncle Bill a couple of bricks to be looking out for her and letting her live with them?

I'm still working 10 to 12 hours a day and the regiment is doing a bang-up job here. We've had two days off since hitting this place. On the first one we held a regimental field day and H & S Co. walked away with everything. We got the cups for the softball tournament, the two-mile relay and the track & field championship. I anchored the relay team and the boys gave me such a lead I could have walked home.

I'm on a new project again. Every time we finish one I catch a new one right away quick.

Most of my swell tan has disappeared because I've had to wear a shirt all the time on the job, but I'm in the pink of condition. Too healthy for any good, but I miss Judy like hell.

The first thing I want when I get back to the states is an ice cream cone. Oh yeah!

I hear 'Command Performance' on the radio almost every week and really enjoy it. And once in awhile I hear that half-hour program in the evenings sponsored by the Army newspaper.

Did my cable and birthday present get there okay? Let's see, that makes you about 39, doesn't it?

Boy, all my old gang are in the Army now, aren't they? Baldy, Champ, George, Jack, Dutch, and myself. All I gotta say is "What in hell are the women doin'?" That practically leaves the old town without a wolf.

I had a nice letter from Aunt Kitty, and a couple of letters from Pee and a box of toll house cookies from Edie (M-m-m-m-m they were good), and Elizabeth sent me a nice bunch of books, which were very welcome. And a couple letters from Aunt Carrie. I really made a haul in this mail, but boy I needed it after four months.

I was glad to hear that Al got his commission. I'll bet Hattie and Al Sr. are proud of him and rightly so. Tell him I said "Congratulations" on the wings.

Who knows, we may bump into each other yet in this war.

I still don't know if I'll see you before this shindig is over or not. But even if I don't, you keep in there pitching. I think your method of helping is real good.

> So long for now, Mother,
>
> Your affectionate son,
>
> *Carp*

P.S. Say "Hello" to the gang for me and a hug for Hattie.

Our mission on The Rock was a well-kept military secret. Just before completing the runway, a plane circled the island looking for a place to land. We fired at him before he got close enough for us to recognize the plane's markings as a British plane, at which point we quit shooting and he landed. He had come from an aircraft carrier and was out exploring, not realizing that the island was inhabited.

July 29, 1942

Dearest Mother,

This will be just a short note in answer to your letter of the 19th. Phoebe ought to be better off in Tucson and on her own again before she forgets how to work.

Apparently some mail of ours was mislaid in June because I sent a money order to the bank and a couple of checks for birthday presents for you and Pee. I'm going to check up on it. In the meantime, I'm enclosing a check for $50.00. Will you send Pee $10.00 for her birthday if you haven't got the other and use the rest for yourself?

I've got my new allotment papers fixed at last, I think, and starting the first of October you'll get a check each month for $40.00. It ain't much, but it'll help you over the edges.

I had a hell of a time today. Got a bulldozer stuck while cleaning out a gravel bank. Then the bank caved in on us. Now the dozer's got tons of dirt on top of it and it's still stuck. Tomorrow we're really going to dig for it.

Had a letter from Kit and he's doing okay. Judy told me that they (Kit and Mary) are going to have an addition in January. Some stuff. Doesn't seem right for Kit to be a pappa.

Didn't Judy tell you that our first girl will be Judith Ann C. (Jackie for short)? But not for awhile yet, Grammaw.

You're getting to be quite the reporter. I'm darn proud of you. How many more from <u>Grit</u>, that I know, are in the service now?

I was in my supply sergeant's tent last night. I think his tent mate is going nuts. He was running around chasing (not swatting) the flies and muttering, "They keep me awake in the day time and I'm gonna keep them awake at night." —He works nights and tries to sleep days. —Who knows? Maybe he's got something.

I'm so glad you feel about Judy as you do. Personally, I'm sure I picked right.

Bye now.
Love,

Carp

Mountain Moved for Base
Ascension Island Airfield Job

By PETER EDSON,
World-Telegram Washington Correspondent.

WASHINGTON, Dec. 28, 1945.—Use of 34-square-mile Ascension Island as a United States air base can at last be talked about. For over a year this tiny British island, 500 miles south of the equator in the middle of the South Atlantic Ocean, has been a stopping point for short-range fighter planes being ferried to southern European and African fronts, and even to the Middle and Far East.

It is perfectly situated for such use, being approximately 1500 miles east of Natal on the Brazil bulge and equidistant from American and British air bases on the southern coast of the African bulge. Its selection as a refueling base for the Air Transport Command came in, in fact, after the generals running the ATC wished that they had such a half-way base, then looked at a map to see that Ascension Island was right where they wanted it. With auxiliary fuel tanks, fighter planes could make the South Atlantic crossing in two hops, easily.

Peter Edson.

But the island was a British possession. That meant making a deal with the British, which proved far easier than the next obstacle encountered—the fact that the island was volcanic, with 2800-foot Green Mountain rising in its middle, an extremely triangular lava rock terrain cut by deep gorges, and no place level or big enough for an airport.

That did not stop the engineers who were given the job of building a field in 90 days. Eighty-seven days later a minor peak that loomed up in the middle of the runway which the engineers mapped out, had been removed. And in its place was a beautiful, 7000-foot, hard-surfaced landing strip that has accommodated hundreds of American planes on their way to the fronts.

* * *

Use of Ascension as a United States air base has been one of the Army's worst-kept secrets. When Gen. George C. Marshall's biennial report was issued, last summer, it revealed that United States troops were then stationed in some 80 foreign countries and island possessions. On a map accompanying the report, showing where all these places were, the name of little Ascension stood out prominently in the South Atlantic. A legend indicated that United States troops had been stationed there since March, 1942.

Everything in the Marshall report was supposed to be off the restricted list and on the record, but efforts to learn more about what went on at Ascension met with flat refusals. Ascension was supposed to be a very hush-hush operation, and the Air Transport Command didn't want anything said about it.

Then, a few days ago, a luncheon-club speaker in Washington, in full possession of all the facts, talked freely about Ascension and said it was all right for the story to be told, without attribution. That's how it got out.

* * *

But this won't be the end of the Ascension Island story. Being another one of these American-built - paid - for - and - maintained bases on British territory, it will become a topic for argument in deciding its postwar use. The strong nationalist point of view is that all such bases, wherever built, should remain as American bases. United States-built military air bases at Newfoundland, Bermuda and other points involved in the swap of old destroyers to the British will remain under the American flag during the 99-year lease, but cannot be used for commercial aircraft.

Some of the leading commercial airline executives are of the opinion that this is unimportant because most of these bases are not on what will be the commercial postwar air routes. Ascension Island, before the war, was certainly no great asset, except for millions of terns and sea turtles which went there to lay eggs. Its human population numbered 300, mostly living in the one community of George Town.

A STOP-OFF FOR OUR FIGHTING PLANES ON THEIR WAY TO WAR

Chapter 4

Leopoldville, The Congo

Originally we'd been told that when we finished on Ascension Island, we'd be sent back to the States. But someone up the ladder decided we were too good of an engineering company to disband. So instead of home, our next stop was Africa, to build and enlarge airfields, starting in Leopoldville, The Congo.

Sept. 1, 1942

Somewhere in Africa

Dearest Mother,

How we do get around. I got your swell letter of Aug. 10 yesterday. That's not bad service to the heart of the Dark Continent in these days, even if we're not exactly in the heart of the place. Anyway, I'm farther into Africa than I ever expected to get.

You and Judy write the nicest newsy letters. I have two from you and one from her since leaving my last station. But it's hard for us to write because we really do have to be careful that no information of military value gets out. I'm especially conscious of it because I am still the censor for my company.

The eggbeater twirled again and I now have a Capt. Nosek as C.O. and Lt. Davis as the other Lt. in H & S Co. Judy knows both of them. I think we'll all work well together and have a darn good company. My job is to handle the motor pool, which interests and pleases me a great deal.

Pee writes to me every once in awhile and I have written to her twice since we started receiving mail. She sent me a lot of these paper-backed novels, which I got just the other day. They are very welcome.

The latest G.I. rumor says that we Reserve Officers will be allowed $150.00 to recompense us for the uniforms which we have bought. It's a graft, but if it's true I'm going to save part of it to buy me a good set of tailored tails when this brawl is over. I've always wanted them and I think that's a good chance to get them.

Did Judy get a letter at the same time you got the check for $50.00 with a check in it for her birthday?

They just stuck me with my third typhus shot and the needle was so long they stuck it in my left arm and I got the shot in my right. Well, almost. Anyway I could taste it.

I'm eating a piece of Nestle's milk chocolate that they sell here. It's made up especially for the tropics and has quite a bit of paraffin in it, but it's still darn good to a guy what ain't had none in a long time.

We've only been here three days, but already we have a well-organized, comfortable camp, with floors in our tents. That's to keep insects from eating us up. (In time, the termites will eat up the floors, but then we'll move on or build new ones.) We've got showers, recreation, supply and mess tents with everything. That's the way this regiment works, quick and on the beam. Don't get the idea that we think we're good. –We damn well know we're good. Just ask 'em about our last job. They'll tell you. One reason for the rush is to get set before the rainy season sets in. Mosquitoes aren't too bad now but they say that later they'll be in rare form.

You've got to stop this praising Judy all the time. She'll have as swelled a head as I, and that'll never work. Personally, I'm kinda partial to her too.

Judy says she's painting her legs and all I gotta say is, quote, "Some legs. I'd sure like to see them."

Have to quit now and censor other guys' mail.

Lots and lots of love,

Carp

Vital African Routes a Problem to War Strategists

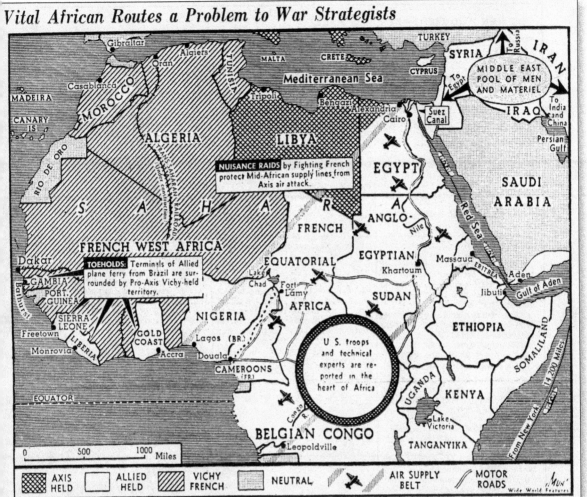

Vichy propaganda, possibly a prelude to severing relations with the United States, brings France's African holdings squarely into focus in this war of continents.

Neutral press sources have carried the story that Hitler has increased pressure on Laval to sever diplomatic relations with the United States to permit German "protection" of France-in-Africa.

The seriousness of such an Axis acquisition cannot be discounted. Nor can the growing importance of Allied holdings in Africa and the good use to which they are being put as American men and supplies pile up there in tremendous quantities for future use against the Axis.

The bulge of Africa has assumed major importance in the Allied scheme of things since planes and critical munitions began to move via air from Brazil across the South Atlantic's 1,600 mile "narrows" to Allied bases in West Africa, thence across Africa's waist to Egypt, the Middle East, Russia, India or China.

Interruption of this steady flow of fighting planes, equipment and technical experts would be serious indeed.

Yet every one of the Allied "toeholds" on the African bulge is a relatively small chunk of real estate surrounded on three sides by Vichy-owned territory.

Dominating the bulge is the heavily fortified Vichy naval base at Dakar. In German hands this could be the ultimate jumpoff for a later move on South America.

Of more immediate concern is the fact that it would threaten the plane ferry landing and would be a magnificent operational base for surface and U-boat attacks on the seaborne traffic to the Allied fronts.

There is no doubt that the Allied high command is concerned over the possibility that Laval will stooge for the Nazis and turn over French holdings in Africa.

It has recently been reported that United States technical troops have been installed in the Belgian Congo and French Equatorial Africa where the Fighting French are in control.

This tends to indicate that the United Nations will make a major effort to counter an Axis-Vichy merger. Fighting French patrols have, with little equipment and makeshift supply lines, ranged far into Libya to dominate the southern part of that Italian colony.

A considerable body of military opinion holds that a desert trained expeditionary force, supplied by cargo planes, could penetrate northward into Libya to menace the rear of Axis troops now in Egypt. The northern portion of French Equatorial Africa could likewise be the jumpoff for activity against French West Africa, and could be similarly supplied.

There is also the possibility that the air ferry route from Brazil could be changed, with stopovers at British-owned islands in the South Atlantic to lessen the menace of Dakar and Vichy territory in Africa's bulge.

It is certain that action in Africa heretofore confined to the Mediterranean coast and East Africa, could well spread to the whole continent.

Both sides have vital stakes in Africa. Transport and operational bases there could quite easily have a direct bearing on the outcomes of the gigantic campaigns in Russia, Egypt, India or China – which is to say the fighting fronts of the world.

THE MEN WHO FIGHT—By ERNIE PYLE

Tough Army Engineers Work At Record Pace in Jungles

Living in 'White Man's Graveyard,' They Build Camps, Airfields, Hospitals, Roads, Bridges and Barracks

Special Radio to BUFFALO EVENING NEWS.

SOMEWHERE IN AFRICA, June 23.—One of the sagas of this war, and one that can't be fully written until after the war, is the career of the —— Combat Engineers.

They have yet to hear the crack of an enemy gun, but their overseas record already is talked about throughout Africa. They have been away from home since the Spring of 1942. They are one of the proudest organizations I've ever come across. They brag about what they've taken and swear they are yenning for more.

These particular engineers build airfields and depots and barracks for other soldiers. But it isn't so much what they have built as where they built it, and how.

No Mail for 3½ Months.

On their first and biggest job they lived for five months in an isolation that few other American troops have known. They worked day and night. The only way they knew when Sunday came was that the colonel would put on a necktie.

They wore out their gloves and worked with bandaged hands. Supplies failed to reach them on schedule, so they went on half rations and then on quarter rations. Each man got only one quart of water a day.

They had no entertainment of any kind and no mail for 3½ months. Some mail did come at the end of two months, but it was all fourth-class, including a sackful of training manuals for troops in Arctic climates.

Kill Two Elephants

These were the first American troops to hit the Congo. They built an immense base camp in record time, when the natives had said it couldn't be built at all. Then, in squads and platoons and companies, they pushed deep into all parts of Central Africa.

They built emergency airfields all over the veldt and through the deep jungle. They built one air-drome from scratch in 20 days. They built hospitals, roads and bridges and set up barracks for the troops that were to follow. But not for themselves.

The outfit has its fun as well as its work. They have killed two elephants. They hunt antelope, deer, buffalo and crocodiles. Snakes don't even count. Monkeys and leopards were accumulated as pets.

Unglamorous Work

One company in a locality where horses abound is called the "Mounted Engineers," because almost every man owns a horse. Another unit is known as the "Mayors of Harlem," since they are in direct control of more natives than Father Divine has followers.

Their work is tough, dirty and unglamorous, and it is done under the most trying conditions. Working in "the white man's graveyard," they have lost only one man —due to a streptococcic infection. One of them said:

"At first, when a bug wandered into the warm soapsuds we call beer down here, we'd throw the beer away. The second week we would take the bug out.

Bugs Flavor Beer

"The third week we took the bug out, squeezed him dry, then drank the beer. The next week we drank the bug. Now we catch them and put them in our beer for flavor."

There were more than 1000 of these tough Army Engineers at the last count.

Their commander is a tall, gangling soldier of the old school. In conversation he is pleasant, and during working hours he is tough. He is always immaculate in his dress, and he remains immaculate even when the tropical sun hits 150. He stands so straight they call him "Ramrod." At work he always carried a silver-tipped swagger-stick under his arm.

Silk was being used for parachutes rather than stockings during the war, so stockings were hard to come by. As a result, the gals used a lotion to make their legs look smooth and tan.

Sat. Sept. 5, 1942

Dearest Mother,

Your letter of Aug. 17th got here yesterday. The first thing I want to set your mind at rest on is the matter of money. I need very little of it here, only enough to play a little poker and to buy myself drinks and meals when I hit town. I have plenty and if I need some I'll write a check. Judy has promised to keep a little in my account at all times and I guess my bills are paid up to the point now that we shouldn't be too hard up. I've saddled Judy with our financial worries and she knows a good deal more about what shape we're in than I do. But I don't think we've got much to worry about now.

I certainly will appreciate any packages I get from home. If they are small enough, they come through quickly. I did get the candy you sent and thanked you for it but that letter or letters was lost.

I know that Hattie won't stop worrying about Al, but tell her to remember that he's doing a job he loves doing. A real job and one that it's a privilege to do. When the Army gives them wings, they are damn good pilots flying damn good planes.

The snapshot of Judy sitting in my lap is my pride and joy. I carry it with me all the time and look at it a dozen times a day. I am lucky.

All the letters and everything have made me think of home a good deal lately. It looks as if I won't see the old Loyalsock Creek at all during 1942. I certainly hope that '43 isn't the same way. I'm real sure we can win this war in time, if we can really start, but who knows how long it will be.

We're only working 8 hrs a day on this job. The siesta hour isn't a joke; it's a necessity. Both Davis and I tried to work right straight thru the other day and both of us were sicker than hell for a few hours. I eat real light at noon too. That's another thing I've learned.

Thanks a lot for renewing the <u>Grit</u>.

Lots of love,

Carp

Miss Phoebe Starr Lose,
Tucson, Arizona

September 12, 1942

Dear Aunt Pee,

The candy and books arrived just before we sailed from our last station. The candy and eats were swell and the books are already making the rounds. They are appreciated I tell you.

I'm awfully glad you got the new dress. Morale is one thing that's got to be kept up. Speaking of it, ours is darn high now because of the mighty nice praise we got, from men who count, on that last job we did. If they give us plenty of good hard tasks it will stay high, too.

I hope you can find the right kind of a job and can stay in Tucson. It sounds swell. I want to see it when this job is over. Boy, after the traveling I've done in the past six months, anyplace in those United States would be heaven to me. –And I used to think that outside of Lycoming County was a long way from home. Nevermore. From now on anywhere that they speak American is home to me.

Especially if Judy is there. –Do I miss that little girl? I think of her all the time that I'm awake and dream of her at night. Who knows? Maybe this war will be over some day.

Don't get me wrong. Outside of missing home, I'm not doing badly at all. This life is okay. See a lot of the world and do some interesting jobs. At present, my job is commanding the service platoon, which consists of a gang of mechanics, grease monkeys, and operators who maintain, repair, and operate the regimental motor equipment. Everything, bulldozers, gasoline shovels, 6-ton Macks and down to quarter-ton Jeeps.

Yesterday morning one of the drivers put one in the ditch. Fenders, grill, headlights, bumper, and radiator all banged to hell. A civilian car's lights had blinded him and forced him off the road. –By this afternoon that truck will be back in service as good as ever. –It's a damn good crew I've got. Our motto is, "We fix anything", and we do. Sometimes it's hard to do out here in the bush, but we keep 'em running.

I'd better stop running at the pen.

So long,
Love,

Carp

September 16, 1942

Dearest Mother,

This letter should be a valuable one. I'm lying on my bunk (that's a hell of a way to write) under a mosquito bar (the mosquitoes don't know if it keeps them out or me in) writing by Coleman lantern (just sufficient light to show the mosquitoes where to attack). Honest they aren't that bad. One landed at a nearby airport one evening and the boys put 40 gallons of gas in it before discovering that it wasn't a B-26 Bomber. –Corny, but you get that way in Africa.

Next morning.

Hi Toots, somehow I must have gone to sleep about that time and here it is the next morning. It was a good night for sleeping. Cool enough for two blankets.

I haven't heard from Judy since she went to New York, but I'm looking forward to a letter in the next mail. Both Segall and Nosek have had letters telling that the three gals got together. I hope she had a darn good time.

I haven't gotten any <u>Grits</u> as yet, but they may be slow or they may be lost, for some of our mail was lost a week or so ago. Anyway I'll look for your articles if I get them. I'm always glad to hear about what you're doing, so don't be bashful.

I was sorry to see Doc Wilcox get transferred back to the other unit and so were the rest of the 38th Officers because he was very well liked here.

Phoebe is babying herself and should be told so. I hinted it rather strongly, but it must have gone over her head. Boy, I can tell her from experience that plenty of work is the only thing to prevent homesickness. And this place is a sight more conducive to homesickness than Tucson, Ariz. But as long as I'm busy, I'm comparatively happy.

There's not much chance of my bumping into Al now. Do you know what sort of an outfit he's with? Light bomber, heavy bomber, fighter, or what have you?

I've made friends with the Motor Officer in the African Army here. He speaks English quite well and is trying to teach me his language, but I'm dumb. He's a very interesting talker and has been around plenty. We're learning each other's slant on things. Yesterday we had a long discussion on how the movies tend to mislead you in picturing so-called average people of various nations. Meeting people like this is the really good part of this war.

Your account of the hotcakes and sausage at Ralph's made me hungry as hell. But all in all we're eating very well here. Much better than at our last station. We ran one regiment mess there and it and the food weren't so good. As good as possible, but much wasn't possible. Here we're running Co. messes and the individual touch, plus a greater variety, makes our meals quite good.

Your speaking of champagne was very apropos. Speaking from experience, I'll say it gives you a very pleasant and lasting jag in a smooth, easy manner. Oh Boy!

Well, Toots, I seemed to have rambled on in this letter. I do like letters from you and Judy so keep 'em coming, please.

> Lots of love and a kiss or two, too,
> to you from me.
>
> *Carp*

P.S.   Dear Toots, Thank you for the hint. I guess I'm just dumb, but I don't want anyone to be able to say that I'm putting something over on Judy. All of the nurses that go to the dances with us know that I'm married because I've shown Judy's picture to everyone who can't get out of looking at it.

The gang has kinda settled down now that the first glow of seeing women again has worn off. I didn't go in last weekend and probably will go only infrequently in the future. We still go in for our drinking brawls though.

Judy still has nothing to worry about from me. I've never seen a gal who can hold a candle to her and I'm not looking for one. I won't write anything I shouldn't and thanks for the tip.

> Love,
>
> *Carp*

The mosquitoes must've gotten through. I ended up with malaria, twice, while in Africa.

On the home front, Mother had moved out of the duplex we'd had in Montoursville and was renting a room from friends on South Market Street in Williamsport (Hattie and Al Ertel – the parents of the pilot, Al, whom I mention several times).

African Mosquitoes Big
Local Officer Writes

AN INSIGHT into the conditions faced by United States soldiers in foreign service is contained in a letter received yesterday by Mrs. Margaret Carpenter, of 722 Market Street, South Williamsport, from her son, Lieut. Grant Carpenter, with the army somewhere in Africa.

"Just to give you some idea of the size of the mosquitoes over here," he wrote, "one of them buzzed in and landed at a flying field the other evening and attendants at the field pumped 40 gallons of gasoline into it before they realized it wasn't an airplane."

Sept. 28, 1942

Dear Mother,

What a nice surprise I got today. Your letter of the 21st, one week delivery. I'm closer to home than I thought. Those pictures of the room are neat. That's a swell room and you've got it fixed up just like home. The china closet made me think of the china that belongs to Judy and me. What was done with that? And whatever happened to my Victrola and records and my rifle?

Your idea of sending me the two sections of the paper is good. I haven't as yet received any papers, but I keep hoping.

Thanks for the clipping on Penn State. I'm looking forward to a good season for them.

Sunday, Oct. 4, '42

Good morning, Mother,

I really got sidetracked on this letter. Tuesday I just couldn't write, I was so bad tempered. I had an attack of toxic poisoning from an infection on my foot and it made me sick as a pup and so bad tempered that it must have been funny. It didn't really clear up until about Thursday and for those three days I wasn't fit to live with.

Thursday I took my gang, the motor pool mechanics and operators, onto a new job. We had to assemble a bunch of trucks. They come to us in a million pieces like a jigsaw puzzle and we put them together.

It's quite a job and good experience because they are stripped down to nothing and you really know all about them before you get them together. We've been working on it since then and have a few more days' work to go.

Thursday night we went in to a club in town for a ping-pong match and next Thursday we have another one. We got beat pretty badly the first time but as soon as we get a little practice I think we'll do all right. I'm battling it out with another guy for the number one position on our team. We're both confident that we can each beat the other. I hope he gets disappointed.

Friday we got some back mail and I got three from you. You're too smart to get left off the Executive committee. They couldn't run Lycoming County politics without you.

Next year I'll try to get home for Judy's birthday. Twenty-two is a very nice age for her to stay at, I think. Maybe I'll just stay 25. It seems like a pretty good one to me. According to the old superstition, my twenty-fifth year should be my lucky one. I hope, I hope, I hope.

How old is Flossie's grandson, Bill Ader, now? About eight or nine? I'm looking for a good souvenir for him, but haven't bit on anything really good yet. I'm so glad that Flossie is feeling better. She's my pet.

Bridge and Poker are a thing of the past around here. It's too buggy at night to do anything but hit the hay if you stay in camp. I'll make up for it when I get home. And bowling, boy how I'd like to bowl a couple of games. And movies, just think of seeing a new movie. We have a show a week, which I always take in, but they average three to four years old and older.

It's now Sunday eve. Oct. 4.

About here I went to chow and then into town to see about a place for some of my boys to play tennis. I found it at a club run by and for some of the British people here. On getting back to camp I found that I was O.D. so I've been busy chasing native gals away from the camp boundaries. They all want to "jig-jig" for two bits. I can't imagine what they mean.

I think I'll hit the hay now for I have an inspection of the guard to make sometime between now and morning.

Lots of love to you,

Carp

I learned that the local gals wanted to "jig-jig" for reasons other than the two bits they would earn. Apparently, if the local Catholic priest/missionary found out a gal had a mixed race baby, he'd take the baby to raise and educate, and would also care for the mother.

Oct. 11, 1942
Africa

Dearest Mother,

My job seems to be getting a little more interesting each day. We've been kinda marking time for the last day or so, but pretty soon I ought to be busy as hell again. We're getting this station fixed up more comfortably all the time. Yesterday they opened up a nice PX where we can get beer, soft drinks, candy, etc., and they're even planning on putting an American style grill so we can get hamburgers. Won't that be something? I am still looking forward to my first vanilla milk shake. Haven't even had a glass of fresh milk since I left the States.

Did you hit the B at the fair? I'd almost forgotten there was such a thing as the Bloomsburg Fair. Did you ride on the Ferris Wheel or see any races? Or did you throw things at ten cents a throw for five-cent prizes? I'm always a sucker for throwing the baseballs at milk bottles.

The natives here use a dug-out canoe like the ones the Indians use in the Everglades and down around the mouth of the Mississippi. They are very fast. I haven't been able to figure out why, but they seem to be faster than our regular canoes. Not as fast as my kayak though. Maybe when this brawl is over I'll build myself another boat, to my own design.

I'm worried about Pee. If she doesn't get a kick in the pants and get to work, she'll find herself in a real fix. Because she couldn't stand it to live with one of her brothers and know that she couldn't afford to get mad and move out.

Take care of my little girl for me.

So long, now.
Lots of love from your affectionate son,

Carp

October 20, 1942

Hiyuh Toots,

I'm trying to catch up on my letters again. You and Judy are the two best letter writers I know and you are darned faithful, which counts a lot. I know that sounds like soft soap, but it means so much to get letters from home that it makes you feel good all over. You ought to see how sick some of these boys look when mail call has nothing for them. That only happens to me once in a blue moon and I know then it's the mail's fault, not yours. I've got three here to gloat over. The first two I got the same day – dates Sept. 24 and Oct. 8. Three days later I got one dated Oct. 5. Figure that out on your slide rule.

So far I haven't seen a lot of this continent, but at that it's a lot more than I ever expected to see, and I will see more.

It rained like hell all yesterday afternoon. I was out in a jeep with no windshield when it started and darn near drowned before I got home. These tents are nice. Just as dry as a bone even in a driving rain like that.

I haven't fired a rifle in a long time, but I now have a Tommy Gun, which I'm anxious to try out. I've fired them before and they're wicked weapons.

Judy has me worried. If she says anything to you about joining the WAACS, use your powers of persuasion to keep her from it, please.

I can't get you a picture of me in anything but cotton O.D. summer uniform. I'll try to get one in that and send it. Don't expect too much. You know me and pictures.

Gee I've used up a lot of paper, taken a lot of time and said darn little.

Anyway, lots and lots of love.
Your affectionate son,

Carp

P.S.   Saw "Tortilla Flat" last night. Woe, am I homesick!

We were enlarging the airfield on the outskirts of Leopoldville. Part of our unit was a thousand miles away, enlarging another airfield. Someone once calculated that if the colonel who commanded our unit visited all of our men who were scattered over Africa, he'd have had to travel over 24,000 miles.

Oct. 27, 1942
Africa

My Dear Mrs. Carpenter,

It is with a great deal of pleasure that I take my quill in hand to address to you this friendly salutation and greeting. I have much of interest to report to you, however that unfeeling chap, that mercenary marrer of meticulous writings, that unmentionable member of the cut-up crew, the military censor to be frank, forbids the passage of such news and compels me to create these little masterpieces of non-intelligence. In short, Toots, here comes another line of bull.

I'm not drunk, honest I'm not. Eleven little scotch highballs aren't enough to make any man drunk. I just feel good. It must be the weather. These crisp October nights when Jack Frost is busy making his usual merry daubs on leaves and stuff, are just the thing to key a man up to that high pitch of perfection. Of course, that isn't exactly the proper description of our weather here. It _is_ rather cool this evening. I suppose the thermometer may have dropped to 75 degrees by now. If you sit perfectly still in the airiest spot you can find for an hour or so, you will eventually reach the point where you are not perspiring, hardly at all. But as we kiddingly say here in Africa, it isn't the heat, it's the damned, bastardly, everlasting humidity. Do I make myself understood?

To again diverge to the seamier side of life, I beg to report that I am in excellent physical condition. Mentally I am quite well balanced. Liquid seems to steady one's equilibrium in these parts. Emotionally I'm in a hell of a shape. I miss my wife and what's more I need a little attention. Technically I'm in fair shape. My job is sporadic as the devil, however. It's a stretch I am kept busier than the proverbial Winged Schikelgruber inhabited by crabs and the next thing I've got <u>Life</u> – no – <u>Time</u> on my hands, or the <u>Saturday Evening Post</u> or anything else to read. I've even read a few <u>True Romance, Spicy Adventure</u> (not bad), and <u>Adventure Comics</u> (darn good).

Mail Call is one of those things we ain't had for the past week so I've got nothing to answer. It's almost bedtime so I think I'll retire. A brief review of this convinced me that I'd better mail it quick or burn it up. It ain't fitten for a mother to read, but you are an exceptional mother so here 'tis.

Lots of love from
Your affectionate son,

Carpy

P.S. All I asked her was "Who held the rats?"

November 1, 1942

Dear Mother,

Boy, we hit the jackpot on mail yesterday. I had thirteen letters and a post card.

If they're taking guys like Sheen, there must be a hell of a lot of guys in this Army. You ought to really work in good at the <u>Grit</u> with all those losses in staff. —I hope to hell this war is over before Bill Ader is old enough to get in.

My foot has cleared up okay, if I didn't tell you before. That's just swell about Pee and her job. I sure hope she keeps it.

I was glad to hear that all my pet articles are being looked after. Judy and I are gonna have a time of it getting organized when this is over, but we'll have fun doing it. That's a nice thing about my wife. She's fun.

We're fixing up a building as an Officers' Recreation Hall, I think I told you. Anyway, yesterday I went into town to the Catholic Mission to get some potted plants for ornament. The gardener filled the back of my truck and promised more if I'd send him boxes or tires to put 'em in. The place is going to look like the jungle room in the N.Y. Museum. The Mission garden has every plant imaginable. All sorts of palms, pineapple plants, banana trees, avocado pear trees and much stuff that I didn't know. The gardener and I couldn't speak each other's language but we got along okay.

The other day we decided that ice cream would taste swell for a meal, but you can't buy sufficient quantity in town for a company. The largest freezer in this section is 6-gallon capacity. So I designed one and the welders made it out of an oil drum and 10-gallon milk can. Two, in fact, so H & S Co. now operates the largest ice cream plant in this part of Africa. Twenty-gallons capacity. Some stuff.

The S.O.S. (Service of Supply) for the U.S. Army is really on the ball. Realizing that radios would be unnecessary to our outfit, they equipped us with drums instead and we just join in on the native telegraph. It works too, so help me. —But no kidding, every once in awhile during the day you hear drums beating in the distance. An odd un-melodic beat. Of course every Saturday night the dance-drums in the villages around the camp beat until early in the morning.

Today is a scorcher. I'm sitting here in quarters with just an undershirt and shorts on and the sweat just pouring off me. I have to rest my hand on a piece of paper to keep from soiling this letter. And in an hour, we've got to put on a parade. Some s--t that.

Signing off now.

Lots and lots of love,

Carp

Nov. 4, 1942

Africa

Dearest Mother,

Is it hot? Can't you feel the heat coming off this paper? Thank God it's Wednesday – half-holiday, and I can park on my fanny here in my quarters. It would be just too much to try to work in this muggy stuff. I darn near can't imagine cold weather anymore. There haven't been more than a half-dozen days in the past eight months that were too cold to go swimming. I'll bet I'll be a hell of a sissy in cold weather the first winter I get back from here. A couple of weeks ago it was a cool, damp day and I was bitching about the cold so the Major told me to look at the thermometer. It was just 74 degrees and felt cold to me. That's no lie either.

Your reports about your job and what you're writing always interest me. I don't comment on it very often, but I'm always pleased when you make the front page, or when you scoop somebody on news around town. The old days when you used to go downtown every morning to market and gather news for Grandfather must have been good training. I got to thinking about that the other day and remembered how you always used to whistle at me as you came in from the walk. Does Judy know the family whistle? She ought to learn it so she can call our kids that-a-way.

Boy this place of ours looks like a fruit stand. My roommate bought three bunches of bananas and has them hung to the rafters to ripen. We grab one off whenever we get hungry. Personally, I've lost my taste for bananas.

> **How did Judy react to my suggestion about college? Honest, I don't think she needs it. I just thought it'd be fun.**
>
> **Lots of love,**
>
> **Carp**

A little about Judy: She and her little sister, Evie, were raised by their Aunt and Uncle, Grace and George Myers. Their Mother had died of cancer when the girls were just six and four years old. Their father promptly abandoned them.

Grace and George were good to the girls, but neither was home very much because they owned a repair garage and truck dealership. George's brother had worked there for several years, but used the opportunity to embezzle, absconding with the funds and leaving Grace and George in an enormous financial hole.

Judy was a good student and also an avid artist. Whenever possible, she would stay after school in the art classroom, painting. She also did a lot of walking. She had had polio when she was four, which resulted in her dragging one foot sideways. But with practice and stubborn determination she managed to relearn how to walk straight.

She wanted to go to college after graduating from high school, but her aunt and uncle's financial straits prevented that. However, George was able to work a trade with the owner of a business school. The man owed George money, so Judy attended his school in payment of the debt.

Upon graduation, she got a job with an investment company and learned about the stock market and how to handle money.

Judy's uncle, Bill Heiss, a professional musician, visited one day. When he realized that Judy was self-conscious about her height, he informed her that she should be proud of it since all the models and showgirls were tall. With that, Judy quit her job, got on a bus, moved to New York City, and enrolled in modeling school. She worked as a model, then landed the job at the 1939-1940 New York World's Fair where we first met.

After the World's Fair closed, the manager of the Chase & Sanborn Pavilion where she had worked offered her a job as hostess at a fancy restaurant he was opening in Florida. Before heading south, she went back to Williamsport to visit with her family and was involved in a car accident. Judy ended up with two impressive black eyes and didn't feel she could accept the Florida job, looking as she did. She stayed in Williamsport and took a job at the Lycoming County courthouse in the voter registration office.

If she hadn't stayed in Williamsport, I would have missed out on the best thing that ever happened to me—getting reacquainted with and marrying that girl.

November 5, 1942

Africa

Dearest Mother,

Mail Call this morning. Two from you and one from Judy.

I'm so glad your cough is under control. You better take care of yourself. I'm the guy who is supposed to be living dangerously, not you.

The Chapter letter from Triangle Fraternity arrived. They still think I'm in S. Carolina. I'll write and disillusion them. What did Judy hear of Gil? Is he reported missing or don't they know anything about him?

What's the situation on gasoline rationing, and sugar and meat and stuff? We aren't rationed on any of them, but once in awhile meat is a little scarce. Nothing like that last job, though. Boy, that took the cake.

Lots and lots of love,

Carp

My fraternity brother, Gil, had been on Bataan and was taken prisoner by the Japanese.

Nov. 14, 1942

Dearest Mother,

This letter was supposed to have been written a couple a days ago. Do you notice how young and weak it looks? It's really terrible to keep letters in suspense like this. I'm ashamed of me, aren't you?

I did rush those pictures to you right quick. I'm sorry about them, but my only comment still is, "Well, they look like me." The funny thing is that I shaved that morning special for the picture. Why do I always look as though I need a shave? Notice the bar on the collar. That's new since you last saw me. The absence of them on the shoulders makes me much more huggable, but darned if I'm getting any more.

Don't I wish I could get me an osteopathic treatment, if it'll cure homesickness? I've just gotten over the worst case of it I've had in my life. For about ten days, there I was, so mean-tempered I wanted to cut my throat. I hope my last few letters didn't show it too much. I tried not to. I kinda miss yuh occasionally, a little. A little like an elephant. I don't ever forget how nice home is, and my folks.

The description of your hat was priceless. I can just see it. —But I hope I'm not right.

You'll think I'm crazy, but last night, the 14th day of November, at about 9:00 I took a shower by moonlight in our outdoor shower, and there ain't no hot water either. And boy did I feel better for it, and did I sleep better. That's the way the weather is around here. Warm, I mean. Don't try it there at home. It's guaranteed not to be healthy.

The mail service may be a little bad for awhile now, but don't worry about me 'cause nothing's going to happen to your favorite child, barring accidents. Speaking of them things (Gosh my English is getting lousy) like a darn fool, this morning I got under one of the skids with which we unload tractors just as it slipped off the side of the truck and it landed across my toes. I'm all for steel safety toes now, because that really did hurt, even if it didn't break any, just bruised them.

And speaking of being your favorite child, I was starting to worry. I thought maybe Judy was now. She can be your favorite girl child – but I gotta be your favorite son. You're still my favorite Mother and Hattie's my favorite assistant Mother and Flossie is my favorite "Old Sock."

I sent Judy a check and instructions as to how it was to be used and I'll repeat 'em to you, especially concerning her, so you can see that she doesn't renege. $65.00 of the check is for Sandy Claws to buy her a matched set of either airplane luggage or rawhide luggage and that's my combined anniversary and Christmas gift. Boy, was I smart to get married on Christmas Day. Please make sure she gets 'em. $50.00 is for you to get you a present from me. $15.00 is for Pee and $20 is for you to buy my usual presents, not forgetting Bill Ader. We thank you, Madam.

Tomorrow I'm starting on a 200-mile jaunt to the next fairly large city by jeep. Ought to be fun and a chance to see some country.

Gotta go now.

Lots of love,

Carp

That 200-mile jeep trip was occasioned by a Merchant Marine getting stranded in Leopoldville when his boat sank in the river. I was selected to drive him back down toward the coast where he could meet another ship.

The road we traveled was not much more than two rutted dirt tracks, so the trip down took most of one day. I stayed overnight and started back to camp the next morning. Along the way I had quite a surprise when a huge baboon erupted out of the jungle, bolted across in front of me and climbed the bank on the other side of the road. There he stood above me, chattering and angry as I drove by in the open-top jeep.

November 22, 1942

Dearest Mother,

After I finished that last note I wrote you, I pushed off on the jeep trip I spoke of and had me a hectic couple of days. Judy heard all about it in the letter I wrote her last evening, so I'll refer you to her files for reference. Speaking of files, I hope you gals are keeping my letters. We're not allowed to keep a diary so the letters I write you are my only notes. By referring to them, I'll be able to remember most of the things I've done. That is, the things I'll dare tell you when this is over.

Gee, I'm glad Judy has quit that job. There's no sense in her doing any work at all unless it's pleasant work that she does to pass the time away. Besides it just costs me money to have her working. Look at the income tax I have to pay. Her idea of going to see Kit and Mary is a good one.

Here's a good literary joke. How many magazines does it take to start a baby? "One Life, Two Americans, and God knows how many Times."

I certainly hope that the election was not in any way a repudiation of Roosevelt. What a hell of a time this is to swap bosses. Is it an erroneous impression I've gotten from newscasts and papers or is it true that a lot of people at home are still wishing we'd win this war? Don't they know that the next 12 months are gonna hang up casualty lists like laundry tickets? They'll make the last war look like an "Our Gang" comedy. –Oh hell, Toots, I'm sorry. You know me, I get hot once in awhile (pretty often) but you know me well enough to separate the wheat from the bullshit. But I wish that a well-known legislative body would get off its respective fat fannies and quit playing politics. Anyway, it's a free country or I'd be afraid to say that.

Put that $65.00 into a very special bond. It's to buy me a set of soup and fish (tuxedo) when this is over. So Judy and I can shine together. Yeah, man.

It must be more and more interesting to you to have all that work to do and you certainly must be doing a swell job to have Mr. Davis speak so well of you. Isn't he the one you had such a hard time proving that your job was worthwhile? I'm looking forward to addressing my letters "M.L.C., City Ed." Won't that be something? I liked the way you settled him when he swore at you. That's the way to handle 'em.

I'm willing to send you a week of our weather in exchange for a week of yours, but I'm warning you, that one week of this and grass would grow out of the sidewalks. You wouldn't get the place cooled down again all winter.

I'd sure like to see you in those cotton socks. And speaking of legs, take a look at Judy's, about up to here, and tell me if they're still as pretty as ever. I'll bet they are, but I'd like to see for myself. What a break my kids are getting, having her for a Mother. Not that I hold that against you, Toots, but couldn't you have carried me like a papoose when I was a baby so I wouldn't be knock-kneed and bow-legged at the same time?

Are Pauline and Anne still at Gordon's? Say hello to them for me, and goose Gordon once. Tell Joe that the Army is looking for men. He better join the Navy.

Give my greetings to all my pals, and lots and lots of love to you.

Your affectionate son,

Carp

In case it escaped your attention, I wasn't exactly "politically correct" in those days. In wartime, a guy (excuse me) a person sometimes says things about their enemy that they'd never say under peacetime conditions. You can think badly of me if you like. But if you'll put yourself in my shoes at the time, I think you might be able to forgive me.

Dec. 1, 1942

Africa

Dearest Mother,

Boy did I get a jackpot of packages this week. Two from you and two from my favorite wife. Idea, wouldn't a harem of 6 or 7 Judys be tough on a guy? But what a pleasant way to die. Whoops, what am I saying? How could your son get an idea like that?

I haven't heard from Judy since a few days before she left for Arizona, and then she didn't know for sure where or when she was going. Thanks a lot for telling me. I know there's a letter on the way, but Lord knows when I'll get it. Personally, I think it's a swell idea. Mary will appreciate Judy's help with the new baby while Kit is out in the field. You'll miss her, I know, but you've got your job and about a million friends and lots of letters from both your children so you won't be too bad off. Which reminds me that in another four weeks it'll be one year since we've seen each other. That's a hell of a long time, Toots. Your letters have been swell. I really do have to get them and you're a brick about writing regularly.

Judy will get a chance to get some of that traveling out of her system. When this is over and I get home, my answer to anyone who says "Travel," will be, "Travel? Hell I've been everywhere – we touched South America on the way down, so that makes three of the six continents. And I hope to get into at least a couple more before it ends." I want to see Berlin and Tokyo, – burned to the ground.

I'm O.D. tonight, so I'm gonna finish this in the morning. G'night.

A nice quiet night for a change. But it's the same everywhere. Monday evening there's just nothing doing.

Three <u>Grits</u> arrived with the packages too. One had a picture of the board in front of the Court House with the Service Roll on it. Is my name on that? It better be. I've got more overseas service than most of those rookies have got in the Army.

You know, I just got to thinking about it, I really can't imagine what it's like back there in the States now. I've often read about the last war and ration cards, and liberty gardens, and war bonds, and meatless days and that stuff, but I've never seen a one of them. Everything was pretty normal when we left. No one had really gotten very excited over this war. Now I probably won't see any of it in this war, so I'll have to wait for the next one to find out what the U.S. is like during a war. What does a Service Flag look like? Do you really have air raid wardens? Or is it really all hub-bub? Is the Home Guard still functioning and, if so, what the hell do they do? You've got to keep your eyes peeled for me on all these counts, so I don't miss anything.

Well, Toots, I gotta go to work now.

Lots of love,
Carp

December 7, 1942

Dear Mother,

Gee, I hope that knee is much better by now. You have got to take care of yourself because I'm too far away to do it. That must have been an awful nasty fall and your padding ain't so good on the knees. Why didn't you just sit down when you felt yourself go? But seriously, Toots, be careful and give that plenty of time to heal. Don't be feminine and take off the bandages too soon just 'cause they look bad.

I'm glad that picture made such a good impression on you. Those snapshots ought to help. The enclosed one shows me at my best. Filthy, dirty, tanned as an Indian and happy and wacky. The gun and canteen were with me during all waking hours all the time we were on that job. I got so used to them they didn't even bother me. It's a shame I've lost that tan.

Your picture is neat but awfully belligerent. Am I going to have to tame you down when I get home?

Got a letter from Judy yesterday, mailed in or near Oklahoma. I suppose she's in Arizona by now. She had her usual start-of-the-trip upset stomach. But sick or well she's mine and I love her.

During the week I was defense counsel for a guy who was court-martialed for being in the native village, which is off limits, being without a pass, and being drunk. My chief argument was that he got confused in trying to come from a place on the other side of the village to the main road along this side and got in the village by accident. Yesterday I was up for a short plane ride and flew over the scene. A creek with no bridges is between the place he started from and the village and he had to get onto the main road to cross it. I got him off with only a month, but if the court had known that, I'd have been in a spot. They call me "The Mouthpiece." The kid has sworn fealty for life because he expected to get six months.

I got the scarf from Elizabeth. It is 15" wide, 7' long and nice and thick and warm. And today the temperature is 93 degrees in the coolest shade I can find. If it gets much colder, I'll need that scarf. —She's a nice girl though.

I hope you get that check before Christmas. I'm now reassured about being your favorite child and I'm glad Judy is your favorite girl-child 'cause I like her too.

Marg (Toots)

All of my injuries have gotten well before I get an answer telling me to take care of them so I have to stop and think back to see what the trouble was. Right now I'm in the pink. But we sure are busy. Even had to work yesterday, Sunday morning.

For dinner yesterday we had stewed chicken, mashed potatoes, stuffing, lima beans, orange ade, devils food cake, and strawberry ice cream. The ice cream was the best yet and was just like Hurrs Dairy's best. Made with vanilla, mixed with strawberry jam, it hit the spot. We now have eight 10-gallon freezers rigged up in the regiment and every company has ice cream on Sunday.

I wonder if there will be a big raid on some Japanese base today? A year ago, they sure smacked us. That evening, Kit and Mary and I went to the Elks in Columbia and really hung on a brawl just to forget that all leaves would probably be cancelled and we wouldn't get home for Christmas. Boy am I glad we did.

I'm wondering if Kit's outfit is practicing landings or are they practicing defense of California maneuvers? If that lucky rat stays in the States all this war, I'm gonna be sore. Because I had the same choice he did and refused it. Actually though, I'm glad I'm over here, because even if we're not in the fighting yet, we are doing fairly important work and Lord knows I'm more afraid of losing this war than I am of a lot of things I know. I don't like the way Nazis treat the women in conquered countries.

Wooee, what a flag waver.

So long now. Lots of love,

Carp

Phoebe Starr Lose
Tucson, Arizona

December 12, 1942
Africa

Dear Aunt Pee,

Had a letter from Mother yesterday and she told me about your new job at the university and how much you like it. I think that's swell. An air-conditioned laboratory in a climate like that, sounds like the perfect set-up for you. It's nice that you've made so many friends too, but I expected that. How is your flirtation with the two Army officers going?

You probably know as much about Judy's whereabouts as I do. I've only had one letter since she left Williamsport. She ought to be having a good time and I sure hope she is. I got a Christmas present from Kit and Mary yesterday and on the card was a line from Judy so she must be right with them. It was mailed "on desert maneuvers, California." I guess they went straight from Missouri to California. Or did they get a chance to see you?

How about sending me a catalogue on Engineering courses, especially M.E., from your University. I'm thinking of taking a refresher semester if this job ever gets completed. How much would it cost Judy and me to live there for 5 months and for me to take a semester's work?

So long now. Have yourself a Merry Christmas and I hope a damn good New Year.

Lots of love,
Carpy

Chapter 05

Dakar

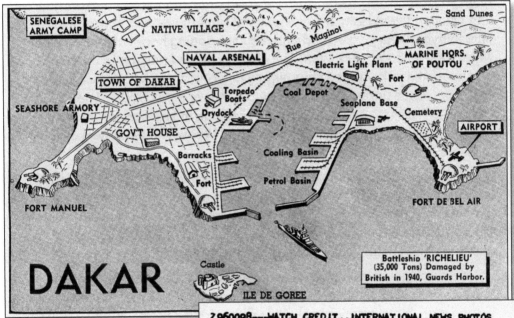

Once we had finished our work in Leopoldville, we headed for Dakar for more work, building and improving airfields.

2960098---WATCH CREDIT..INTERNATIONAL NEWS PHOTOS
    SLUG...(DAKAR)

        DAKAR---A THREAT ENDED

NEW YORK.....THIS IS A CLOSEUP MAP OF DAKAR, THE
STRATEGIC BULDGE ON THE AFRICAN COAST THAT IS ONLY A
NON-REFUELING AIRPLANE HOP FROM THE SOUTH AMERICAS.
NOW AS A RESULT OF A BLOODLESS VICTORY, THIS VALUABLE
BASE, WITH ALL ITS FACILITIES, MAY JOIN THE CAUSE OF
THE ALLIES. SUCH IS THE INDICATION MADE BY ADMIRAL
DARLAN, FORMER MAINSTAY OF THE VICHY GOVERNMENT, WHO
WAS CAPTURED IN ALGIERS. (E-11-24-42)-NOON

December 24, 1942

Dearest Mother,

'Twas the night before Christmas and all through the ship guys like me were sitting around writing letters to gals like you. The writing is worse than usual because this old tub really vibrates. We checked out of our old station last week and are due to pull into some port this evening, still in Africa. What a country in which to spend Christmas. I've slept raw every night on the boat and not even a sheet over me. You'd freeze to death if you tried that at home.

The day we shipped out, our packages caught up with us. One from you, one from Grace, and one from Edie and three from Judy. I had to open them right away because I wouldn't stand the idea of this baby getting torpedoed and me abandoning here without knowing what was in those packages. I've already played one game of chess and used the poker chips four nights in a row. Two nights successfully and two nights unsuccessfully. I also got two more <u>Grits</u>. I get a big kick out of reading the news about local lads in the service, but I still can't recognize your writing except that I know the fields you cover. I think you're doing a swell job too.

Mail has been avoiding us for the past few weeks again. My last letter from you was Nov. 29 and the last I heard of Judy was a letter postmarked somewhere in the Middle West. I guess it'll be some little time before it catches up with us so I'll just hope that Judy got the check in time to mail you your share for Christmas.

It still gripes me the way they hand out those commissions in the States. In all justice, I've got to admit that your friend Mark is a good man, but commissions and promotions are so tough to make out here that it doesn't seem fair. We have a couple of fellows in this outfit who would make damn swell officers and have been accepted for Officer Candidate School and aren't sent back because they claim we have no quota.

Our guys have a funny conceit that tickles me. They claim that they are selectees not draftees, and they're proud of it. Their reason being that when they were called they were selected, but now-a-days they're just drafting anybody. And I sure agree that they are a damn good crew of men. There's not much in the way of an engineering job that we can't do and I wouldn't be scared to take these guys into a scrap either. You can count on them.

This has certainly been a long 'three months tour.' I hope my next three months on Foreign Service isn't this long. Maybe you won't understand that, but when we started out on that first job, it was with the idea that we'd be back in the States in three months. So— I sure hope that before next Christmas I'll have had a leave in the States, or that the war is over, which I'm afraid won't be.

This has been an awfully poor letter. I guess I'm homesick. Actually I'm not too unhappy. So don't worry.

Lots and lots of love,

Your affectionate son,

Carp

December 27, 1942

Dear Mother,

Maybe this letter will be a little more cheerful than that last one. I'm feeling my usual joyful self again. Man have I been doing lots of sleeping on this trip. I sleep so much in the daytime that I can't sleep at night so I have to sleep in the daytime, if you get what I mean.

We stopped over Christmas Eve in some little port and moved on again late Christmas Day. Destination still unknown. I'm remembering all the things Judy and I did a year ago when we went to the intercollegiate ball. We ran into some friends just as we were going in and then as we were leaving the shindig, we bumped into Jeannie who was slightly high, and she informed Judy that if Judy hadn't grabbed me off when she did, she was going to.

A year ago tomorrow night, Kit and Judy and I gassed up at Joe's gas station there next to the market on Market St. and then took off over the mountain for South Carolina. This will make the first full year that I haven't even seen the valley of the Loyalsock and a year since I've seen my favorite mother. I hope to hell it isn't another year before I see you again.

Christmas was pretty quiet here on the boat. The officers and a lot of the men sang carols Christmas Eve, but Christmas Day we had nothing unusual except an enormous turkey dinner which was unusual only considering the place.

The poker chips have been in regular use every night except last night. None of us were quite up to it last night but we'll probably be back at it tonight. So far my luck has been averaging out as usual. Win a little, lose a little and keep fairly even in the long run.

The library on this boat is practically non-existent so I've read every scrap of reading material I could get from one of Zane Grey's to James Cain's "The Postman Always Rings Twice." You've probably read that last. This morning I even leafed thru "The Fellowship of the Horse" by some stuffed shirt of an English Colonel and for pure unadulterated horse manure, that took the cake.

Give my love to the mob at home and lots and lots for yourself.

Your affectionate son,

Carp

December 30, 1942

At Sea (rough)

Dearest Mother,

Can you feel this baby pitching? It probably shows up in my writing. Last night was the worst though. It was so rough when I went to bed and this tub was pitching and rolling so hard that the smoke was rattling as it went up the stack.

Funny thing about this rough weather, I feel swell. I sure am glad I don't get seasick because I think that would be too much.

My poker last night was very successful. I played for three hours and didn't win or lose a penny. One time during the game, I was about twelve bucks ahead and once about four behind, but the last hand brought me up just even.

I wish we'd get some mail soon. This idea of not knowing for sure where to send Judy's letters gets me down. I finally compromised and decided to send 'em home and trust that Grace knows where to forward them.

Day before yesterday it was nice and smooth and a gang of us were sitting on the deck reading and watching the ocean when a whale surfaced and spouted about a half mile away. I didn't see him, but I started watching and pretty soon another one showed up less than a quarter mile from the ship. We could see him quite plainly and I watched him for quite a while. You could only see his back when he surfaced, but judging from that, he was pretty big. We see lots of flying fish and quite a few sharks.

I was shooting the bull with one of the new 2nd Lieutenants who arrived here recently and he ruined my morale. He was telling me of Washington now and how you have to salute every uniform you meet. But what got me is that he told me that officers, captains and majors are stationed in front of public buildings to act as M.P.s and make sure that the officers salute each other. We don't salute anyone around here except in a military formation and by God we're doing a hell of a lot more toward fighting this war than those brass hats in Washington.

We have some of the same trouble over here. In the regiment we have sufficient officers to organize, plan and operate any job which the regiment might be called on to do. But then they send a staff over here to take care of that organizing. A staff of men who don't know the regiment, don't know the type of work and don't know their asses from first base and expect them to run things. Boy do we get hot under the collar.

Well I guess that's my quota of bitching for today. I'll do more later.

That knee of yours ought to be pretty well by now. I hope some of those letters I expect to get will tell me how you are.

Lots and lots of love from me to you.

Your affectionate son,

Carp.

January 8, 1943
Africa (Dakar)

Dearest Mother,

We reached our port a week ago today and landed the following day. It took us until the middle of the afternoon to get out to our campsite and then you should have seen us move. By dark, we had our tents set up, temporary latrines dug, a temporary kitchen up and doing business and were very comfortably fixed, i.e. for us. That's the way a rugged bunch of veterans like the 38th go to work. What I mean, I'm really proud of this outfit.

A few days ago we had a big mail call and four swell letters of yours caught up with me, Dec. 4, 7, 14 and 17. I read them all twice the same evening I got them. You write the nicest, newsiest letters, so now I'll try to answer in detail.

I haven't heard yet whether Judy got to see Pee or not, but she said she was planning to. She seems to be having a real nice time. Anyway I hope so.

The clipping about the way people are taking the war was good, but didn't impress me nearly as much as a lot of little things you told about in those four letters. They really made me feel good.

Your letter about Ed's job and your talk with him was good news, but I'm afraid of one thing: This regiment is just plain too damn good. Too many of the officers are real engineers and practically all of the men are too experienced at engineering construction work. They won't send us back because we're too valuable over here. That may sound like bull, but I've heard too many officers in other branches of the service say that the 38th is the best engineer outfit in the Army. We haven't seen the job yet that we can't do. I'm not gonna like being a Lieutenant the rest of the war, but I am gonna know I did my part.

I thought you'd like the snapshots. They were all censored and passed as you'll note by the stamp on the back and therefore are okay for any purpose. I took a lot more but couldn't send them because they contained items that would be military information in the wrong places. I wrote to young Bill Ader a letter and told him you had some snapshots that he might like to see.

Boy what I'd give to see Judy in that red velvet housecoat. I hope it's got a zipper. Did you get everything you wanted for Christmas? I hope so. —I think I got every one of those kisses on Christmas Day. The idea on Bill Ader's Christmas gift sounded swell to me. Did he like it?

I'm getting just as tanned and dirty here. The sun and wind burn you beautifully because it's just cool enough that you don't need a sun helmet and the sun gets a chance at you and we're right along the coast and you know what a sea breeze will do. Now that we're getting used to the change in temperature it's swell. But the first few nights I darn near froze to death. The weather reminds me of Indian Summer. Chill at night, but warm in the day.

Your letters give me the best picture of things at home. That treatment of Tom K. should have started early. They should send him over here. You go AWOL and you're liable to starve to death, and when you come back they let somebody else carry your rifle with orders to shoot if you don't work like hell or if you try to get away. Get out of line here and a court martial will step all over you.

More damn fun. Lieutenants Tuck, Van Hoy, Roth, and myself went into town the other night and investigated all the Houses. Purely a visual inspection. No samples. I never in my life saw anything run quite as open and above board. One good-looking little blonde sat down on the edge of my chair while we were having a drink in one of the houses and looked us over. She spotted Van Hoy, who is a damn good-looking kid and immediately went over and sat in his lap and did her damnedest to make him. We questioned her and found out that it would cost about 70 cents for a quick job and $4.00 to stay all night, but none of us stayed. I'm sure seeing the world and all its sights.

That's a hell of a paragraph to write to a fond Mama, but I know you got a nose for news.

So long now, Sweet. I'll write again soon.

Lots and lots of love,

Carp

January 17, 1943

Africa

Dearest Mother,

I've got to apologize for being such a brat and missing writing for so long, but honest, Toots, we aren't doing a thing that can be written in a letter. I've been to town only once since my last letter and then as Provost Officer and not a thing happened. We're working 12 hours a day 7 days a week and sleeping and eating the rest of the time. Not even time for poker now-a-days. My appetite has improved immensely and I feel so much better than I did at our last station that I've got to admit I'm delighted to be where I am and working the way we are.

You must be writing most of <u>Grit's</u> local news now-a-days. You and the other cub reporters. –What the hell kind of a cub are you?

Speaking of Marge always reminds me of how you picked her out as a girl I'd like to date. But if you remember, it was about that time that Kitty was cutting my throat so regularly and she cut it with Marge before I got a chance to ask for a date. Anyway, Marge is a nice gal, but I like Judy better. That Christmas outfit you picked out sounds like a honey. I'm awfully glad about it.

If Bill Ader uses that case as much as I use mine, he'll be using it a long time and darned glad to have it. Major Genthon still carries one given him during the last war.

Evie will need a lot more than room for four pictures for her suitors. She's a darn pretty kid and doesn't seem to be too intent on deciding right now.

Your letter about Mr. Brown fairly stuttered, but I'm so darn glad you got to talk to him. I don't even know his first name or anything about him except he's a swell guy and he and I got to shooting the bull together a lot of times back at the other place. He's an officer in the Merchant Marine, but I can't tell you any more. I warned him not to tell you anything except that he'd seen me and I was well.

That seems to be all the news that's fit to print.

Lots of love from,
Your affectionate son,

Carpy

P.S.   Lots and lots of love.
P.P.S. In fact bushels.

January 29, 1943

Africa

Dearest Mother,

Gosh, it's me again. Yeah, I know. I'm a rat. But I don't mean to be. It just happens. I always think, now today I'll write my mother a nice long letter. And then today is gone and I'm dead tired and tumble into bed and then it's another today and the same thing happens.

We had two mail calls within a couple of days. I'm so glad you liked the little souvenir. It's real ivory and real Africa. The kinda modern weirdness was what caught my eye.

You and me too on that wish for '43 to bring me home.

I'm glad you didn't stew about me because it doesn't do anybody any good. When I don't write it's because I'm moving or working like hell. If I get sick, I'll have time to write and if I get bumped off, Uncle Sam will let you know in a hurry, but don't worry about that because I won't get it 'til my number's up, and then there's no use of worrying. You know me, Toots, you taught me to look out for myself a long time ago.

I hope Pee is over her attack by now. She sure is allergic to Christmas.

I'm awful proud of the way you're doing with that newspaper work. It's fun when you can see yourself advancing, isn't it?

Your opinion of Judy ain't a bit better than mine. I think she's swell too. And what's more, I miss her like the very devil. Boy what I'd give to get home a while. Mmmm. Just homesickness kicking me in the pants, when I get time to think about it.

Boy those new gas-rationing rules are something, aren't they? That's good, I think, as long as I'm over here.

I got my Triangle Review yesterday and discovered that I'm in England. Boy, how I get around. The news of Gil was that he was a Captain on Bataan and was last heard of on Cebu. I'll bet he got out of there too. He'll be a General yet, you wait and see.

Yesterday I saw something that I've read about and never expected to see. A swarm of locusts passed over this area. It took 3 - 4 hours to pass and they didn't eat every green thing, but they made a hell of a good start at it. They filled the air and covered the ground as far as you could see. Clouds of them were so thick that they threw a shadow like a real cloud. They didn't bother us in the least. They don't land on a person and they fly as you approach them so you're always moving in a little open space. But they didn't do the native gardens a bit of good. Bushes were so covered that they had locusts instead of leaves. The birds had a feast on them, but there were literally millions of them. It was something to see.

We've had a couple of rather warm days lately. It isn't the heat here as it is the sun. Boy how that sun beats down on you. You can sure feel the heat of them thar rays. But it cools off nice at night. I still think it's a swell climate.

What did you think of FDR being up at Casablanca? The radio reports sounded like the Allies mean business in this war. I hope so.

Well, Sweet, that's all for now.

> Lots of love and a hug and a kiss,
>
> Your affectionate son,
>
> *Carp*

January 30, 1943

Dearest Mother,

I'm listening to a short wave broadcast from England while I'm writing this note. How music does bring back memories. A pianist just played "Marcheta" which always reminds me of the Boy Scout prayer to that tune and the summer camps up the Loyalsock. What a thrill that used to be to sleep in a tent for a week. Phooey! It was a lot of fun in those days though, but I must have been an awfully intense little rat because I can remember how hard I was bucking to make patrol leader and how everybody seemed to me to be against me that one summer. The time I grew so fast. Remember how Johnny and I used to read every night? A book a night was our regular quota.

Interruption in the line of thought. I'm enclosing a money order for $75.00. Will you please invest this in bonds in Judy's and my name and put them in an envelope in your safety deposit box marked 1942 income tax? I've decided to take advantage of the fact that I don't have to pay those until I return to the states. I'll send more money for the same purpose next month.

Now to get less mercenary. The enclosed two bucks is to buy a Whitman's valentine for you, if you will be my valentine. Will yuh, huh, please? You will! Oh Boy.

We're just as busy as ever. I don't like to brag, oh yeah, but we do work like hell.

This is Saturday night and Saturday night in Africa is the night the natives all throw their parties. I can hear the drums in the village back of us just a beating away. Funny but it isn't scary like it is in the movies. It's just kind of human.

There just isn't anything to do around this darn place. Just to show you how dead it is, every woman you see on the streets is pushing a baby carriage and got another one due in a few months. There's just nothing else to do. Oh well.

I told you we got some new lieutenants the other day. Well one of them turned out to be a Ruppert boy from Williamsport. I'm getting a snapshot of the two of us taken and I'll send it to you. We have more fun sitting around saying, do you know so and so, or boy, how I'd like a swim in the Loyalsock today. He went to St. Joe's and knows Mary and Rox and the gang.

We've been chowing especially good lately. Lots of fresh meat. I sure hope it keeps up. Then again it may be my appetite but I don't have any trouble stowing it away. The change in climate did wonders for my eating ability.

Boy they're playing all my favorite records tonight and all my favorite bands too. Bing Crosby and Artie Shaw just did their bits.

The news sure is good, isn't it? Oooh – there is Artie Shaw's recording of Star Dust. Remember my high school graduation? We had a class song to that tune.

Well, Valentine, I guess that's all for tonight.

Lots and lots of love from
your affectionate son,

Carpy

P.S.   Be sure and let me know when you get this money order.

February 4, 1943

Africa

Dearest Mother,

Tempus has been fugitting again while Carpy has been working, but not as bad as she sometimes does. Anyway, in the interim, I got paid and am enclosing 2-$100.00 money orders to be put into that income tax fund. That should purchase ten bonds with a little spot left over, right? That's of the $25.00 variety, which I believe cost $18.75. Now if I am right, I'd like you to take that extra $10.00 and buy some little gadget which is or will be near and dear to your heart. Thanks, Pal. I will keep heckling you for verification of receipt of these things until you tell me you have received them because I don't want 'em floating around Davy Jones' locker uncollected.

Now for the news that practically ain't. We're still working at top speed, but we're hoping to start taking Sundays off again soon. In fact, we're working so hard that it's practically unheard of for an engineer to write a letter home any other time than in the evening. I'm different. I'm writing mine right after lunch. All the other lugs in my tent are siesta-ing and old Sol is out there just a beating down as usual. Boy, but he is strong in these parts.

I got invited out to lunch by some people with whom I was doing business yesterday. He is a mechanical engineer and has worked all over Africa and his wife is the daughter of a Chinese diplomat. She speaks a half dozen languages and is smart as a whip. Mighty good looking gal too, to have two sons 14 and 13 years old. She speaks American and her husband and I talk by sign language. We under-stand each other quite well too. The Major and I are going out to their place for dinner some evening next week.

I'll truck on out to work now. I'm getting to be one the best big truck drivers you ever saw. After the war I'm gonna get a job trucking freight between New York and Chicago.

Lots and lots of love, Toots,

Your affectionate son,

Carp

February 8, 1943

Africa

Dearest Mother,

I hit the jackpot again. Three letters from you yesterday. Oh boy.

I like your new writing paper very much. Anything, just so I hear from you regularly.

I'm getting too many correspondents. Truthfully, the only people I give a damn about hearing from are you and Judy. We just don't have time to write much, so I write to you two and ignore the rest.

If you had a piston to blow you could very easily blow one. All it requires is a super abundance of hot air. Oooh – that was nasty, but you stuck out your chin and asked for it. And you are a news-paper reporter.

Boy I don't feel as if I've been married a year. It just hasn't seemed like a year that I've been out of the States. When I get the blues it seems longer, but generally we've been so busy that time just swoops by.

I got a little bitching to do. And I'll do it to you because you're my safety valve. Two or three times in the last couple of weeks I've had a chance to listen to the radio for a couple of hours in the evening and it's made me slightly sick at my stomach. The English short wave programs are pretty good but the American ones are too few and too lousy. It gives us a big pain in the neck to get a verbal pat on the back from a smooth voiced announcer or guest star who is sitting on his fanny back there earning a ceiling salary of $25,000 per annum. We don't mind his sitting, but trying to tell us what heroes we are is what rankles. Even if we were, we'd rather be patted on the back by guys who really know what we're doing. And the new war songs, peee-ew. Do they ever wave the flag and pull the heart strings.

That's two things we don't like about 'em. There's a lot more patriotism in 'swinging' a piece than in swinging Old Glory. Why don't they put out some good programs with good catchy tunes? The few good new ones and the old favorites are what we want. The old favorites may make us a little homesick, but they don't make us sick at our stomachs a lot. American newscasts are generally good and the comedians are good 'til they start waving it. That's my opinion anywho. And a lot of guys over here agree.

Our girl writes awfully nice letters, doesn't she? She's nice. I'd sure like to see her again soon. No such luck, though.

Did I say this climate was pleasant? It's cold in the mornings. During the day it warms up like a nice warm November day. An outdoor shower about 4:30 in the afternoon is pretty rugged but you can stand it and it gets you clean. Of course, the weather does vary and sometimes it's much warmer.

Boy do I feel old. I just got a letter from young Ed Foy and he signed it "respectfully yours." I'll mow him down. If he weren't so unmowable.

Well, Sweet, that's all. Lots of love.

Your affectionate son,

Carp

P.S.   Did you get three money orders in two letters total $275?

Miss Phoebe Starr Lose,
Tucson, Arizona

Feb. 9, 1943

Africa

Hi Pee,

Or should I say 'lo Pee? Anyway, Hiyah.

Long time, no hear, then blooey, three letters in one mail call. The one you lost, the replacement and one written a couple of weeks later. Also got the Univ. pamphlet. Thanks, Pal. It depends on how jobs shape up after the war. If Jones & Laughlin will put me right to work it's a deal. Otherwise I think I'll take a half-year of school. Provided I can talk Judy into supporting herself while I do it, and if she can get a job where I go to school.

I sure hope that damn asthma of yours is better. It seems to me that you must be allergic to Christmases. You are getting in a rut about spending them in bed. Better luck next time.

Judy seems to be getting over the wanderlust. Her last letter mentioned the possibility of her going back home again. We've missed connections on letters lately so I don't know if she got down to see you or not.

I thank you for the gifts you sent me but have to admit that they didn't arrive. I think Davey Jones got some of my stuff. I know you wouldn't forget your nephew though, so thanks.

Don't let the censors bother you. They don't censor much coming to us and I know you won't be handing out military info.

This afternoon I wandered over to where a half dozen of my men were knocking together a temporary cook shack. After watching them for five minutes, the sergeant in charge walked up to me and said, "For Christ's sake, Lieutenant, will you get the hell out of here so we can get something done?" –Oh well, the non-comms run the Army anyhow.

So long, bum. Don't let that picture of me bamboozle you too much.

Lots of love,

Carp

February 20, 1943

Africa

Dearest Mother,

Oooh what a hangover. I had dinner with some Navy boys on their boat last night and then we went out to show them the town. I didn't drink so much but I sure feel it this morning. To top it off I had to stand reveille this morning and it darn near killed me.

Boy what a meal they tossed us. Not so fancy but well cooked and tasty and topped off with apple pie, and after we did the town we went back and had sandwiches and cocoa. Their wardroom and neat quarters looked swell to me but I suppose it gets rather confining after ten or more days at sea.

I'm happy again. We had a movie the other night and will have two or more a week from now on. And I have the job of fixing up our ice cream freezers again.

Interruption February 22

Back again and only two days later. It's now 23:00 hours and I've just come in from seeing "King's Row". Good show too, I thought. And at 1 o'clock I go on a shift. Twelve hours shift again for officers, reminds me of our first job. Those long hours in the morning are nice for cogitation – and other things too, but why think about the impossible?

We had a nice mail call the other day and I got two more swell letters from you. Something leads me to believe that some of the letters I wrote you in January will not reach you. But particularly I'd like you to tell me if you did or did not receive two letters containing money orders. One for $75 and the other for $200. That was my income tax dough so I hope it arrived. I do have receipts for it so it doesn't matter too much.

You sure do put in a busy Friday afternoon. And walking up and down steps is supposed to be conducive to a nice slender chassis.

I hope you are right about Judy being happy wherever we could be together. My conceit agrees with you too. At least we always have been happier than a couple of bedbugs when we were together. Confidentially, Toots, you have an awfully nice daughter-in-law. I sure as hell do miss her. Fifty-one weeks now since I last saw that little Jill of mine. By the time you read this it will be well over a year. On the night of March 14th, your baby is going to get himself skunk drunk and I mean plastered as a wall, along with all the other officers of the outfit who sailed from those United States a year ago on that date. I intend to do my best to completely surround one fifth of a gallon of Canadian Club which I am saving for the occasion.

Snow is something I vaguely remember. Last winter I saw never more than 1/4 inch of it at any one time. This winter just forgot to come around. No snow whatsoever.

It's probably pure coincidence that they censor more of Judy's letters than yours. Of course, some of the things I say to her are strictly censorable, but not from a military point of view. I try my best not to disclose military info but it's good that they censor these on down the line because a guy is liable to let something slip without realizing that it's important.

I'll have to get back in practice on my bridge if I ever expect to play in your league again. I'll never forget the mistake I made in believing Judy when she told me she wasn't very good and then how rough on me it was when she proved how good she really was. Oh me, such is married life.

Judy has an idea she wants triplets now. Maybe I'll be like the Englishman in the story and be forced to comment "Roomy bitch isn't she?" Oh well, anything would be fun if I could be there to cooperate.

Lots and lots of love,
Your affectionate son,

Carp

Feb. 27, 1943

Dearest Toots,

We were all excited today. The rumor was around again that Martha Raye and her U.S.O. Troupe would be in to give us a show, but no dice as yet. I hope it's more than a rumor. We could do with a show. Though I shouldn't bitch. We've had a different movie every night this week and all good ones. The two best were "King's Row" and "Pardon My Sarong." Boy did Will Hays slip up on "Pardon My S." or else they're shipping unedited versions to us, which I don't believe the Purity League would allow. Some of the cracks were terrific and one of the dances was real Mmmmmmm.

Your Valentine was cute and I think Ogden Nash would have been proud to claim that. Judy sent me a swell Valentine too. Hers was a ration book of A-1 priorities on hugs and kisses which I've got coming to me. Could I do with some loving?!

Hiho, she will be here. Martha I mean!

I'm glad about Bill Ader getting that letter. I'll write him another this week.

Judy is all primed up now about having a family. She used to say she wanted a year or so for us to have fun together before starting, but I guess seeing Kit's and Mary's has changed her mind. —I wonder if mental telepathy is really any good?

Send my congratulations to Al. That sure is swell news. Tell him I know just how he feels. I got a stiff neck the first two weeks just watching the sun shining on mine. It's probably the only time in your life when you feel good about changing gold for silver. ((Gold bar 2nd Lieutenant, Silver bar 1st Lieutenant, two Silver bars Captain, gold oak leaf Major.))

Interruption

It's now the next day and Martha didn't show up, so we had a movie, "Allegheny Uprising." Then I went to work.

Your two daughters-in-law ((Judy's sister Evie was with her)) seem to be having fun out yonder. My last letter says they're getting set to truck off to California in a few days.

I'm looking forward to next week and going on day shift again. This going without sleep for a week makes me bad tempered. Today being a day of rest. More fun? All I have to do is keep an eye on a couple of emergency jobs.

Our Special Service Officers got hold of some musical instruments the other day so now somebody practices all hours of the day. The drummer and sax player are now working out "Melancholy Baby." Last night after the show we had a good jam session. A couple more weeks of practice and we'll have a real swing band.

Boy that was a good mail call. It's a shame we can't have one every day.

> Anyway, lots of love and lots of love,
> Your affectionate son,
>
> *Carp*

Judy had gone out to Phoenix to help Mary with the new baby while Kit was out on maneuvers. Her sister Evie met up with her in Arizona and, after Kit got back, Judy and Evie headed west to California. They found an apartment in Hollywood and got jobs to support themselves. Judy worked as a sales clerk at a high-end department store called Bullocks.

Africa

March 5, 1943

Hello Sugar,

Stationery by Ballard, ideas by Carpenter, published after the movie in a tent.

By the way, don't let 'em put that little wife of mine in jail. Between us we screwed up the income tax proposition 'til I'm sure she'll be late paying it. It's all Uncle Sam's fault anyway because his mail service is so lousy.

Thanks a lot for getting those bonds for me. I know I don't have to thank you, but I was brought up to be polite.

Well Martha was here and put on a show the boys really appreciated. Ruppert and I had our picture taken with her and if it's any good we'll send it home if the censor will allow. That's a lot of ifs.

Carp & Martha Raye

Saw another movie tonight called "When Johnny Comes Marching Home." Boy is that rubbing it in. I've seen a movie every night for the past two weeks. Some fun. I was just thinking that we've been here more than two months and how the time has flown. The days and weeks just pour by when you're as busy as we've been. Personally I like the days to really race by as long as I'm away from home.

So Flossie's boy Johnnie Weaver is a doughboy now? It would be funny to get him in my platoon. That's one thing I don't want is to ever get any of the hometown boys under me.

Your political fight sounds like fun. I'm betting on you.

So long now, Toots.

Lots and lots and lots of love,
Carp

Sunday, Mar. 14, 1943
Africa

Hiyuh Toots,

I'm a few sheets to the wind but still flapping. One year ago today we left those good old United States for parts unknown. Now we're quite familiar with the parts unknown and we're still away from the States. Every time we take a drink to celebrate the past year, we pray that it'll be the last year overseas. I'm now sporting a campaign bar (African). I can't picture me as a veteran of a foreign campaign. Some stuff, eh sister? Okay, okay I won't get so familiar.

We had the afternoon off today and I had more damn fun. Four of us took a rifle and a couple of Tommy guns and our pistols out on a reconnaissance. We jeeped about 30 miles along the beach and across country. I got in some target practice with a Garand rifle too. A trip like that does us good because it helps you keep your eye in on shooting. That Garand is a honey of a gun and old Tommy ain't so bad. I like to shoot him with tracers. It's fun to watch where you're shooting. But the pistol is still my hoodoo. They say that shooting a pistol is all mental and I guess that's my trouble.

Judy's last letter to me made good time. I hadn't realized that Evie was planning to stay out there with her. The two of them ought to make out okay and have a swell time too. I sure hope so.

Got my <u>Grits</u> up to the 1st of Feb. now. There are so many guys in the Army now that I hardly ever recognize any names in that 'news about service men' column. But it's fun looking for guys I know.

We had a band from an outfit stationed near here to entertain us the other night and boy I mean they were good. Made me think of the night just before I left for the Army when Baldy and his date and Judy and I drove to the dance at Berwick. How I'd like to go dancing with that gal again soon.

I've heard a rumor that 18 months is to be the limit for troops overseas without leave. Have you read anything about it? If it's true, I'll do this last six months standing on my ear.

The weekend in Muncy must have been a lot of fun for you. Maybe I ought to introduce that 50-cent poverty poker to this gang. The funny thing is that since I've played real poker, I can't play 5 & dime. I always lose my shirt at 5 & dime because I always figure that since it only costs another dime to see another card, I'll take a chance, and taking too many chances is what kills you in poker.

It's kinda funny about Bill W. not being in the Army, but I'll bet there's a good reason. I'd sure hate like hell to be back home and not in the service. I know just how cruel unthinking people can be. And the worst offenders are people at home who aren't doing anything.

Have you noticed how full of propaganda the movies are now-a-days? Everything we see has somebody waving a flag in it. –Phooey!

So long for now, Toots.

Lots of love from your best boy friend,
I hope.

Carp

Africa

Mar. 19, 1943

Dearest Mother,

Got your letter of Mar. 11 yesterday. Your stories were swell and new too. Nice work, Pal.

A letter from Judy came in the same mail and had two marvelous snapshots of her in it. Boy I am lucky. She is the prettiest and nicest girl I've ever known. Wasn't I smart to marry her? I still wonder how I did it. She is a real beauty and she writes the best letters, just what a guy wants to hear. –Apparently she and Evie are having fun in California and I hope so, but she says that nothing is real fun unless I'm there and I know how she feels because I feel the same way.

We haven't had a chance to see the picture "Casablanca" yet. I'm hoping though. We did see "Random Harvest" the other night and "Pied Piper" a few nights ago. Both were very good, or so I thought. The "Pied Piper" was the best propaganda I've seen yet. Most of it consists of waving the flag like hell and spouting phrases. Which is just so much bullshit to us.

I think that movies are an essential industry, but I don't know how many guys would agree with me. Too many of them don't think far enough ahead or back to realize what the ingredients of a good movie are. And stars are certainly a big factor.

Gotta go to work now. Lots of love to you, Toots.

Your affectionate son,

Carp

P.S.   And respectful too.

Africa

March 28, 1943

Dearest Mother,

It was swell of you and the mob to celebrate our first year overseas with us. I didn't really get skonk-dronk as I'd planned, but I sure was nice and pleasantly lit. Barring a radical change in plans we'll be here, come '44 because they've got that much work lined up for us, and I'll still be a 1ˢᵗ Lt. dammit. That's what really hurts. You go overseas early, work like hell, and some 90-day wonder back home is drafted, goes to O.C.S. and makes Captain before you get a chance to draw a deep breath. Yeah, I know, I'm bitter. Okay I'll stop bitching.

Last night we saw Bette Davis in "Now Voyager." How that lady can act – Mmmm. I think Paul Henreid was in it too, but my vote goes to Humphrey Bogart. He's one of my very favoritest stars. Did you ever see him in "The Maltese Falcon" or any of those detective pictures? He's really good. Tomorrow night we're having "Pride of the Yankees." The whole gang has been looking forward to it.

We're working as hard or harder than ever – no – just as hard. But in addition to regular work, Ruppert and I are training a new group of truck drivers for the outfit. I have to teach them what we call 1ˢᵗ Echelon Maintenance, which is the elementary driver maintenance, and Rup is teaching them the advanced stuff. My boys claim they'll make a mechanic out of me yet. Then I'm teaching a refresher course on military subjects to our non-comms and in my spare time I'm defending a guy on a court-martial. It's the third time guys have asked me to defend them. I think they believe I'm a shyster lawyer. And tonight I'm O.D. – more fun.

Nope, I haven't taken up smoking yet.

Why don't you teach Hattie how a clock works. I'll bet she could learn. If her son could learn to fly a plane, then a simple thing like telling time shouldn't be too difficult.

Did you ever take a look in the cockpit of a modern plane? That array of instruments will scare you half to death.

I'm just itching to see "Casablanca." Ingrid Bergman is very pretty, but not nearly as pretty as Judy. It's funny how I never went for big girls until I married one and now the little ones have no appeal for me. If they aren't over 5'6", no dice.

How often do you have a practice black-out and for how long?

Gotta go to work now.

Lots and lots of love,

Carp

Here are two excerpts from later editions of the Army's newspaper called "Bonjour" "Somewhere in Africa" that Carp references in his letter.

U. S. ARMY "BONJOUR" SOMEWHERE IN AFRICA

VOL. I, No 22   APO 622, c/o PM, MIAMI, FLA.   AUGUST 21, 1943

38th Engineers Win High Praise

FROM COLONEL HILL

Headquarters 38th Engineer Combat Regiment
A.P.O. 622, c/o Postmaster, Miami, Fla.
DCH/sar
14 August 1943

MEMORANDUM:

To the Members of this Regiment.

Buried as we are in mud, disappointed in failure to make tangible progress according to our own ambitions, we are perhaps inclined to be discouraged in the thought that we are forgotten and neglected.

Let the following letter, copy of which was sent to us by the Inspector General. ATC, AAF, encourage us in the knowledge that our efforts are recognized and appreciated. And let it spur us on to greater endeavor and additional achievement.

Every member of this regiment has cause to be proud of himself, and of the part he has played in earning this fine commendation.

I congratulate you.

DONALD C. HILL
Colonel, 38th Engineers
Commanding.

News from Home

◆◆ Spokane, Wash. - Truman Jones received a letter from Sgt Keith Walser, serving overseas. The censor had deleted everything except this postscript: "I don't know if this will get through the censor or not. Now you know everything I know."

◆◆ Dunkirk, N. Y. - Herbert F. Cristy was hospitalized for injuries received while painting a porch. He fell 12 feet, landed on his feet and apparently suffered only from the jar. Then a plank tumbled down, struck his head and knocked him unconscious.

◆◆ Knoxville, Tenn. - He met her in Nashville and the meeting was grand. It was so grand in fact that Pvt Tom Phillips of Knoxville married the girl the next day. Then she disappeared, said Tom, and now he doesn't even remeber her name. "I have an idea," Pvt Phillips said, "that she married me to get my allotment pay."

◆◆ Sicily. - When the British Army rolled by one farm here its happy owner, freed from the Axis yoke, gave an officer one of his cows. The Briton had the bovine loaded on a bomber and flown to Cairo.

◆◆ South Pacific. - Lt William F. Fielder Jr., former Ohio Northern University football star and now an ace with the 13th Air Force, has been awarded the Navy Air Medal for shooting down five enemy planes.

FROM GENERAL SMITH

In reply refer to ;
IG/ATC 2014

19 July 1943
Subject: Recommendation for Citation for Meritorious Service, 38th Engineer Combat Regiment.

To : Adjutant General, War Department,
Washington, D.C.

1. It has come to the attention of this office that the 38th Engineer Combat Regiment has been recommended for meritorious service in the construction of air fields and associated installations at…, in Central Africa, and in…

2. A recital of the accomplishments of this Regiment constitutes an epical chapter in the history of the American Army.

3. All the more admirable qualities of American Soldiers have been shown in abundant measure. A high standard of duty, and devotion to that duty, has been evidenced continually through the long months since March 1942.

4. The energy, fortitude and self-denial, coupled with the magnificient leadership of this Regiment, combined to accomplish tasks which lesser men would have found impossible to consummate.

5. Professional competence, as Engineers, of officers and men in all their undertakings has been a marked characteristic of the Regiment.

6. The Air Transport Command has reason to be grateful to, and proud of, the 38th Engineer Combat Regiment. Without their construction, this Command could not have performed, when and as, it has.

7. It is sincerely to be hoped that the recommendation, in which this Headquarters so heartily concurs, will be approved and the citation published. Such a citation would be a source of great gratification to the officers and men of this Command who have been aware of the contribution of the 38th Engineer Combat Regiment to the war effort.

For the Commanding General,

C.R. SMITH
Brig. General. U.S. Army
Chief of Staff

THINGS TO WATCH FOR :

That when Italy drops out of the war, Turkey will drop in on the side of the Allies and play a prominent part in the conquest of the Balkans.

After the fall of Italy an attempt by two of the smaller Axis partners to sue for peace. Probably Rumania and Bulgaria.

THE WIDEAWAKES

By Robert Peter Duffy.

The Monday night round table symposiums that end with this column ready for the Tuesday noon deadline was held this week without Larry Babine. Larry decided to try a little of that hospital stuff that I found so enjoyable on my recent vacation there.

Every city seems to have its sore spots. This camp is acquiring one in that partially filled hole in front of the recreation hall. We were quite curious at one time when it was being dug as to its purpose. We never found out. Before it is finally filled I suggest that they remove those locally purchased stones that they covered up.

Those more or less comfortable benches that made their appearance in the Wideawake theater about four weeks ago still lack brothers and sisters to seat all of the customers. The plans on the cement blocks have a habit of being a bit unsteady and do not lead to the complete enjoyment of the films. I suggest the Colonel pay another visit to the theater and this time I hope he sits on the left side.

We have had a real pleasure this week of hearing the RAF swing band three more times. At the Rajahs, at the beach, and at the Wideawakes. It is undoubtly the best aggregation of jive boys that I have come across since leaving the niterys of Manhattan. Incidentally Wilbur, I thought we were ready too, but after hearing these boys I realize that we need many, many more rehersals. These messed-up rehearsals certainly don't help either. How about some cooperation, boys ?

We think that the boys who worked on the new beach, the PX, the bathhouses, the latrines, the bus service, should be complimented on their fine job. In comparison to the other beaches around here this G.I. job is "Jones beach" in miniature.

At the dental inspection this week Jim Crounse of "B" Company was given a "four" on his teeth – both of them. While on the subject of dentistry we hear that some of the boys are going to spend their Sunday mornings having their theeth cleaned. That's the spirit. If more men would spend their time taking care of their wants, we might get this war over with a little faster.

This week Lt Grant H. Carpenter was transferred to "B" Company. The boys in H&S think he is a pretty swell guy and it is definitely "B" Company's gain. H&S would like him to drop over every once in a while and say hello. We wish you the best of luck, Lieutenant.

The promotions for this week are :
From Sgt to S/Sgt : Robert F. Maddux.
From T/5 to Sgt : John A. Rourke.
From Pfc to T/5 : Homer S. Scott; Clifford Storz; Joseph S. Stasko; William O. Gentry Jr; George T. Corder.
And that's all for this week.

Africa

April 3, 1943

Dearest Mother,

Now that I've censored a hell of a bunch of letters I should have lots of ideas for a letter to you. But I suppose a composite letter from the boys wouldn't be too interesting to you.

Something has been bothering me for the last couple of days. I keep dreaming of a nice big vanilla milkshake. Do you think you could wrap one up real well and send it to me? I'd even pay for the stamps. No kidding, but I'd darn near sell my soul for a glass of sweet, fresh milk. The drug stores in this part of Africa aren't all they're cooked up to be. No cokes, no sodas, and no milkshakes. Darn few drugs too.

Did I tell you that one of the boys in the company has a nice new pet? A seven-foot python. He wanders around camp with the little fellow wrapped around his neck. The other day he was showing him to a group of boys and a fly landed on the nose of a guy directly in front of him. Brother python spotted said fly and nabbed him almost instantaneously. He also got about an eighth inch of the nose. The amazed look on that boy's face was worth the price of admission. That snake doesn't like me worth a darn and when I go near, he hisses at me. I think he senses that I'm scared of him. Yeah, I know, I'm a sissy, but I still don't like snakes.

Our C.O. has been away for four or five days so I'm acting C.O. in addition to my regular duties and it keeps me some busy. In addition to that I have been a little under the weather, caused, no doubt, by overindulging in some good Scotch which we were lucky enough to lay our hands on. I'm getting more and more to be a scotch and soda man.

Judy wrote me and mentions the possibility of her going to New York from L.A. As I've said before, anything she decides to do is right by me, but it will be nice to have her in N.Y. where I know that if I should ever get home I'll be able to see her quickly. Speaking of getting home, I don't know if I'll really like it or not. This idea of practically no gas, and everything rationed doesn't appeal to me after being where we have as much gas as we need, and free movies three times a week, and no rationing of food.

That room of yours must be just swell. The eighteen ashtrays should be almost enough. Even for a chain smoker. I still have those pictures you sent me and every once in awhile I think how nice that room is.

I'm enclosing a copy of a local newspaper the boys have started here. It's all censored, as you'll note in the filler in the top front page. Or what do you call that blurb?

Did you hear about the Coca Cola salesman who got in with a bunch of WAACS and knocked Seven Up?

You seem to be getting more interested than ever, if that's possible, in your job. I think that's swell. I'm always bragging about my newspaper woman mama.

A new lieutenant and I were out shooting again the other day. I'm improving with both the rifle and pistol but it'll take me a long time to get back in the shooting form I was in that last year in college.

> Lots and lots of love
> from your wandering boy,
>
> *Carp*

Africa

April 6, 1943

Dearest Mother,

I got your letter of the 28th today and the one for the 24th the day before yesterday. The reason I didn't answer you yesterday was that I was writing Flossie a flip letter. Your letter of about the 21st, telling me what happened to her hasn't arrived yet, but I've deduced that she had a bad fall and injured her back. Am I right? I feel just like you do. It isn't right, but I didn't say so to her. I just kidded her. Could she use 50 bucks? I'll send it in a day or so when I get paid and if you can use it for her, do so. She's my pet. We gotta look after her, 'cause she looks after us when things go wrong.

I kinda urged Judy to go to New York. I know you like to have her around, but I'm a little scared of Williamsport for her without me around to laugh off the edges. We'll both be back when this is over.

You're right about its being a long year, but as you say, it has passed quickly in a way. That's because we've worked so darned hard.

Just imagine a gallon and a half a week? I used to run that through my Ford just warming it up on a cold morning. I'd better stay in Africa away from all that dreadful rationing. I'm not kidding you, Toots, I'm kidding myself. I still can't picture the United States during wartime.

Judy said she and Evie did without meat because it was so hard to get. Is it that bad at home?

Lots of love,

Carp

Judy and Evie took the bus back from California to New York City, since trains were too busy moving troops and war materiel. Early in the trip, they got off the bus during a scheduled stop and ordered some food from a lunch counter.

While they were eating, they noticed that the three Mexican Army officers who'd been on the bus with them did not seem to be able to get served. They walked over, asked the men – one of whom spoke English reasonably well – what they wanted, then ordered lunch for them.

When the two got back on the bus, they found the officers had rearranged their seating so that they would be sitting next to Judy and Evie. The girls learned that the officers were part of an exchange program with the American Army and were on their way to NYC also. The officers stuck close by throughout the trip and the girls acted as their interpreters and guides.

This one is a V-mail, and it's typed – the first typed letter in quite a while – since he left the States.

V · · · — MAIL

Africa, April 19, 1943

Dearest Mother,

I got this V-mail form because they issued instructions that only V-mail would be sent out of here by plane, but today they changed it and regular mail will go as usual, provided we limit it. Mail from home will come in as usual so keep writing. I think our mail to you has been delayed quite a bit lately but I don't know why. I write pretty regularly, but I do miss occasionally such as when we don't get mail and I have nothing to answer. Then we get a bunch and I have a lot to answer, like today!

We, the Officers, played softball against A Co. yesterday morning and got the pants whipped off us. I pitched for the officers and while I ain't good, I ain't as bad as the 25 - 4 score indicates. Talk about your errors, we made 'em. But it was fun and good exercise. In the afternoon, I took my basketball team in and practiced them so I made good use of my day off. We're getting a whole day a week off now or did I tell you?

Judy wrote me a swell letter from New Orleans telling me all about the trip from California to there. She and Evie are having a swell time, but seem to have difficulty finding quarters in the larger towns. Her letters are so happy and full of life that it does my heart good to get them. Last night I dreamed I was back home and that she and I were driving home for a leave. Boy do I hope that comes true soon.

I'm glad to hear Flossie is feeling better. Give her my love and the enclosed fifty bucks.

So Pee's gone religious? Oh boy. The only thing the Army has done for me is lessen my respect for churches and preachers. Or maybe

---

I've run into an especially chiseling bunch of chaplains.

Take care of that cold, Toots. It just won't do for you to get sick so I have to worry. That's purely a selfish request, but you'd be surprised how many guys crack up over here from worrying about home and not from the work or climate. I'm lucky, knowing that you are enjoying your work and living comfortably and that Judy is having such a much better time. That's a big part of morale.

Will you see if you can find a half dozen packs of Durham-Duplex razor blades and paste them to a card and put 'em in an envelope and send to me, please? If you could get one of those Durham-Duplex stropping devices, I sure could use it.

I'm awfully proud of the job you're doing and you know I like to hear about it. Your description of the blackouts and everything that they're doing was swell, and I'm sure glad to hear about it. Just think of it, I still don't know what it's like in the States during war. I've never seen a WAAC. That letter was a big help. I think what you're doing for them is swell too. That publicity means a lot.

Lots and lots of love,

Carp

Africa

April 24, 1943

Dearest Mother,

I'm acting as Justice of the Peace now and trying to arbitrate a horse trade. One of my boys traded horses with a native and gave him so much to boot. Now the native claims the deal was never consummated and he wants his horse back. What I need is a little of Solomon's wisdom. I'm afraid that on horse deals, the soldiers get the worst of it. At least, judging by the looks of some of the plugs I've seen around here, that's the case.

I'm training at nights, trying to get in shape for a little cross-country jaunt that's coming off in a couple of weeks. If I get in shape I think I'll enter the meet. But I'm getting old, Sister Nell, and my joints, they creak like old joints always do.

This afternoon I'm taking the company out on the range for a little practice. You know how I'll enjoy that. Anytime I get a little shooting practice in, I'm enjoying life.

I was all pepped up here about six weeks ago and thought sure that things would break so I'd have a chance at Captain this year, but everything seems to be in a rut again and all indications point to a non-promotion year. Oh well. Some day I'll get a 90-day wonder for Company Commander and then I'll have something to bitch about. No kidding, Toots, I really enjoy the life. If I must be in the Army, then this is the best place for me. Interesting work and more or less in my line. It's just my pride that bites me now and then.

I'm sure getting restless though. This sleeping alone bothers me. Must be the climate.

We had a good movie the other night, or did I tell you? Ida Lupino in "The Hard Way." Boy she can act. As good as Bette Davis, I think, and twice as good looking. Tonight we have an old one, "Rise and Shine" with Jack Oakie and Linda Darnell. I'll like it because Linda Darnell looks so much like Judy. But it'll make me homesick.

Tomorrow is Easter and we're going to have a big meal. Turkey and trimmings and cake and ice cream. Some change over last year. Last year we ate Type C rations out of a tin can and in the afternoon I went on a 12 mile reconnaissance (by foot) over the roughest country God ever poured forth on the face of the earth.

I wore out a pair of shoes the first ten days on that job. Then I got wise and had my next pair hob-nailed.

If Judy stops in Williamsport, give her a nice friendly pat on the bottom for me. You know the kind I mean. I'd rather deliver the pat myself, but you know how that is.

> Lots and lots of love,
> *Carp*

Africa

May 9, 1943

Dearest Mother,

I hope you got a Mother's Day corsage today from your favorite child. I am your favorite child aren't I? You know I'm proud of you.

This afternoon my tent-mate and I went for a little joy ride up-country. Boy does it get hot back in those parts. It was like driving thru an oven. The movement of the jeep didn't cool you a bit. It just burned your face and hands. Gee I'll be glad to hit a nice temperate climate again.

I got your letter of April 28th. I'm so darn glad that money was a help to Flossie. She's real folks, but you knew that.

What do you think of the shindig in North Africa? Pretty good. Hey Gal. Where you betting we start next? I don't think it'll be Italy, but I may be wrong.

Lots and lots of love to you, Mother.

Carp

Africa, May 22, 1943

Dearest Mother,

In front of me is one of these Dymaxion globes as they printed in Life Magazine. It's a pretty slick idea and gives you a quite good view of this old world in its proportions. From where I sit, it isn't really so far to little old Broadway. But the swimming isn't good. These over-the-pole air routes are certainly going to make a big difference in world travel after this shindig is over. Sixty hours by air to any point on the globe now, and probably less as the war goes on. And boats make me sick anyway. I think I'll do all my travelling by air from now on. Judy is going to have to buckle down on her Spanish if I'm to work in South America afterwards. I've finally admitted I'm just plain dumb on languages. They don't touch me, or at least they don't sink in.

Interruption... while I went to the movie. We saw Gene Tierney in "China Girl." Highly imaginative, but it appealed to me. She is something of an actress. At least she did this quite well.

Our theatre is about the best in Africa, I think. It's open air with a seating capacity of about 600. The ground is graded to form a sloping bowl and the seats are arranged in a semicircle. Benches really. The screen has a floodlighted stage in front of it and the entire theatre has a windbreak about 10 ft. high made of thatching. The wings and background of the screen are of thatching too. Quite tropical.

The projection room is set on stilts in the rear and looks like a native hut with a couple of small windows. Out front of the theatre they have a board that shows what's playing and what's coming. Very modern and up-to-date.

This post is getting civilized. The 38th will get sissified if we stay here much longer. Swell movies three times a week. A marvelous PX where you can get American beer, candy bars, chewing gum, cookies, crackers, all kind of sweets, a lunch bar where you can get hot dog sandwiches and coffee and they say we'll have ice cream and cokes in a few more weeks. All kinds of snacks too. There won't be any use in coming home, what with every-thing rationed.

Goodnight, Sweetheart. Be a good girl, but have a good time. Give Judy a kiss for me when you see her and remind her that I still love her.

Lots of love to my favorite Mother,

Carpy

Africa, May 23, 1943

Dearest Sugar Plum,

Just about the time I get to bitching because mail calls have been few and far between, one shows up. Today I got one from Pee and yours of May 12 & 16.

I went down to the beach for the afternoon; only stayed in the sun an hour and a half because this sun is treacherous. I don't think I got a burn. The beach is swell. You'd love it. Nice and sandy and the waves are only a few inches high. It's so well protected. You can wade out a good 200 feet before it gets over your chin, nice level slope all the way. But the water is just now beginning to warm up. It was just nice today. This evening I'm settling down to some good, steady letter writing.

What I want done with that $65.00, now that you bring it up, is to send Pee $15.00 for her birthday, give my Mother $25.00 for her birthday, send Judy a corsage and take her out to dinner on June 25, just to remind her that she's been married a year and a half, and save the rest for contingencies that I may write you about. Will you do those, please? And out of curiosity, will you price star sapphires for me? They're Judy's birthstone. Don't tell her.

I hope you get your raise and I sure think you deserve it. That's a dirty trick they're pulling. Don't ever worry about me. One thing the Army does for you is take care of you. I've always got a place to sleep, plenty to eat and wear, and enough free entertainment. What money I spend on myself is for laundry and eats at the PX, purely unnecessary, but very nice. If it weren't for my poker, I could get along on $20.00 a month.

Your comments on public opinion about the ending of the war were good. I always like you to tell me things like that because you are well-informed. As for this generation (younger) I don't remember ever hearing you bitching. Every generation, the older pans the younger, but they seem to turn out all right. Used to tickle me when they said we were soft. Maybe we are. We ride to war in jeeps.

Your method of living from day to day is the only answer to this existence. I don't worry about the future because it doesn't do any good and besides, it'll come out all right. It always does.

Just now ran out of ink, but I'm okay now.

Every time you tell me how nice my wife is, I just say to myself, Hell's bells, Babe, you knew I'm fussy and could be depended on to pick only the best, and besides, wasn't I lucky that she decided to like me too? Gee, but I miss her. You too, but in a more mental way.

That's too bad that Flossie feels she isn't getting well fast enough, because she really must be doing okay. I keep wishing for her.

Love,

Carp

Phoebe Starr Lose
Tucson, Arizona

Africa

May 29, 1943

Dear Phoebe,

I'm ashamed of myself. Four weeks in a row I've heard from my nice Aunt Pee and haven't gotten around to answering 'til today. I'm a bad boy.

Yesterday was our 2nd anniversary and we had a big feed to celebrate. Roast Turkey, mashed potatoes, filling, giblet gravy, cranberry sauce, biscuits, butter and jam, green peas, ice cream, four cans Pabst per man, and cigarettes and cigars. Don't you wish you were in the army instead of being a poor, rationed civilian?

Did you hear about the Mexican Army officers Judy and Evie met on the bus? Judy got a letter from one of them so now she's learning Spanish. I've heard Mexico City described as one of the nicest cities in the world. Would you be able to get a job there if you didn't have a good command of the language? It would be an interesting experience to live there awhile. But don't let anybody kid you that anyplace in the world is quite as nice as the poorest of those United States. My travels have turned me into the most rabid American you ever saw. From now on, any spot in the United States is home to me.

This country has really warmed up since we hit here in January. I'll bet it's even a little hotter than Tucson. Couple of Sundays ago I drove back into the desert a little ways. Even in a moving jeep you burn up. It's like driving through an oven.

Sorry, but the cookies from Altman's never arrived. Packages over 8 oz. come by boat and the chances of their reaching me are pretty slim.

Boy when I read about that S/Sgt. and his wife living next to you while on furlough it made me homesick. I'd give a month's pay for a 10-day leave with Judy and that ain't hay. I think Judy would give another month's pay for the same leave. Man, I'm getting sick of the tropics after 14 mos.

Cousin Bud and Jane may know what they're doing, but I could give them some good advice based on long experience. If I were anywhere in the States, even waiting orders, I'd have Judy with me. We'd live in a one-room shack and be damned happy just to be together. They'll learn, but it's tough to learn by experience. It used to make Judy so mad when Mary and Myra bitched about only seeing their husbands a couple of times a week.

Boy, what a lot of bitching I've done. Honest, things aren't quite so bad as I sound. We have a pretty darn comfortable post here now. Swell Post Exchange where we can buy most anything, so we're really in the best shape we've been in since we left the States.

Leafing through a "Field and Stream" magazine, I found an account of deer hunting in Muncy Valley. It spoke about Williamsport and about the Loyalsock Creek. What a thrill just to read about that country.

Love,

Carpy

Following are a few paragraphs from a letter written by Aunt Edith Flack to Marg (her sister) in May of 1943, from Kansas:

I know how Judy feels about Williamsport with Carp away. I'm so glad that you and Judy are friends. I'd say I was proud of you, but it might give you a swelled head, so I won't.

Yesterday when I was up street, I was trailing a sergeant and his pop and mom. There was a boy about ten years old on the corner and he started saluting. The soldier stopped and gave the child a very military salute. The boy beamed. I beamed, pop and mom beamed and everyone in the vicinity beamed.

Lots of love,

Edie

Africa, June 1, 1943

Dearest Mother,

I'm really stymied for news this evening. We're working straight thru again and I can't tell you about that and other than work I haven't done a darn thing.

Maybe I'll bitch a little. The sand fleas are driving us nuts. Boy how those little bastards can bite and I mean we've got 'em. The mosquitoes too, but not so bad as we had 'em before. We take quinine as a protection and it makes my head buzz and ring. I can hear bells ringing for fair.

A funny and maddening thing happened to me yesterday. We broke a glass jar that is used on an attachment to bleed the brakes on trucks. An ordinary Mason quart jar like we used to have a thousand in the cellar. I couldn't find one in town so I went to a ship in the harbor to see if they could give me one. They had one all right, but I had to go clear to the Captain of the ship before they'd give it to me. I was disgusted enough to spit. We're used to bumming and lending and chiseling and stealing anything and everything that we need to do the job – and then to hit a piker like that. I had a notion to give him your address and tell him that you'd gladly give him one if you knew it had helped me a little.

This is just a note. I'll do better with a letter to answer, but I send you lots and lots of love,

Your son,

Carpy

June 2, 1943

Dearest Mother,

That note last night was so short I was ashamed to send it.

One of the boys in the company is pretty good with leather goods and made a real nice shoulder holster for a .45, so I bought it from him. I'll be all set to be a gangster chief when I get home. You know me. I always am a sucker where guns are concerned.

The movie last night was an old one, "A Yank in the RAF." I saw it with Judy, just before we left the States, so I just sat and dreamed through it. The way Betty Grable got out of a car reminded me so much of Judy. All beautiful legs from shoes to high heaven. That leather seat was always a big help because I could just slide her across to my side and save walking around. Besides, it gave me a chance to admire those legs.

My class ring just caught my eye and started me thinking. I wonder how far over the globe those fifty-odd rings have spread out? I'll bet you'd find them in some odd sections of country. Mine is sure getting smooth and worn but it's still a good-looking ring. Two more years and we'll have our tenth High School anniversary. It doesn't seem possible. I'm sure hoping this war is over and we're home by then. Now I've got to go to work.

Lots of love,

Carp

Africa
June 6, '43

Dearest Mother,

Mail call yesterday and I got two swell letters from my Mother. Boy you've got me all excited over this birthday present. The idea of the picture is swell but you didn't need to worry that I'd forget what you look like. Shucks, Toots, you're my favorite Mother. Those good wishes and prayers are nice too.

I hope Hattie's dream about Al coming home comes true. Boy I dream of the day when I hit those States again. Only thing I don't like is going thru torpedo junction again. Those tin fish make me nervous. Maybe I can get to fly home.

That pleasure-driving ban sounds like a beaut. You'd know where the gas is going if you saw this outfit work. 24 hours a day seven days a week on all trucks and equipment takes a lot of fuel.

Am I burned up. Every time I read about that coal strike in PA my temperature goes up four degrees. Boy, would I like to have those bastards working for me in this hell hole. Any noon I can show you the thermometer between 110 and 120 degrees and up country where some of my boys worked, it goes to 135 and 140 degrees. I'd make 'em mighty happy to dig coal for the wages they're getting.

I had a touch of Malaria last week but I'm okay this week. Man what a jag that quinine gives me. If the fever didn't make you feel so rough it'd be fun. I was on quarters one day so you see it wasn't bad. I even worked that day.

Some Victrola up the way is playing "Because." Memories of Christmas '41. I'm an old married man for sure. Year and a half in a few more days.

Lots of love to an awfully nice Mother.

Carp

Phoebe Starr Lose
Tucson, Arizona

West Africa

June 12, 1943

Dear Aunt Pee,

I hereby retract any and all derogatory statements I may have made about or to you in the days of my youth. In fact I forgive you for blackmailing me about aforementioned remarks. Your neat card and letter arrived in the last mail call and are appreciated. That card is the berries. You're an awfully nice girl. I thank you!

You ought to get in the Army and stay healthy. My hay fever has been cured and I don't have time to catch a cold so the only thing that bothers me is a couple of bouts of malaria and they weren't too bad. I've only been sick enough to hit the hospital once since leaving the States and that was only five days for the fever. Not bad for a poor, sickly youth. This outdoor life and good plain food certainly doesn't hurt a guy. I hope your bronchitis has improved.

We're working regular as hell still, seven days a week, 24 hours a day. I've been just about nuts the last few weeks. Work always seems to come in bunches in this maintenance game.   No time for swimming and it's sure hot enough to really make it nice.

It'd really be something if Olive and the gang would go to Tucson. I can't see Mother leaving Williamsport though because she seems to be too set on that job and it is really a swell chance for her to get set for life. I sure would like to be back carving me out a niche in Jones & Laughlin. Except I'm afraid the rationing would get me down.

Lots of love from
Your neffoo

Carp

West Africa

June 13, 1943

Dearest Mother,

Here it is Sunday morning and I've just censored about 50 letters, so I'll sneak in one of my own. Just a little one because I wouldn't want to gyp the government too much.

I've got a hangover, dammit. Last night I got a bottle of peach brandy and one of some other kind of liqueur from Col. Jones. Price was $6.00, but I matched him, double or nothing and won. After the movie Rup and Mac and some of the boys were drinking cognac so I opened up the brandy. Four or five shots of it, just before going to bed and it didn't hit me 'til after I got in bed. Then I really got high, but this morning, I'm paying for it.

We saw "Bringing up Baby" last night. You and I saw it about four years ago, didn't we? Just before the show they played a censored version of a song which we've been singing since our first job. It's to the tune "Bless 'em All".

Oh they say there's a troop ship just leaving

Bound for those U.S. shores

Heavily laden with time-weary men,

Bound for that land they adore.

Now there's many a striper* just ending his time,

There's many a twerp signing on

But there'll be no promotion

This side of the ocean

So cheer up my lads, ---- 'em all.

---- 'em all, ---- 'em all, ---- 'em all.

The long and the short and the tall.

---- all the sergeants, the topkicks, the bums,

---- all the corporals and their ----ing sons,

For we're saying good-bye to them all

As back to Ft. _____ we crawl.

For there'll be no promotion this side of the ocean,

So cheer up my lads, ---- 'em all.

*non-comm

Pee sent me a real nice birthday card that she made herself. Verse, illustration and all. Or did I tell you?

Lots of love,

Carpy

West Africa, June 21, 1943

Dearest Mother,

This typewriter was sitting on my desk so I figured I ought to make use of it and, after all, what better use can I make of it than to write to my chief booster? I've just finished a good hard morning's work and have fifteen minutes between recall and chow. That is, a good hard morning's work for Africa. Other climates wouldn't think much of it. It's a little cooler today than usual. Here it is noon and the temperature's only 90. It'll probably do better later in the day. Just a thought, if it ever hit 20 below as it does around home, half those in this part of the country would kick the bucket in 24 hrs. I sure hope I can come home in the summertime or I won't be able to take it.

Last night we had a pretty good show. Judy Garland in "Me and My Gal". I'd like her in anything. Just like my Judy. I'd like her in nothing at all. Vaudeville sure put out a lot of good songs. Every time we have a picture like that, you hear the boys whistling and singing them for months after. That song "Mary" from "Yankee Doodle Dandy" is number one on our hit parade right now.

One of those interruptions came along again. I
went to chow and then back to work in the afternoon
right up until suppertime and after supper we played a
ball game. As usual, I sparkled. Made three runs and
caught all the flies hit into left field. All two of
'em. We lost anyway.

After the game we had our usual poker session. The
night before, I lost about 20 bucks in an hour before
the show. Last night I started out with only 17 bucks
in my pocket, but I ended up with $70.00. One time
in the game, I was down to my last two-bit piece.
Tonight I'll probably lose my ass. That's the way with
poker. But it's the best entertainment we've got here,
next to the movies.

"Casablanca" is showing here sometime this week. I
hope it's as good as you say it is. Anyway, I know
Ingrid Bergman will be good. "Stage Door Canteen" is
still my vote for the best I've seen this year.

Did Judy show you the item taken from Kaltenborn's
broadcast? About the "Rock"? A General who inspected
this area a short time ago said that the job we've
done here is the best of its kind in the world. The
only trouble with building up a rep like we're getting
is that it will probably keep us over here longer. I
still think we'd be a good outfit to supply cadres for
new outfits so the advantage of our experience can be
spread out. You think so too, don't you? Judy does,
I know. Ain't it a shame we don't run the Army? We
could do such a swell job.

Sunday they gave us the day off for a change.
Nice change. I slept late, 'til 9:00 believe it or
not. Then, since some of my maintenance gang were
working, I had to go out and check up on them and in
the afternoon I was out with them again for a while.
But it was still a day of rest and a lot better than
a full working day. We had vanilla ice cream for
supper. The first in three weeks. That was, and is,
a treat too. But I'm still thirsting for a milkshake
and some real milk. Fifteen months is a long time for
your little boy to go without tasting real milk, after
drinking two quarts a day for the previous 24 years.
Which reminds me that in three days I'll be 26 – one
foot in the grave and the other on thin ice. Gosh,
when I think how old 26 used to look to me. I thought
you lost all interest in everything, including women,

when you got that old. You don't though. Funny, ain't it? Or ain't it? It's fun anyway, as I remember.

There I go again. I'd better quit now. Lots of love to you, Toots. I like you lots. Keep those morale boosters coming. They help lots. I probably get the best news reports from Williamsport of anyone in the Army.

Your affectionate son,

Carp

Miss Phoebe Starr Lose
Tucson, Arizona

July 19, 1943

West Africa

Dear Pee,

I was awfully glad to read the last paragraph of your letter and find out that the storm was not fatal to you. Speaking of thunderstorms made me realize that I've seen not more than two in the past 18 months and only one was bad enough to notice.

We get so tired of hot sun but I must admit that the last ten days or so have been quite comfortable for these parts. Only in the middle of the afternoon does it get hot enough to really bother you. At night however we still sleep under either a sheet or nothing. Rain bothers us quite a bit though. I don't mean that it rains so much, but when it does, it's a mess because we have to go right on working in it – and it pours here. The ground gets about six inches of sticky mud and raises hell with our work. The last storm we had I drove my jeep through what looked like a mud puddle and it turned out to be bottomless. My left front wheel went all the way under and I had to get a gang of guys to lift me out.

That sulpha-drug treatment sounds like it might be the answer to your prayer. I sure hope so.

So long now.

Your loving neffoo,

Carp

Africa, July 22, '43

Dearest Mother,

I'm a brat, I know, or else confused. Did I write you a letter Monday or didn't I? If I repeat myself, I'm sorry. I've been catching up this week and wrote to Baldy and Pee, and Kit and Annabelle, and nobody I should have.

Judy has pepped up tremendously. Every mail call now I get a couple of swell letters from her.

Did I tell you about swimming all last Sunday and having a whale of a good time? The surf was just rough enough to make it really rough exercise. I was so tired that evening I could hardly move.

How do you like the Sicily job? Seems to be going good.

I'm tickled pink at how well Flossie is getting along. It's just swell. I owe her a letter now, but she won't get mad if I'm a little late answering. She's nice, just like my Mother.

Have to go do a little work now.

Lots and lots of love,
Your affectionate son,

Carp

Somewhere

Aug. 12, 1943

Dearest Mother,

Thrill, thrill. Al Jolson is to make a personal appearance here tonight. If I can get up enough ambition, I'll walk over to see him. If there was to be a movie too, I'd go for sure.

So Judy reads "Love Stories?" That's a vice I never knew about or has she just taken it up since her love life has dropped off so badly? Maybe she'd better mail me her old copies, that way we could get a vicarious thrill. One of my sergeants gets 'Cosmopolitan' and I read it from cover to cover each month. It's almost as good as 'Love Story' and has better pictures, I think.

How many carats is that stone going to be? Boy I hope she likes it. It'll be a couple of months before I can pay back that money, due to the way poker has been treating me lately, but it really won't matter too much.

Now it's August 19.

Monday I started a new job. It's a steel fabrication job and my crew is pretty small so I have to get in and heave and grunt with them when we're putting a plate in place. It's heavy work and I've been just worn out when the day was finished. Today we had the morning off to hold a parade in honor of one of our men who was presented the Soldiers Medal for heroism. The area Cmdg. General made the presentation. The fellow who got it was one of my H & S boys. Maybe you remember me telling you about a kid who got mixed up with some high-powered electric lines one day last winter and this man got him loose. Well, that's what the medal was awarded for. We're all right proud of him.

Judy sent me a snapshot of her in shorts standing by the Ford up at the cabin. Boy is that wife of mine a beauty. The prettiest legs I ever did see and the cutest face. Mmmm, will it be fun to wake up mornings and see that again. She's a real beauty. I'm so crazy about her and so in love something should be done about it. I just about burst with pride just because she's my wife.

Al Jolson was here last week and I was very snotty about whether I'd go and see him or not. I finally broke down and decided to take a chance and was properly squelched by enjoying his show immensely. Just Al and an accompanist. He cracked a bunch of wise ones and sang, "Mammy" and "April Showers" and "Melancholy Baby" and "Sonny Boy". He's got a swell voice and can really plug a song. He's much better in person than on the screen.

Lots of love,
Your erring boy,

Carp

The steel fabrication job I mentioned was the building of a 6000-foot runway east of Dakar near the town of Rufisque. We were building it on sand and couldn't use usual construction methods, so we made it out of steel using 5 foot long by 1 foot wide metal plates, which hooked together.

Dear Toots

Chapter 6

The Gold Coast

After we finished up at Dakar and Rufisque, we shipped out to the Gold Coast. "Shipped out" isn't accurate. We flew this time.

Central Africa

Aug. 27, 1943

Dearest Mother,

How's my enquiring reporter today? Your vacation is just about over by now. I sure hope you had a good time.

I didn't go out of camp the morning after I mailed that letter, but I did get away Wednesday morning and got here in the evening. Nine hours of flying is the longest I've had to date. The trip was kinda tiresome toward the last because we were above the clouds and couldn't see a thing and it got darn cold.

This post is the best I've seen yet in Africa and is even better than Jackson, S.C. was. Of course, it doesn't have Judy, but except for that it's nice. The meals are really good. We get lots of fresh fruit. Oranges, tangerines, bananas, alligator pears, pineapple, papaya, or practically anything you want. We have movies regularly and darned comfortable quarters. Two men in a room, double deck bunks with innerspring mattresses and all the comforts of home. We sleep under at least one blanket at night, which is a pleasant change. Each two rooms has a houseboy who makes the bed, cleans the room, takes care of your laundry, shines shoes, or runs errands, and calls you "Master" when he speaks to you. This morning he saw me writing and asked if I was 'writing my wife home.' I think he's Pennsylvania Dutch.

The guys in this barracks are a swell bunch. All of D Co. officers and some from other branches. They play poker about every night so I'm in the groove.

I just sent my houseboy over to the PX for Coca-Cola. What a life. This is quite the racket.

The work here is well organized and will be interesting I think. So far I'm just getting oriented and have no regular job yet.

> Lots of love,
> Your affectionate son,
>
> *Carp*

Central Africa, Aug. 31, 1943

Dearest Mother,

This place is terrific. The cheapest lumber around here is mahogany. So the company mess hall has a floor, walls, roof, beams, and tables all of mahogany. And it isn't a small building either. The pay-off is the latrines. The latrine shed and even the seats are mahogany. What a life. When they build a fancy house around here, they use a mahogany frame and sheet it with expensive yellow pine from the States. That's class. The native carpenters are slow, but good. They do really nice woodwork.

Our quarters are really something to write home about. Did I tell you that my bunk has regular coil springs plus an inner spring mattress? It's kinda tough getting used to it. Boy, if only Judy were here.

I hope you got that ring okay for Judy. I'll enclose a note with this for her on her birthday. Is it her 22nd? The note can't be sealed because of censorship so will you seal it, please?

I'm anxious to hear about your trip to Laporte. How is Gramp anywho? You know, I'll bet he's kinda proud. It's a hell of a note we didn't make you one first.*

Just think of what we have to look forward to. Mmm, such thoughts.

I'm so glad Hattie heard from Al. He's really seeing England like I'm seeing Africa only there's not so much of England.

So long now, Toots. Lots of love,

Your affectionate son,

Carp

* Grant Sr.'s son, Don, from his second marriage had had a child with his wife by then.

Central Africa, Sept 8, 1943

Dearest Mother,

We got the good news about Italy this afternoon about 4:30pm. That's certainly a step in the right direction. It shouldn't help German morale either. I know mine is up tonight. It came so suddenly that I can't quite assimilate the idea yet. And I can't figure just how much it's worth. But it seems to me that as soon as we can fully occupy Italy and start operations from there it will have tremendous value. After all it is a darn good bridgehead. Now another one in the lowlands should certainly do wonders. Who knows, Toots, another 12 months may see this European phase ended. I don't see how Germany can last any longer. She's certainly going to take an awful pounding in the next year. I'm anxious to hear what rumors are running around tomorrow. This should start a hell of a bunch of them. I'll bet we move everywhere from the States to Italy to China. Some fun, traveling by rumor.

I was looking at a job downtown yesterday when some lieutenant whom I'd never seen before hailed me and asked if I could change some money for him. Neither of us had the right change so I said, "Here, I'll lend you two pounds and you pay me back when you get into camp." I wrote my name and address on a card and we parted. I didn't have the faintest idea who he was or if I'd ever see him, but he looked honest so I thought it was worth a gamble just to see what would happen. When I came in last night he'd already stopped in and given the money to my roommate and he came back in the evening to thank me again. It just goes to show you.

We're having a camp rifle match and I'm coaching Co. D. Tomorrow we go out for our first range practice. I always enjoy anything like this and I think we have a pretty good chance to win. Anyway we'll have fun trying.

Monday we had a retreat parade to celebrate Labor Day. I think I can send you a snapshot of the company showing me being very military. If so, you'll get it.

At the movie Monday evening they served us free ice cream, doughnuts, and Coca-Colas. What a post. It's got the States beat all hollow. Except it ain't got Judys or Tootses. That's about all I miss.

Four years ago this time I was in Philly to see about that job with the Pennsy R.R. –for which I couldn't see well enough. Now I've done 18 months foreign service in Uncle Sammy's Engineers and done some mighty good work. Somehow I think the Pennsy was wrong and I'll always hold it against them a little, even if it did turn out for the good. I wonder what the job situation's gonna be like after this brawl.

Mail call has been weak as hell lately. So I still don't know if you got my message about the ring. I sure hope you did and that she likes it. It'll always be something she can hock if she ever gets hungry enough. Not that I expect her to get that hungry.

It seems like a lifetime that I've been away from Montoursville. I'll bet it does to you, too.

> So long now Toots.
> Lots and lots of love.
>
> Your son,
>
> *Carp*

Central Africa
September 12, '43

Dearest Mother,

The letter you wrote the night you got back from Laporte came in today. It sounds as if you had a real nice vacation. I'm so glad. We have mail call about every second or third day and it's very seldom that I don't get at least one letter and, like this morning, I often get four or more. If you just keep writing me two nice letters a week, I'll be a happy boy. If you write more it'll make me feel like a brat for not writing oftener and I do write as often as I can, almost.

Marg, Laporte, 1943

I know just how you felt that rainy day because I've spent one there. Only that day, Aunt Carrie was baking and the results were delicious.

The fellow with the fractured wrist tickled me. I can understand just how he felt. I'm always a little jealous of those boys who have seen real action. Everything we've done has been so peaceful and humdrum. But really, down inside, I guess I'm thankful both for you and Judy and, too, because I really don't think I'm the hero type.

I won't accuse you of being a liar because I don't think you are, but you must have led Mrs. Fisher on scandalously for her to make a statement like that. I'll bet I haven't ever spoken a dozen words to her and only have seen her four or five times in my life. Or could it be that I'm 'a nice boy' because I had a nice puppy-love affair with her pretty daughter? Could be. Mothers are funny. I'm glad I'll never be one. I'll just be a proud father, I hope.

Pee sent me a couple of copies of a little magazine called "Letter" put out by Ada McCormick. Isn't that her boss? Anyway, they stunk. Or at least that's my opinion.

Friday night we had a British ENSA show, which is their USO and I enjoyed it very much. Some real good singing especially.

Your affectionate son,

Carp

Central Africa , Sept. 15, 1943

Dearest Mother,

Your letter of Aug. 20th just got here in the last mail. It must have caught the wrong plane somewhere because it was scorched so badly on three sides that the envelope had to be put in another envelope by the postal dept. However I could read all of it so here's an answer. I'm so glad you got the letter telling you to order the ring. If you'll tell me what form to use I'll send you authority to cash some of those bonds. I can't send any money from here because I have Christmas plans for all my pay between here and December. – Now I'm anxiously awaiting your report on how she likes it.

I know darn well you're worth every bit of what they're paying you and more too. I'm glad Dick said that. It's always nice to get a compliment from a fellow worker.

Judy sent me a couple of nice snapshots again. Only trouble with them is you can look but can't touch. Mmm, but I crave some good solid necking. That proves I'm getting old. There's a new name for it now.

My rifle team got off to a bad start yesterday and we were 7th out of 14. Today we pulled up to 4th and Friday we're going to make 2nd. The leading team is too far in front to be caught, but they've had a hell of a lot more practice than we have. –Alibi.

Lots of love from
Your affectionate son,

Carp

Central Africa Sept. 20, 1943

Dearest Mother,

Here it is two days after Judy's birthday and I haven't yet heard how she liked her present. Disgraceful mail service.

In answer to your question: Descriptions of the countryside have to be pretty vague. The best I can say about this is that it's typically bush country. The jungles of Africa are few and far between really. Even my first station had relatively little of the jungle about it. As for wild flowers, I've got to admit I haven't noticed very darn many. Flowering trees are quite profuse but flowers are scarce.

Your story about the farmer was good. He really is doing a job isn't he? About ten times as much work as most of us are putting in. Of course, I'm not speaking for the lads in Italy.

Talking about Flossie's meals just made my mouth water. One of these days I'm gonna sit me down to one of them and just about kill myself eating.

So the Army and Tom K. couldn't get along. What's he doing now? I'll bet he gets a good defense job and starts really making the dough. He should have been sent to Leavenworth for the duration and then let out to compete with the men coming home for jobs. Instead of being allowed to get in on the gravy now. It ain't fair.

We don't see enough newspapers here to know how they're handling the news, but our pet gripe is still the movies. They gripe us most because they so calmly insult your intelligence. They run over you with a freight train and then back it up and show it to you again and a deep bass voice from the rear says, "See, you stupid people you were hit with a train." A perfectly good movie that we saw last night, "Edge of Darkness" with Flynn and Sheridan, spent two hours and ten minutes showing us the kind of fighting people the Norwegians are; and then to end the show they give us Roosevelt's voice saying, "Now my children, since you've failed to grasp properly what we are trying to show you, may I explain that the Norwegians are a fighting people and are anxiously awaiting a little help from the Allies." It makes one slightly ill. The movie itself was good, or so I thought, but that last scene was the crowning touch. Phooey. Some one of these days I'm gonna write me a fan letter to a producer and it won't be flattering. I wish my bitching to you would do some good, but you never do anything about it.

My rifle team didn't quite come up to my expectations. We ended up a poor third. The boys were rather downhearted but at least we had fun.

Is Al flying or doesn't he ever say anything? He's a fighter pilot, isn't he? He should be having some pretty good hunting but I suppose he doesn't say much for fear of worrying Hattie.

Love,

Carp

Central Africa
Sept. 26, 1943

Dearest Mother,

I wonder how many letters I've written you since the summer of 1935? I wouldn't be surprised to find that it's a quite large number. Four years of college and two-and-a-half of war.

Just another statistic. Poor Judy, too, had nothing but a postal romance all along. I'll bet I've written a couple of small encyclopediae to you two gals, let alone all the other women in my life.

I'm on a very high upswing today. I've just been checking newscasts against the map and it has dawned on me that the Russian army is knocking hell out of the Germans to put it mildly. At their present rate they'll be knocking on the Polish door before Christmas. The German people must be beginning to get a little nervous. The handwriting on the wall is getting clearer and clearer. Next week sometime when I'm down in the dumps all I'll be able to think of is how much longer I may have to stay in Africa and stay a first lieutenant, but today I'm in the clouds. My hat's off to Russia and England. What a battle they've put up.

I've ordered a little native-made, real gold bracelet for Judy for Christmas, but don't say anything about it. They do some very pretty work here.

The weather here or rather the temperature has been perfect. Warm but not too warm and nice at night for sleeping.

Tell Kenny for me that only a damn fool would want an army-trained man for president. Just take a look at history. Taylor and Grant were flat tires as president and Washington and T.R. were essentially politicians turned soldier by force of circumstances. The training and background aren't conducive of good presidential material.

I'm getting tired of this post already. There isn't enough work here to keep me properly busy and that's bad. There's plenty of work, but it's so well organized that the men really need little supervision so I just piddle around making work most of the time and I hate that.

So long now Toots.
Love,
Carpy

Phoebe Starr Lose
Tucson, Arizona

Central Africa

Sept. 26, 1943

Hi Pee,

The war news is good. It looks now as if I may see Judy again before I reach 30. What I mean is what the Russians are doing to the Germans. Today's news reports say that they're crossing the Dneiper at a number of points and that's only about 150 miles from the Polish border. They'll beat the English and Americans into Berlin yet. I can't help but wonder what the Germans think of the news. I don't think the Italian situation is enough to worry them yet, but I'd hate like hell to know that the Russians are moving as fast as they are if I were one of der Fuhrer's boys. Of course, this is one of my optimistic days, but I really don't believe the Germans will last another twelve months. The Japs are an entirely different proposition though. But once we can really concentrate on them and throw in really heavy amounts of men and equipment it will change the situation pretty quickly.

As for Christmas Sweetheart, you might try the candy if you're sure it won't spoil. I appreciate the offer of the painting but you know how I appreciate art.

Your coyotes make Arizona sound wilder than this country. We've got jackals here, but they're cowardly animals and don't sound off. This new post is too damned civilized for wild life.

The weather there is a lot hotter than I'm having but it's starting to warm up here and in another month it ought to be pretty hot. Of course we have the advantage of a pretty steady cool breeze off the ocean.

So long now. Mind your P's & Q's.

Your neffoo.

Carp

Central Africa, Sept. 27, 1943

Hello Sugar,

Mail call again last night and two from my Sweetheart and one from my favorite mommy. The description of Judy's purse was luscious. I'll bet she really likes it. I'm still waiting for a letter from her after the 18th so I can't quote her on that.

In my hurry Sunday, I neglected to answer a question in your letter of the 20th, so I'll answer it now:

Those booby traps are tricky. I'll enclose an account of one from Sicily that's taken from "Yank." Some psychologist figured out this one. What a dirty trick.

Newspaper clipping:

" ...told about two GIs who saw a nice-looking Italian gun resting peacefully on a table. One of them suggested it might be a booby trap. As a test, he gently attached a long string to the gun and went all the way back to a nearby foxhole. Jumping in, he pulled the string. Nothing happened to the gun but the foxhole blew up. There was a mine in it. The other GI, watching the whole thing from the distance, now has the gun. It's a good gun."

Even if your September 20 letter was a bragging one I enjoyed it. You can brag about our Judy all you want to. I don't send home as much money as I could so I'm well fixed and whenever I want some she always sends it to me so don't let her talk like that.

What's this beatin' you took on the election mean? Is the country swinging back Democratic again?

You must have done a swell job on that Water Co. lumbering story to get John to change his mind. I'm proud of you.

Your observations on women in the war tickled me. One of my pet peeves is this practice of praising up the American workers for doing so much for the war effort and talking about how American production lines are winning this war. Certainly they are. Without American production the Allies would be in a hell of a fix. But who wouldn't like to fight this war in a defense plant six days a week, eight hours a day with time and a half for overtime, rather than man a gun against the enemy in Russia or the East Indies or Italy or just doing ordinary Army work in Africa. I'm not bitching about being here. This is my job and I'm proud to do it and lucky it isn't worse, but when it comes to credit for winning this war my hat's off to the English and Russian people who really saved the American hide. They didn't do it for us alone but we sure as hell aren't producing for their benefit either. – Boy have I changed from a rabid isolationist.

Gee, but I'd like to see that cute little daughter-in-law of yours. Sometimes I get so homesick for a little plain 'n fancy necking, I could blow my top.

I'm really proud of the way you're doing with your writing. Maybe someday you'll be a sob-sister for some big New York Daily. I'll bet you'd like to do a political column on Washington or even Harrisburg. That'd be better because you know all the political big-wigs in the State.

Let me know more about this assistant proposition. It sounds swell.

Lots of love,

Carp

P.S.   Annabelle wrote me the other day and gave me hell for not telling her about lesbians in the days when I was educating her to the facts and pitfalls of life. Seems she's run into a few lately. – I hate like hell to have to admit to a lack of any concrete knowledge, but I never appealed to 'em so I don't know much. – She still seems to be getting a kick out of being in the Army.

So long again,

Carp

October 16, 1943

Dearest Mother,

Saturday afternoon and no races so instead of sleeping, which is my natural inclination, I'll write a letter to my favorite Maw. I can't understand how it is that I always owe you a letter. It couldn't be that a nice woman like you could have a lazy brat for a son so it must be due to the weather or somethin'.

Boy for about two weeks I've been homesick and griped as hell. I think my letters home have been stinkers. Judy hasn't introduced divorce proceedings, has she? I told her when I left I'd never divorce her so long as I'm overseas so she's stuck. You know it's funny. But absence does sometimes make the heart grow fonder. I think I'm crazier about that child bride of mine now than I was when I left home. Letters from you two are really the only thing in life over here.

It doesn't seem possible that this is October and pretty soon you'll be bitching about the cold. Only a couple of months ago it was too hot for you. Now take this climate for a change or rather lack of change. I'm sitting here in my undershirt. Windows wide open and a fairly cool breeze keeping me just comfortable. The temperature must be about 80 degrees in here. Just nice. I really hate to think how tough on me it's going to be to get back to Pennsylvania. If I hit there in the winter I'll practically die. Good thing I'll have such a nice, effective bed warmer. Great invention, those things. Bed warmers, I mean. They're sure nice on a cold winter night. Tish, tish what a mind.

Well Snooks, I'll break it off until I hear from you and then I'll write a nice long one.

Love,

Carpy

Central Africa
Oct. 17, 1943

Dearest Mother,

Last night when I came in from the movie I found three swell letters from my Sweethearts. Two that Judy mailed in New York and yours of the 8th. It's now Sunday afternoon and I'm listening to a swing broadcast from England, and a bunch of old numbers.

Did I tell you that I saw a WAAC the other day? She should be a great addition to this army. She looked strong enough to do a harder day's work than I can. I wondered if she wouldn't maybe take over my job and let me go home and work in a nice clean office. She was a Second Lieut. I saw a couple of men salute her and she returned it, but her salute was strictly G.I. No snap.

The new paper sounds neat. I sure hope it means more writing for you. They aren't going to eliminate "News of Men in the Service" are they? That's the one thing I read very carefully. You've really made a success of that job of yours. I'm proud as hell of you. My editor mother is the way I speak of you.

I'll bet you'd sure like to be here. It's a nice hot summer afternoon. I'd be at the beach if I wasn't so damned lazy, but it's too comfortable here in quarters.

I'll close this now with bushels
of love from
Your affectionate son,

Carpy

Central Africa
Oct. 24, 1943

Dearest Mother,

Your hospital story is ancient as the hills. If I've got to stay in Africa you at least ought to send me good jokes. First thing I know you'll be trying to tell me, "That ain't no lady..."

The PX opened their big beer garden this week. Naturally the Engineers built it for them and some of my gang installed their ice cream machine for 'em. So every day I went in to inspect the job and check the results. I've had more ice cream in one week than I ever expected to get in all my stay in Africa. How do you like that for rough Army life? An ice cream machine. Real boughten ones, not the kind we rigged up in Leo. This place is a country club. I'm so sick of it I could spit and I'm not kidding either.

We had a bunch of good movies this week. "Mr. Smith goes to Washington," "Man Hunt," and "Mutiny on the Bounty." I'd never seen "ManHunt" and really enjoyed it.

The Oct. 4 <u>Time</u> had a column on Mrs. Roosevelt's report to the Mothers of the country. It interested me because it seems that she really did pick up a lot of points that the soldiers are wondering about, thinking about, and griping about.

Time for chop now so I'll break up this Bull Session.

Lots and lots of love from
Your affectionate son,
Carp

Central Africa
Oct. 31, 1943

Dearest Mother,

Don't ever get mad at me and stop writing when I let my correspondence lag. I don't do it deliberately, it's just that the days kinda slide by and I always promise myself I'll do it tomorrow. Well today it's tomorrow so here's the letter.

I've just come back from the beach. It's without a doubt the nicest one I've ever seen. Miami would gladly trade. Clean white sand and lots of it and the water shelves off so gradually you can still touch 150 yards out. And the breakers are swell for surfboards. Just off the edge of the beach there's a grove of about 20 acres of beautiful palm trees. It's strictly a beautiful setting. And was it nice today. Mmmmmh. Doesn't that make you jealous? Don't you wish you were in Africa? I don't. I'll take dirty, cold Williamsport and my family in exchange for the whole darn continent any day.

This has been a red-letter week. Friday night I was invited to a dinner dance that an Officer's club here was giving. I didn't have a date, not knowing many gals in these parts, but I went anyway. There were about 40 officers and about 25 girls, American and British nurses, and Red Cross girls. All the dances were tag so a wolf like me had a hell of a good time. The best in fact since some of the similar parties we had in Leopoldville. I think it was the third time I've danced this year and the first time I've danced anywhere near as much as I would at a dance at home. My legs were stiff and sore as hell next day after the unusual exercise.

Thursday night I saw "San Francisco" with Gable and MacDonald. Remember it? I really enjoyed it. Not a flag was waved in the entire thing. Those old shows get a real turnout. And we really go for 'em because they don't even hint at a war.

Judy wrote me a swell long letter all about her trip. Whatever she does about the ring is right by me if she gets it. But I do want her to have it.

I was very interested in what you had to say about the R.O.T.C. That's one thing that we've all been worrying about. Fear that we'd be over here for the duration and that they'd then put us in the Army of occupation because we're engineers and there will be a lot of work for engineers. I hope to hell you're right.

In answer to your question: Your letters haven't been censored in over a year, and as for my own, the fact that we censor company mail all the time makes us pretty careful on our own.

I'm glad to hear about the over-subscription of the war bond drive because the news of the coal strikes and other strikes isn't the best morale booster in the world. We have a thousand men in the outfit who would be glad to give up their soft cushy $60.00 a month to go back home and slave in a coal mine in the good old U.S. at present pay scale. But they're patriotic boys who wouldn't feel that they were sacrificing a thing.

Have the Republicans wised up and decided to let Wilkie run them, yet? They'll be as extinct as the auk if they don't pull their heads out of the sand soon.

Have you heard the definition of a "she wolf?" It's a girl who will trip a man and then beat him to the ground.

So Montour still has football? I'm glad to hear that because I'll vouch for it that the game does the boys who play it a hell of a lot more good than the small harm of a broken ankle or two. You know what it did for me in the way of giving me self-confidence and teaching me to handle myself. Which reminds me that some of the guys in the company saw me centering a ball the other day, so now they want me to play center on their touch football team tomorrow night.

> Lots and lots of love to you, Chicken.
> Your affectionate brat,
>
> *Carpy.*

P.S.   I love my wife, but Oh you kid.

Central Africa, Nov. 4, 1943

Dearest Mother,

It's payday for my labor gangs so I've got a few minutes of the working day to myself. But at one o'clock I'll have to go over and spend the rest of the afternoon witnessing the paying. It's a pretty lonesome procedure, but I get some fun out of it by studying the different types of native features. Most of them here are of one type. They're rather short and well built. Their faces are quite square and pleasant and they all have wide mouths full of sparkling teeth. The tribal markings vary from three small diagonal cuts on each cheekbone to long slashes all over the face. One of my best headmen has markings all over his puss. Makes him a tough looking hombre.

A few of the men are representative of a lot of different places. A couple of tall slender Senegalese work for me. Some Moroccan natives with a lot of Arab blood are here. Some big, tough-looking babies from Kenya are in the gangs, mostly as headmen. And a few Congo and French Equatorial natives drift in. They're little fellows and if they're from back in the bush they have sharp-filed, blackened teeth. About one in every 15 or 20 can write his name and boy is he proud to sign that payroll. We make X's for the rest; that's why I have to witness it.

We had another good movie last night. A comedy called "Young Ideas" with Mary Astor and Herbert Marshall. I really enjoyed it. They didn't wave the flag, mention the war, or even so much as sell a bond. It was wonderful. I think Universal produced it. They are the best at it because they play up the war less than any of the other studios.

I'm reading a hell of a good book now too. Judy told me about it and when I ran across a guy with a copy of it I snatched onto it. "A Tree Grows in Brooklyn" by Betty Smith. Actually I guess it's a rather sad story, but she tells it so well and gets all the humor out of every incident in it that it just keeps you enthralled. The Aunt in it is my favorite. She isn't bad, she's just fundamentally kind. She can't refuse anybody anything and besides she likes it. You really ought to read it. You'll like it too, I know.

I'm going to send you a couple of little bracelets that are to be my gift to Judy. One will be along in a week or so and the other some time in December as soon as it's made. Will you get a nice little jeweler's box for them? They're handmade of native gold and I think she'll like 'em, I hope.

As usual this morning I visited the ice cream plant. Now I'm darn near too full to eat. My weight has settled at 160, which isn't too bad for the tropics. I really feel fine and get a hell of a kick out of the softball and touch football we play. It's really too warm for the football, but we get a shower and drink a gallon or two of water after the game and it really makes you feel better. The exercise I mean.

Just to make you jealous. It's beautiful, fine, hot, swimming weather right now. Don't you wish you were here?

Love,

Carp

P.S.   Love. C
P.P.S. Love. C

Central Africa
Nov. 6, 1943

Hello Sugar Plum,

Your day of doing nothing but what you want to do sounded swell. After the war I'm gonna inaugurate a series of those days and nights.

I think Grandfather would be real pleased about publishing those articles in your paper. You know I've lost my copy of "The Vanishing Trout." I lent it to someone and it never came back. I'll watch for the copies you're sending me.

Gosh, Phoebe wrote that she's sending a Christmas present. I thought I told you to pass the word not to send me anything. It just clutters up the mail and is useless. If either you or Judy sends anything I'll divorce yuh. If I need or want something I'll ask for it, like Judy's picture, but anything else no. Letters are all I want and in quantity.

You're doing okay on that score, but I'm a little bitched at my wife. Don't tell her, because then she may start writing duty letters and they're worse than nothing. —Don't mind me, I've been in Africa too long.

The enclosed money order is for Christmas presents. Will you send Pee $20.00 and buy my usual presents with the rest. Aunt Edie, Uncle Bill, Bill Ader, and you know who all. Get together with Judy on family presents. She is going to get some for both of us and I'll fix it up with her. The two bracelets will be all I have for her. I hope she likes 'em. Gee that paragraph sounds bossy doesn't it? I don't mean it to be Toots, really, I'm asking a favor, please.

The radio is just playing Mandalay. I always did like Kipling. "There's a Burma girl a sitting and I know she waits for me." –Hell I never could quote right, but his stuff's always got such a rhythm that I like.

Lots of love from
Your affectionate son,

Carp

Central Africa, Nov. 22, 1943

Dearest Mother,

Judy came across with some more writing paper so I'll start right away to wear it out. I know just what you mean about that fountain pen not allowing you to stop. This one of mine gets the same kind of a spell every once in awhile.

I just laughed when I read about what a nice day it was back home. Shucks, Toots, they're all like that here. Yesterday afternoon I went down to the beach as usual on a Sunday afternoon. It was swell under the palms, but hotter than hell out in the sun unless you got in the ocean and it was just perfect. The kinda water I could stay in for hours, and you know I get cold easily. If I wasn't selfish I'd wrap you up a bottle of this sunshine and send it to you. Maybe I will. We've got lots to spare.

As some dope once said "It's a small world." I was going to work Saturday afternoon and somebody hailed me as I passed the P.S. It was Gene Entz. I hadn't seen him for more than three years. He's a Lieutenant in the Air Corps, a pilot, and was just passing through on his way to a new station. We roamed around camp all afternoon, had dinner together and then went over to the officer's club and threw the bull over a couple of high-balls all evening. He left early the next morning. It was an awful lot of fun just to talk over old times and compare notes on who was doing what and where. He looked swell and seems to be pleased that he's getting into it at last, but he said he wasn't looking forward to twenty-months of it.

Did I tell you that ((half-brother)) Don Carpenter wrote me so I now have his address? I wrote him a resume of the past year or so and he is going to report on what he's been doing.

The bombings on Europe must be having a terrific effect but I don't think Germany will quit until we establish a foothold on the mainland near Germany. Then, I think, she'll fold quick. Anyway I hope so. That foothold is going to require a lot of men and a lot of planning. Last week I heard they hit Berlin with 350 two-ton bombs in one raid. That wouldn't do any place any real good.

I'm sweating out that leave now, waiting for Roy to come back and for the money order from Judy to get here.

Lots of love from
Your affectionate rat,
Carp

Central Africa, Nov. 25, 1943

Hi Toots,

Monday afternoon, right after I wrote you I got a bunch of mail. One letter from you, two from Judy and the pictures of her. Boy, are they swell. I can't make up my mind which I like best. Guess I'll keep both of them. She's a beauty, isn't she? Gosh, I hope it's not another two years before I get home.

I've had a hell of a busy week. Work has been pressing and everybody and his brother has been bitching at me to get his special job done 'on time.' Yesterday I was about ready to blow my top.

I'll tell you all about today if you'll promise to forget it because otherwise you won't believe any of my horror stories about the hardships I underwent in the African Campaign. Anyway, it was

Thanksgiving Day, so they gave us the afternoon off. Which was quite a break because up until last night we expected to work. For dinner (noon) we had turkey with all the trimmings, even down to stuffing, cranberry sauce, and pumpkin pie. It was a really delicious dinner and I made a blooming pig of myself so after dinner I slept 'til four o'clock. Then I went up to the company and played about half of a touch football game against the Q.M. boys. We won 18 to 0 but I didn't help much because I was still too full of dinner. Well that wore off the meal pretty well and a shower fixed me up fine so at six-thirty I was back at the company and we had a light supper of cold turkey, pumpkin pie, ice cream, doughnuts, cocoa and Coca-Cola. I stuffed myself thoroughly again and then went down to the theater where the local police band played us a concert. They're a darn good band and as colorful as can be. It's an all native band with a white conductor, about thirty pieces. They play marches marvelously, classical music quite well and popular not so well. Their costumes consist of white shirts with a red and gold monkey jacket over it. Tight knee-length blue shorts with red braid. Olive drab leggings and bare feet. Oh, and a red fez with a tassel to top the ensemble.

Well, next week this time ought to see me started on my leave. Hello Cairo, here I come, I hope. I wish to hell I had some one to go with me. Preferably a girl named Judy, but I'd settle for Baldy or Kit or Wimpy.

G'night now Sweet.

Your ever loving chee-ild,

Carpy

Chapter 7

England

I never got that leave to go see Cairo. Instead we received orders to move out again. We boarded a ship and sailed down the coast of Africa, stopping in Liberia, where we picked up more soldiers. We turned around and sailed back north, all the way to Gibraltar. I'd like to have seen Gibraltar, but they kept us on the boat for the almost-week that we anchored there. Next it was up to England. We sailed up the river past London before finally getting off that boat.

Phoebe Starr Lose
Tucson, Arizona

December 26, 1943

Hi Pee,

Twas the day after Christmas and all thru my head, the Gremlins were working. Boy, I wish I were dead.

You know it's a funny thing, I had about six quick ones and they never fazed me, but that seventh one sure upset the apple cart. What a beautiful shine I had last night. I had two quarts of Canadian Club so every time a guy came in the room he had to drink a toast to Judy on our wedding anniversary and naturally I had to drink with them. Considering the situation, it was a good celebration.

We're on the move again. I left my last station about the first of the month and am heading for APO #640. Lord only knows where that is. We're at an intermediary port now which is a break because it made it safe to get lit up for Christmas. I like to be perfectly sober when I'm at sea. It's been a good trip so far. This is a swell big ship and the food is excellent. My only complaint is that we're not going home. Twenty-one months over here and my homesickness is just as bad as ever. At least I can say I've seen the world. 13,000 miles by boat, 4,000 by plane and ten countries. Boy, will I be a homebody when I get back to the fireside.

Your Christmas present reached me last so I saved it 'til Christmas day to open. It was swell Pee. You're a nice girl. Those mittens are neat. It was smart of you to figure out that I'd need them. The cake was wonderful. Did you make it with your own little Lily Whites? The potted meat and nuts we're nibbling at. They make good midnite snacks.

Your friend Elizabeth sent me a box with some toilet articles and good books. She's always sending me nice long letters with newspaper clippings and books and stuff. Not exactly always, but regularly, every couple of months and I forget to write her. So why don't you write her and thank her for me? I'll write too, I hope.

I remember your saying that you were making out better and had developed quite a gang of friends. I was awful glad to hear that because I know you were pretty darn homesick for awhile. The pet mouse sounds real cute. He must be pretty smart. I hope you don't catch him.

Lots of love from,
Your neffoo,

Carpy

Jan. 8, 1944
England

Dearest Mother,

I got your letter of Dec. 14 last night and am slightly confused. It'll probably take the rest of my mail to unfuse me.

I'm glad to hear that your influenza is better, which I didn't know you had and I hope Judy's cold is all okay.

As to your writing, I think you're having the same trouble I do. You think faster than you can possibly write and then you try to write that fast. If I slow down, I can write a fairly legible hand. I hadn't noticed the change in yours until you mentioned it, but it has changed. It's still a very legible hand, but smaller and I'll bet faster.

You probably know by now that I got lots of Christmas presents. Two from you, one from Judy, one from Pee, one from Edie and Bill and The Readers Digest from the Company. I've already written and thanked everyone. The bathrobe and slippers from you and the raincoat from my Judy are my prize possessions. Speaking of possessions, now that we're in England, all the guys are going to have to buy uniform blouses to replace the ones we were ordered to leave in the States. Luckily, I got one in Africa and have it with me.

I'm glad you found something nice for Judy for Christmas. Did that other bracelet ever arrive? The answer to that question is probably on its way to me now.

Jan. 9, 1944

I had to go on O.D. last night and didn't get this finished.

I was tickled to hear about Bill Ader going in the Boy Scouts. I know just how he feels about it. If I get time, I'll write him a note one of these days.

Judy's written a lot about the Bishop girls. I'm glad you met their mother and liked her. It must be a nice family. Having nice friends like that, new ones I mean, will be a big help to Judy to keep her from getting too blue or lonely.

I've got a change in my address for you. I'm no longer in Co D, but am now in 1 BN HQ. I have been commanding D Company, but my job now is 1st Battalion Adjutant. It should be interesting, but not as much fun as running a company. The job rates a captain, so if I keep my nose clean for a couple of months, I may rate a promotion. Just keep hoping, but don't say anything.

I need some new razor blades. Will you try to send me a few packs, please? Put them on a card – i.e. tape 'em on and slip them in a letter. One pack only lasts me two weeks here because I have to shave every day.

I, personally, can't see where the meeting between Churchill, Stalin and the President did any good. It undoubtedly solidified the Allies war aims and plans, but as to any definite program of action after the war, I don't think they have any.

These bombings that Germany's getting now delight my heathen soul. I always like to see a bully who started something get the hell beat out of him and they are getting it. I'm bitter, yes, because of the bastardly German race I've lost two years and more out of my life.

So you weren't flattered by Norman's proposal? Well anyway, he proposed to you the first time before he went off his nut, maybe this is a sign that he's coming back to rationality. Could be.

As to your Dec. 5th letter, I wrote you a letter the same day you wrote me if I remember right. Because that was the day I cracked up on the motorcycle. Did you get my letter telling you that I'm all cured of any injuries from that accident? I've grown all new skin and my ankle doesn't bother me a bit. I'm lucky, that's all.

Gee Toots, I'm glad you got something nice with the Christmas present. Your description of Judy's face when she gave it to you was swell. Gosh, but I'd like to see her grin at me. She thought up the card by herself, but she said just what I'd have said. Haven't you noticed how you pick up phrases and mannerisms of someone whom you love or admire a great deal? I know I use pet phrases of hers often. The suit and hat and all sound really neat. I'll bet you do knock 'em cold.

You are writing more and more stuff all the time, aren't you? I'm just as proud as a peacock about my newspaperwoman Mother.

Keep me informed about how long it takes my letters to get home, will you? I'll do the same. It may boil down to using V-mail, but I'd honestly rather wait a little longer for a real letter.

Did I tell you about taking the company out for a hike yesterday and going thru a small village near camp? It was absolutely the prettiest place I've ever seen. Not more than twenty or thirty houses all with gabled, second story windows and all just as neat as a pin. I really enjoy just walking thru town, drinking in the sights.

Lots and lots of love,
Your affectionate son,

Carp

The motorcycle accident happened when I was heading back to that last camp in Africa and met up with an on-coming truck that was taking its half out of the middle of the road. I was forced to swerve onto the shoulder of the road where I hit a pot-hole and blew out the front tire.

England, Jan. 13, 1944

Hi Toots,

Yesterday another love letter came wandering in. The one you wrote Dec. 30. It brought me up to date with gaps. I gathered that you've found a satisfactory apartment and are moving in today. And it must be somewhere near the Montoursville bus line. I hope you wrote me a full description of the place.

Gee, but Doc Wilcox is a lucky guy. Boy what I'd give to be home on leave. Don't get me wrong, I'm not homesick, much. I hope he gave you a really good picture of the works. You know he and I have a pact. Anything one of us says, the other backs up implicitly. Ruppert and I have a similar deal. Is Doc on leave or has he been transferred back to the States? Did he know anything of the part of our gang that we left there? Speaking of warm baths, I had my quota on the boat and I'm really getting to enjoy hot water for shaving. It's a swell idea. I'd almost forgotten.

I think I understand what Doc means, and I know how you feel, but I agree with him. People in the States do know that there is a war going on because of the sons and husbands overseas and to a small extent because they can't get certain luxuries. But they don't get the full picture. I think you're probably better informed than 98% of the people, but I know you haven't seen bombed areas or any of the countries I've been in and 'til you've actually seen them, all the pictures and descriptions in the world won't give you the real picture. I think that's what Doc meant.

People at home have been touched by the war in a personal way, but we've seen it as both a personal picture and also the big impersonal scene. There's a difference. – I guess that doesn't explain what I mean but it's the best I can do.

Last night I broke down and went to town with a half-dozen of the officers. We went to a skating rink and skated for a couple of hours and had a swell time. My first time on skates in more than three years and I never was too good. But no spills. The town is weird. The blackout is absolute and no fooling. The M.P.'s showed us our way around because there are no advertising signs or anything and to walk thru the town you'd think it was deserted except for the unusually large number of people walking thru the dark streets. Bicycles are my biggest hazard. I forget to jump out of the way. —It still amazes me to see more than three white women in one place. I can't get civilized.

This is short because I've got work to do, but it's got a lot of love and kisses.

Your brat,

Carp

This one is addressed to Marg at her new apartment, which was actually in the Grit building, 228 W. Third St., Williamsport

England, 26 Jan. '44

Dearest Mother,

That was an awfully nice Christmas letter. Judy wrote me on the same day and I got 'em together. It sounded like a very nice Christmas under the circumstances. Both of you gals did all right on presents. In fact we all did because I got a swell bunch of presents just after we sailed, as you know by now.

Thanks for Val's address. I don't know when I'll get a chance to look him up. It's really quite a difficult proposition because of regulations against disclosing military locations in any way. And if he's as busy as I am, he's damn busy. I've worked two nights this week and expect to work tonight. That's the hell of an office job. What I need is a W.A.C.

That new suit of yours sounds really snazzy. Judy raved about it.

I guess the bracelet won't arrive, but it's no loss so we'll skip it. She wouldn't have worn two anyway.

Gee, I'm glad Bill Ader got his Boy Scout equipment and liked it so much. He'll make a darn good scout.

Now it's New Years already and I do appreciate the good wishes in your Jan. 2nd letter. You're probably well settled in your new apartment by now. It ought to be really swell and handy. —Those red curtains sound rather dangerous, you'd better be careful.

You're in the same ward with Judy, aren't you? I'll bet you'll make a good committee-woman and I'll bet you can handle both sections too. We always were a good tribe for mixing low and high-brow friends. Generally, I prefer the low.

Gee Whiz, Pal, if the Office of War Information will let you print it in the newspapers then I ought to get a copy of it. I'm interested. —Have you forgotten? Your mail to me is not censored. I hope you've got a full file of letters so I can bore my kids with it ten or fifteen years from now.

I went to town last Friday and took in a dance but it was pretty boring so I haven't been back. What I need is a good love affair, but my conscience holds me back. Maybe one of these days I'll get the best of it and break down. Okay, okay. So I'm just like the old man. Well maybe, but I don't think so. But it's been too damn long. Don't bother to write and give me hell 'cause it wouldn't do any good.

The best thing about England so far is the food. Boy do I eat. You wouldn't believe it if you saw me. I go back for seconds darn near every meal. And it's darn good food. On Saturday I had the best steak I've had in months and on Sunday the best chicken since leaving the States. Real tender chicken. Not birds that had been run to death.

I'm going to ask for something and it may be impossible. If so, skip it. If not, well I need brown shoe polish. A big can or two. And I'd like a half dozen candy bars. We're rationed down to one can of shoe polish for two months and two candy bars a week. Well for shoes and an appetite like mine, that's rough. And don't forget razor blades, please.

I've heard that candy is scarcer 'n hell in the States, so maybe I'm asking the impossible. I don't know 'cause it's been a long time.

It's time for work now so I'll break it up and start earning my salary again.

Lots and lots of love,
Your affectionate son,

Carpy

Feb. 7, 1944   England

Dearest Mother,

For a change, a nice typewritten letter. What a thrill. I haven't written many of these in the last couple of eons. Gosh, something's going to have to be done about my writing so often, or did I say that wrong. Well, there's been nothing to write about anyway. I've been busy as hell at all kind of piddling jobs. This life is killing me. Reports, reports, reports. What an office soldier I am.

Uncle Bill Flack wrote me a nice letter that I got today. He was quite flattering, it almost embarrassed me. I'm afraid that The Rock job has been talked up to a lot more than it really was. It was fascinating and I'll probably bore hell out of everybody talking about it, but a lot of it was just run-of-the-mill, ordinary work.

I went to the bi-weekly dance Friday night and had a good time. I hadn't realized how much I'd missed dancing and small talk. You know, it's funny, but I'm so out of practice at the art of making conversation that I remind me of how tongue-tied I used to be at social functions when I was a sophomore in high school and just starting to date.

My Jan. 17 <u>Time</u> magazine arrived today. And as usual, I pored over it from cover to cover. The "Letters" page always has some good stuff in it. One that interested me was a letter concerning the unfairness of persecuting loyal, American-born Japanese.

It also had quite an item about the WACs and their failure to meet expectations as to the number of volunteers they could get. They gave a number of reasons for it but kinda glossed over the reason I think is the chief one and that is that most American men don't approve of it. You may remember the letter I wrote Judy about it when she mentioned something about joining. The wife of one of my sergeants joined without telling him and he was fit to be tied. He cut out her allotment and quit writing to her so when it changed from WAAC to WAC, she quit.

This soldier vote bill is still getting a big write-up in our daily <u>Stars and Stripes</u>. Most of the comment here is that Congress is sure giving them the dirty end. My opinion is that Congress just doesn't give a damn except that it is a good political football. So far both Frank and Wilkie have been quite cagey about following all the various moves. I'm betting on Frank. He's the smartest politician of the whole gang.

The lads from Russia are still going great guns. "God Love 'Em." The quicker they reach Berlin, the better.

I'll bet the little old Jappers are starting to sweat too. The Gilbert and Marshall moves were mighty big steps in the right direction.

> Lots and lots of love
> from your brat,
>
> *Carpy*

My dislike for the WAACs was probably unfair, but it was also widespread. The Censorship Office kept track of comments in soldiers' letters to home and found that over 80% of the soldiers disliked the idea of the WAACs. That's probably because we didn't realize at the time what a good job the gals were doing.

The WAACs (Women's Army Auxiliary Corps) was the result of a bill introduced by Congresswoman Edith N. Rogers of Massachusetts in 1941. She didn't feel it was fair for the Army to accept women volunteers to help with the war effort, as they had during the First World War, without being able to pay them and provide them with housing and food. But she couldn't get the bill taken seriously until after Pearl Harbor. Even then she had to give up on the idea that the women would be a PART of the Army and accept that they would be an Auxiliary Corps working WITH the Army.

In the spring of 1943, there were Congressional hearings to discuss how to encourage more women to join. One way was to be able to offer them equal pay and protection. To that end, in July, a new bill was signed into law making them a part of the regular Army – the Women's Army Corps.

At that time, the women were given the option of staying on as WACs, as an official part of the Army, or going home. Three-quarters of the women stayed, and, after many months of recruiting, many more signed on.

9 Feb. '44 England

Dearest Mother,

I've got two more nice letters to answer and I'd better get at 'em because I'm going on a new job tomorrow and it may be a little time before I dig out sufficiently to start corresponding again. One dated Jan. 26 came in yesterday and one Jan. 21 came today. But none from Judy. It looks as if there is a conspiracy to keep us from getting each other's letters. You'll have to be our go-between. Give her a nice big kiss for me and tell her I kinda like her a lot. And I'm still being a good boy, dammit. The flesh is willing but the spirit is weak.

You're sure running on a busy schedule when you can't make a dinner date except a week ahead. Put me down for a Tuesday night sometime in '45.

I haven't gotten in touch with Al yet but from talking around, I got the idea that he's not so far away. It's really tough to make contact here though because you can't so much as mention nearby towns as places to meet except maybe London; and Lord only knows when I'm gonna get time for a pass to London.

I'm afraid that English accent is out of the question. I can imitate a few phrases, but I still can't talk like 'em.

Do you think you could get a restaurant license to increase your coffee allotment? With all those early morning guests, you're going to need it.

I saw snow the other morning for the first time since that winter in S.C. And just about as much as we used to see there. Not real snow, just a flurry.

The boys in Italy are hitting rough weather even with that new beachhead. That move tickled me. It was so characteristic of this new type of warfare, which the Germans thought they had a monopoly on. It's the Allies now-a-days who are pulling the unexpected and the Nazis who are catching it on the chin. The boys in the Pacific are really cutting chunks out of the Japanese defense lines too. But the Russians are my pals. They keep steadily chopping up pieces of the Wehrmacht (defense forces of the German Army) and masticating them.

Do you ever see any English newspapers? I think they'd interest you, especially if you could follow them for a couple of weeks. Single copies kinda leave you up in the air. This country has real freedom of the press and except for essential military censorship, they print what's happening, why it happened and what future results may be expected from it and good luck to the guys responsible. They criticize (usually constructive) anyone whom they see fit to pan from Winston on down. Columns of argument between the politicians on various questions intrigue me. They give both sides of the question right from the feed bag.

A lot of OCS officers are hoping to make the Army a career, but damn few of us who are reserve officers are interested. At least that applies in this outfit. All we want to do is get back to civilian engineering. We're making good money now, but that isn't the only thing in life. I'd rather be making less on a properly run civilian construction job. Army snafu kills me.

Grace is sure my pal and I sure do appreciate it. But I think that she and George are just about the nicest folks that Judy could possibly have had. Judy's mother must have been a swell person.

I get a kick out of your raving about your apartment. It must be really nice. I'm darn glad.

Lots and lots of love from
your affectionate brat,

Carpy

P.S.　Gosh oh gee. I almost forgot Valentine's Day.

Roses is red,

Violet's is purple,

I like you lots,

But my poetry's tur'ble.

Will you be my Valentine?

Feb. 23, 1944

Dearest Mother,

I've just finished my dinner and am dashing off this note to you and I mean dashing. Mail from you is still coming thru quite well but Judy's letters seem to be held up. However I did get a couple of packages from her. One had some uniforms and one had stationery and photographic paper.

The letter containing the article about Doc and me got here yesterday. It also had some good philosophy from my favorite Maw. The letter that evoked that philosophy from you was written when I was in a rather low mood. So far, I'm pure, and while I may not remain pure, I'll at least remain particular. I'm funny that way.

One thing very pleasant has happened to me. I've met the most delightful family. Four women, oh boy! The mother is 60 some and the widow of an English General. The oldest daughter is about 38, single and a very forthright gal, reminds me of Phoebe. The second daughter, Essex, is about 30. Married to an English Major who is out east. They have a three-year-old son. The youngest daughter, Francoise, called "Gay" is about 24 and single. Reminds me of June Konkle with Bea Mason's wit. Boy she can snap 'em back at a guy. When I want a date I take Gay out, but usually I go to the house and we sit around the fire and play games or talk. We play charades, and checkers, and "Who am I" and stuff like that. The house is always full of British and American Officers and their dates and the people who go there are my kind of people. They've been swell to me and always urge me to come back again soon. So I do. It's the kind of a house that you don't knock on the door, you open it and walk into the hallway and holler. –You've probably gotten a pretty good impression of the Barters by now and you'll undoubtedly be hearing more.

This job has been hectic but fun. We've made camp twice since starting it and are now living on the job itself. There really isn't much to it except for getting supplies and tools, but it has kept me busy as hell in the daytime and, nights that I didn't go down to Barter's, I've slept. That's why no mail. There's no place to write in our barracks and at night it's plenty cold. So bed is the only place to be. I'll be moving back to my regular job in a few more days and maybe you'll hear from me a little more regularly, I hope.

The best thing about this job has been that I've had a bunch of my old "A" Co. boys cooking for the detachment, and we've literally eaten like kings. Hot biscuits, apple pies and things like that in addition to regular, well-prepared meals.

Lord only knows when I'm gonna get a chance to go to London, but I'm angling for it. I'd hate like hell to have to say I'd been in England and never seen London. But I certainly have seen some beautiful country and towns. The town the Barters live in is beautiful. It's real old, even for England, and has wide, rambling streets and the prettiest stone houses with stone fences in front of each house. Nice well-kept shrubbery and a whole appearance of being all posed for a picture. It's neat.

Time for work call, so I'll scram.

Lots and lots of love from
Your erring brat,

Carp

Evenings spent with the Barter family are among my most pleasant memories. To try to thank them for their hospitality, I would go to our mess cook and get sugar and cocoa, which I would then take to the Barters so we could make fudge.

February 26, 1944   England

Dearest Mother,

I'm now back with the battalion HQ. We finished up the small job I was on so I had to return to the fold. I'd just as soon have stayed. That's the best job in the Army. Commanding a platoon on a job away from the regiment. I sure hated to leave that hotel room I was staying in and come up here to a tent. But it is a quite comfortable tent. It's got the nicest fat-bellied stove in it you could ever want and in fifteen minutes I can have it so hot everybody has to move out. The last two mornings the boys have loafed in bed and let me get up and start the fire. Even that hasn't been too bad 'cause I move around fast.

Over at Barter's the other night we were playing "Truth or Consequences." One question was asked of an English girl as to the characteristic of the Americans she most disliked. Her answer was, their slouching walk. She elaborated that they walked like a bunch of Lascars carrying the weight of the world. I blushed.

I can fully understand how much you like your little apartment and housekeeping it. It's all yours and for you, so you have a different idea about working in it. Besides it must be an awfully handy little place.

To change the subject abruptly, a remark my sergeant just made reminded me of a topic which used to burn me up. From censoring mail, I used to get a pretty good idea of how true or untrue a soldier's girl was being. And it really used to get the boys down when they'd hear from home that their best girl was running around with some 4F defense worker. There just wasn't anything they could do about it, but things are different now. The usual comment is, "Well if she wants a 4F'er she can have him. There are plenty of damn nice English girls who would gladly marry an American man." And a lot of guys have married English girls, you read about some American marrying an English girl in practically any newspaper you pick up.

I get a kick out of Gay Barter. She's very, very pro-American. She says that if she doesn't marry an American over here during the war, she's going to the States afterward and catch one in his native habitat. She was engaged to a Polish-American RAF pilot, but he was killed over Germany in the fall of '42. She'll get herself an American too, because she's a plenty all-right dish. Kinda a pert little brownette. She's about half brunette and half blonde, if you get what I mean. In Truth or Consequences, I asked her if her hair was really that color and she took the Consequences.

I discovered from a letter of Judy's written before she got my request that candy bars are rationed to one a week. That's even worse than England. It's hard to believe.

I'll break now Toots. Lots and lots of love to the nicest Mother in the world.

Your brat,

Carp

Postcard from Essex Spencer, addressed to Mrs M. L. Carpenter

THE GREEN BROADWAY WORCS.

From E. Spencer,
Southwold,
Broadway,
Worcs, England

27/2/44

Just a postcard to show you what our village looks like and we hope to see you here visiting w\us after the war. G. is very well and looking so fit and we have great "fudge-making" parties. My mother, sisters, and I all join in sending best wishes to you and Judy.

My small son loves G.!

Essex Spencer

March 6, 1944

Dearest Mother,

I got two swell letters from you yesterday and one today, but last night I was just too darned tired to answer (I got in at 5:00 AM the morning before) so here I am tonight as chipper as a lark and bubbling over.

The first item I want to answer is about your new job. That is just the best news I've heard in a long time. I'm awfully proud of you, Toots, and happy about the whole thing. You must be doing very good work or they wouldn't have done this. I know that when I read your stuff I have to keep remembering that you wrote it 'cause it sounds just like a newspaper. S'funny. You've learned newspaper writing awfully quickly, I think.

I'm glad my letters are getting through so well. As you may have noticed, the service in this direction is spotty as hell. And Judy's letters have an awful time getting here. The last I have from her was dated Feb. 7. I'm awful glad about the pin. That you like it and it matches. It's supposed to be gold but I don't know much about the stuff. But I did think it was a pretty thing. I studied over earrings and necklaces but decided you wouldn't wear either, so the pin was the best bet.

The guy who came in to protest your article about girls marrying soldiers was probably right. I suppose there are a lot of nice 4-F guys at home, but not from where we sit.

I'm going in to London on Thursday on a 4-day leave, and I'm going to take in about four good stage shows, one good movie, "For Whom the Bell Tolls," as much dancing as I can find, and lots of sleep.

I was up to Barter's again Saturday night, the night I got in at 5:00 AM. Fred went along with me and we had another perfectly grand evening. An English Lieutenant and his wife and three other American officers were there so we had kind of a party again. Gay's going to meet me in London for part of my leave. She'll stay with some friends and show me the town. And don't worry about me and the bombings. I sleep under so many covers it would take a direct hit to bruise me.

You want to get a little more rest yourself. You're going an awful clip.

I have some news that's just the opposite of your good news. I got fired the other day. Orders came out transferring me back to line duty with Co. F. I asked Donovan why and he said he hadn't been satisfied with my work so— I'm kinda burned up, because that was the first intimation I'd had that I wasn't satisfactory, and I had only two more days to go to make me eligible for promotion. But this is the Army and there's nothing to be done about it. I'm in a good company and I like the C.O.

Lots and lots of love to my
favorite mother.

Carp

P.S.   Don't let it bother you. I'm more burned up than anything.

March 12, 1944

Dearest Mother,

Would you believe it, your own favorite brat is here in London writing a letter to his favorite Mother. It's a nice feeling and a nice town too. One very nice feature of it, from my point of view, is an excellent subway system. I have a neat map of London that also has all the subway lines on the back of it so I've been travelling all over the city with no trouble at all. Anytime I get a little confused, somebody always offers information to straighten me out and I have a wonderful time. Only differences between New York and London subways are escalators and the people sleeping in them. London tubes are so deep in the ground that they have one or two escalators at each stop. They have three decker bunks against the wall at all stops and every night you can see whole families sleeping down there. The kids love it.

To start out, when I got on the train, British reserve went to hell. One chap offered me a newspaper before we'd been riding a minute. We were in one of these 1st class compartments like you see in the movies. Six people in seats opposite each other. Another chap let me read a magazine he had, and a nice gal about 40 talked to me most of the way in. She had lived in Philly during the early 20's and then married a Canadian and moved to Canada and then England.

When we left the train she gave me her name and address and invited me to tea. Her home isn't far from camp. Thursday afternoon, I went to a matinee and saw "Something in the Air," a good musical comedy, modern. In the evening I saw "The Dancing Years" about Vienna before and after the last war. All the songs were waltzes and were grand. –Friday afternoon Gay came down and in the evening we went to a revue called "Sweeter and Lower." It was too. I loved every minute of it. After the show we had dinner and danced at the Lansdowne Hotel until midnight and then went on to dance at the Coconut Grove until the wee small hours. Friday afternoon and yesterday afternoon I bummed around town and saw some of the sights. Leicester Square, Trafalgar Square, Picadilly Circus, The Thames embankment, Tower of London, Waterloo Bridge and stuff like that. Gay had a date for a dance in a town near London last night so I was on my own and went to see "Strike a New Note," another revue with a cast of newcomers. It was swell too. One of the best numbers in it was "I'm gonna get lit up when the lights go up in London." You've probably heard some of the controversy over it.

This afternoon if Gay gets back in time, we're going to the Grosvenor House for tea, then dancing, otherwise I'm going to see "For Whom the Bell Tolls."

Tomorrow I'm going to see some more of the sights and then go 'home.' Dammit.

The Germans have been very kind about laying off London while I've been here. If they'll stay away tonight it'll be perfect.

Lots of love,
Your brat,

Carpy

P.S.   Mar. 14, 1944

Two years over here today. Arrived back from London last night. It was swell. I'll write more later.

March 27, 1944

Dearest Mother,

You're going to get gypped again on this letter. It'll be a note because I'm so tired I can hardly see.

Yesterday was one of the nicest days I've had in many a long month. It was beautiful, kinda like those rare days we get in late May when it's just so nice out it's unbelievable. And I did everything to get full enjoyment out of it. I slept 'til 8:30 which was two hours extra sleep. Then I walked down to a riding academy near camp and went riding for about two hours. Two of the new lieutenants in the company were with me. It's unbelievably beautiful country to ride through. All up and down hill with paths thru the fields and woods everywhere. You're always coming round a corner or out on a hilltop right over a pretty little village of a dozen or so picturesque stone houses with slate or thatched roofs and that atmosphere of having been there for at least a couple of centuries. The stable where we ride was built in 1653, but the house is quite new. 1711.

In the afternoon, Mots, one of the new lieutenants and I went for a hike. We did about eight or nine miles over and around these same hills. I was fagged when we came in and all set to take a shower and relax and write a few letters, but Tuck and Mots talked me into going in to the show with them. So we took off. The movie got out early so we went Pub crawling and ended up with eight of the 38th Officers at a little Pub on the outskirts of town. All of us just a little happy and singing Beer Barrel Polka, My Old Kentucky Home, and such with the other customers. They were all extremely nice to us. It was a hell of a lot of fun.

Yesterday and today were just too energetic for me. I worked like a buzz saw all day today and tonight I'm practically out. So I'll stop this and say good night.

Lots and lots of love.
Your affectionate son,

Carpy

P.S.   If you should find a small money order enclosed, it's to buy a favourite mother a nice Easter present with lots of love from her boy.

P.P.S. Your letter of Mar. 12 arrived two days ago. None from Judy in 18 days now. She's okay, isn't she?

I'll have Gay look for an Englishman for you. I haven't been up there for a week now. Maybe I'll get up this week.

I'll have to give you a real answer to your letter later. There are some things on which I want to expound.

G.H.C.
That's me
Carp

This one's in the form of a little, bitty V-mail. It was handwritten, then reduced in size by a microfilm process.

V · · · — MAIL

Mar. 31, 1944

Hi Toots,

A fortune teller told me this was going to happen, but I didn't believe her. One afternoon while in London, I stopped at this place and had the palmist read my hand. She told me the usual crap and also said my transfer would go thru and turn out well. I told her she was crazy because I hadn't asked for a transfer, didn't want one and didn't expect one.

This morning they told me that I was being transferred or rather had been and that I should report here today. So three hours later I was on my way, and here I am at HQ S.B.S Opr. Section APO #519 c/o Postmaster, New York, N.Y. –

I haven't the least idea why or what I'm to do so I hope the second part turns out. I'll write when I know more.

Love,
Carp

HQ S.B.S. Opr. Sect.
APO #519 New York

April 4, 1944

Dearest Mother,

Your wandering boy is still in a hell of a fog over this change in status he's just performed and talk about homesick, boy. Only here's where I get shot, I'm not nearly as homesick for home as I am to see that old gang. Boy I'd give a month's pay to be back with 'em. Of course I'd give a year's pay to be back with you two gals. This business of being on a staff and not with an outfit just doesn't appeal to me. Or maybe I'm just lazy because I've had a job pushed in my lap that is a honey. I can't tell you about what it is but it's sure gonna worry me into gray hair. I'm getting around England a bit on it, so it isn't too bad.

The part of England I'm in now isn't nearly as pretty as some parts I've been in. Or maybe I'm just bitter and too busy to look. But the station I left was just about as pretty country as I've ever seen in my life and just about the nicest people too.

I wrote the Barters a note to explain why I wouldn't be seeing them so very often. I'll miss them a lot. Especially Essex. She kinda adopted me. By the way, I think she may have dropped you a card just to reassure you that your little boy is in good health, excellent spirits, and fine fettle, whatever that is. I'm going to have to manage to get up to see them once in awhile if I possibly can.

English books will always fascinate me from now on because I can picture the country now. I've lived in a manor house and I've tramped over a country estate. In fact when I came down here I stayed three nights at some big shot's country place. One evening I walked around the place and saw a number of rabbits, quite a few wild ducks, and more ring necks than you could shake a stick at. And there is a stream about the size of the Warrensville Mill Creek that flows through the place and kinda curves around in front of the house and has trout in it.

Yes, English girls do have marvelous complexions, but they all have rough, red hands because the only soap they can buy is a utility soap that is pretty hard on them.

That was swell news to hear that Pete hasn't forgotten me. I'm kinda counting on him to put me to work in the wire rope business one of these days.

Don't ever say you write piddling letters. I love every bit of your letters so keep 'em coming even if I don't do so good.

I'll close now. Lots of love,
Your son,

Carp

As the Allies prepared for D-Day there was a need for "skids" (pallets) to be used in moving equipment and supplies for the invasion. My job was to coordinate with the British Timber Control people to get the lumber to build those pallets. Each evening, around 7:00, I'd get a call from British Timber Control giving me a dozen locations where lumber was available to us. I had an Army trucking company working for me, whom I'd call and assign to pick up the loads. The trucks would bring the lumber back to where the pallets were to be built by American prisoners. Yes. American prisoners. Not all of our guys kept their noses clean and some of 'em got locked up.

One of the biggest problems with getting the lumber from and to the right places was that there were no road signs and no signs for any of the villages. Signage had been removed to make it harder for German spies to gather information or, in the event that the Germans invaded, to make it as confusing as possible for them. As a result our trucks were frequently lost, so I spent a lot of time finding them.

Most days, my driver and I would go out looking for trucks and locations and would try to keep things moving. As a result of that job, I covered a hell of a lot of Southern England.

Every once in a while the Timber Control people would send us a couple of train cars of lumber, which was nice because they couldn't get lost.

HQ S.B.S. Opr. Sect.
APO #519 New York, NY

Dearest Mother,

What a job this turned out to be. It's after eight and I'm still in the office waiting for a report to come in so I can finish my operating schedule and go to quarters. For the past week now I've been finishing work anytime between six thirty and eight thirty. And what's more I start about seven-fifteen in the AM. It's rough and tough in the E.T.O. But I'm enjoying myself. It's interesting work and I'm so busy the time passes quickly.

My quarters here are the most comfortable I've had in England. Practically all the conveniences. Good hot water in the bathroom right next to my room, shower 'n everything. A thundering good officers' mess. Two movies a week, right here on the post, so I can go to 'em and still be near the phone. A room orderly who makes my bed, shines my shoes, sends out my laundry and cleaning and takes care of me in general. It's great.

Now to go political on you. I see that the Republicans don't want Wilkie. I hope they get a good man, because if Roosevelt goes back in, there will be hell to pay. This year, for the first time, he's going to have a Congress that is dead set against him and that just doesn't work with a government of our type. Witness: Hoover. So the Republicans had better elect their man if things aren't to be thoroughly snafued.

Boy what a bunch of fighters those Russian lads have turned out to be. They'll be in Berlin long before we are. –The Navy is really making up for Pearl Harbor too. That raid in toward the Philippines was a beaut.

I'm happy about their at last putting DeGaulle in as the top Frenchman. He's been top man in my estimation for a long time. Giraud always was connected with the Vichy-France in my mind. Nothing definite, but I couldn't get that feeling out of my mind.

Did my little donation toward a pretty Easter get thru in time? I hope so. I worked all day yesterday and it looks like I'll be working Sunday for awhile. Maybe I'll get home a little quicker that way.

I'm over my homesick spell now. Just as soon as I got acquainted down here, it went away.

Lots and lots of love,
Your affectionate son,

Carpy

HQ S.B.S Ops/Sect.
APO #519 New York

April 18, '44

Dearest Mother,

I've got two letters to answer. The first one, you told me about getting a letter from Essex. I knew she'd written you but I didn't know how quickly the letter would reach you. She's just as nice as you think. In fact the entire family is swell and I'm mad because I'm too far away to get up to see 'em now. But that's my home in England and whenever I get a chance you'll find me high tailing it up there, even if only for a twenty-four hour pass. I just wish that you and Judy and I could visit them after the war, because they're real folks.

By now you know all about my London trip. The black-outs are quite a shock when you first hit England, but after three months we're used to them and it seems natural. It's surprising how quickly you learn to get around in the black-out. And speaking of hearing planes and trying to imagine what it would be like if you knew bombs were going to fall, the average English girl can tell you by the sound of the engines if they are American, English or German bombers, and make no mistakes about it.

Letter two was a nice one telling about the apartment and Flossie, Cora, and Mame visiting you. That must have been fun. I get a special enjoyment out of letters like that, that tell me that you are living comfortably and that the gang of you 'girls' still get together pretty regularly. They're all my favorites, but Flossie is my favoritest.

Gosh it seems impossible that Larry Klepper is in the service. I hope it's over before he has a chance to really get in. Truthfully I can't worry about the Heim boys not being called. They're all too old to make very good soldiers. Honest, Toots, I'm twenty-seven and that's getting pretty old for combat work. These kids from 18 to 24 are the ones.

I hope your proposition with the job works out all right. I can't begin to give you any advice but what you've done so far seems right. Just sit tight and develop a big stick to hold over their heads.

Judy said in her last letter that she wasn't feeling very well. Your later letter said you were going over to see her, but didn't say how she was. I have enough faith in you that I think you'd tell me if she was really sick so I figure it can't be too bad. Don't let me down.

Gosh but I have been working. Tonight I thought I was done at 7:30 but two long distance calls came in before I could get out of the office and it was after eight when I came down here. That little old jeep of mine is sure covering ground by leaps and bounds.

Mother, I've slipped so bad on writing letters lately I owe everybody so do me a favor. Just write a note on the bottom of all your letters to everybody, "Carp sends his love." Thanks, Chum. And I do send you lots and lots of love and kisses.

Your affectionate son,

Carp

HQ S.B.S. Opr. Sect.

April 25, 1944

Dearest Mother,

I like the little editorial on anti-British prejudices. The guy is right, too. It is going to require a definite program of education to correct the situation. I think I've been very fortunate in meeting and getting to know some awfully nice English people, the Barters, their friends and few others I've met in my travels. And my little sojourn at another Army base or two had already started to cure me of my prejudices. But I still get in battles with dumb Yanks and I do fight occasionally with the English. They always move slow and sure, and sometimes I need a little push to get this job done. But we eventually get it done.

I think you're right about sitting tight and waiting for developments on your job, but maybe I'm not right. My belief is that if you're worth a raise, you'll get it, but sometimes I wonder if the Army works that way. I'd have a hell of an inferiority complex if I thought all the captains I meet are better men than myself. My consolation is that at least I know I can earn a living as an engineer and I wonder about some of them.

I like that song, "When the lights go on again," but as you say, it kinda gets you. It will really be something to walk thru an English town some night and see lighted windows again. But it isn't good to see 'em now. You're just inviting trouble. And you don't see 'em either.

Sometimes I've wondered what newspapers and radio commentators talked about ten years ago. It must have been the depression. I don't see how they interested people enough to buy a paper. You ought to look thru your back files someday and see what had the lead ten years ago today.

Thirty days seems awfully short after going thru North Africa, Sicily and Italy. What the hell are the four million still in the States doing? It'd be just as easy to send one of them over as to send Shorty back here. That policy burns me up. I've run into hundreds of guys who have been overseas, invalided home, and shipped over again as soon as they got out of the hospital. Give the U.S.O. club boys a chance is our motto. – Enough of the griping.

Life in the E.T.O. (European Theater of Operations), Judy didn't know what it meant, isn't too rough on me. I now scale 170 pounds in ordinary indoor clothing. They call me muscles around here.

I've got to go jeeping now. Lots and lots of love,

Your affectionate son,

Carpy

May 2, 1944

Dearest Mother,

I wrote the first word of this letter about three hours ago and then the phone rang and I've been cracking ever since. When things hum around here it's a real buzz.

The description of the apartment rearranged to focus on the new flowerpot was good. I wouldn't say you were cracked, but surely thee art a little mad. You are a good writer of human interest stories, though. You not only can write, but you've developed a good nose for news stories, especially human stories. That is due partly to your training in picking up gossip for Grandfather, I think.

Old Joe is asking for trouble when he picks on our Flossie. He sure did monkey with The Buzz saw when he started that. And if my Buzz saw mother needs any help, I'll gladly send her a couple of grenades and a book of instructions on booby traps.

This European Theater of Operations is quite a place. It has another word to go with Snafu and Tarfu. It is Fubar and ends out 'F----- u- beyond all recognition.' That's the final stage of snafu.

Kipling had the right idea. It really is lovely in England in the spring. If only I had Judy here to help me enjoy it, it would be perfect. Speaking of Judy, there was a U.S.O. show here last night and one of the girls reminded me of Judy. (Any really pretty girl reminds me of Judy). She had the same beautiful mouth and chin and when she grinned she had that same wicked, knowing grin that Judy's got. To top it off she had dark hair and big brown eyes. She was purty and could she sing and dance.

I talked to her after the show and told her she reminded me of my wife, only my wife was better looking. –The show was darn good. Much more to it than the ones I used to see.

I haven't seen any heather as yet. Or if I have, I didn't recognize it. The countryside abounds with birds, but I don't know their names so I don't know what I'm looking at when I do see 'em.

How I'll ever locate Don ((Carp's half brother)) is a problem. He can't write anyone, even Essex, and tell where he is because all mail has to have a return address and you may not connect an APO with a town or county.

Judy's letter on Easter day was swell except for one little paragraph about wondering how long she could stand this messed up marriage of ours. It sounded like things were getting pretty heavy at home again. You'll keep an eye out for her, won't you?

> Lots 'n lots of love,
> Your affectionate son,
> *Carpy*

May 4, 1944

Dear Toots,

That return address of mine means that I'm now in the Chief of Operations' Office at Southern Base Section Hdqtrs. Strictly an office man, that's me. That's a lie. I'm not strictly in the office because I have been getting out around the country quite a bit. As long as I can do that, I'll be happy. But if they keep me pushing a pencil all day I'll sure be a sad sack.

That raise sounded swell. You've almost doubled your salary in a little more than three years and that ain't bad. Is that raise a result of your one-woman campaign for a new and better job? I agree with Mr. Davis. They'll have a hard time finding as smart a girl as my old lady.

Just think, Toots, I'm now on my second hitch. Three years of active duty and 26 months of those years in foreign service.

Speaking of Judy, and you were, she still calls me Grant in her letters. What does she call me when she's talking to you?

Your letters are always full of some of the gang from Montour visiting you. I'll bet more of them have been up since you moved into the new apartment. It delights me to read about it because you sound so happy.

Love,

Carpy

May 13, 1944

Dearest Mother,

Your favorite son is dragging his bottom tonight. Boy I am tired. I jeeped about 230 miles today and a jeep isn't the most comfortable riding thing in the world. But I feel good because I got a couple of things straightened out that had been causing me more darn extra work. It was a bit on the cool side today, but yesterday was beautiful. I did about a 100 miles yesterday and it was marvelous. Gee, but I do get a kick out of this beautiful English countryside. It surely would delight your heart to see it. I know you'd love it too.

Two letters from you and one from Pee were waiting for me when I got in tonight, including the long lost one with the blacksmith shop and library articles in it. Those articles were really swell, Toots. I'm awful proud of yuh.

I haven't been able to get up to see Essex and tribe since I was transferred. My travels haven't been near there and 100-odd miles is too far to go on a 24-hour pass, which I haven't had either. But last Sunday I had dinner with the Turners, another nice family I met just before I left the outfit. After dinner, or rather before tea, several of us took a hike through some of the prettiest country in the world. So help me it is. It looks like something you read about in a nice English book. A narrow winding lane along the side of the hill with stone walled fields on each side and trees shading most of the lane and then back to the house by way of the mill stream in the valley. And it's got trout in it too. Good sized ones.

That's swell about Johnny Weaver's promotion, but it just proves what I've said right along. Flossie must be so proud of her boy.

Tomorrow is Mother's Day. If the PX doesn't fail me, you'll get a bunch of flowers and if my telepath works, you'll get a whole lot of love and kisses. I'm a lucky guy to have you for a mother-in-law for my wife and I know it. I'm awfully proud of you, Toots, as you may have guessed.

You've done a wonderful job to have gotten as far as you have with the paper in the last few years and it just goes to show what having good parents will do. So there must be hope for me.

You've probably read in the papers quite a bit about the WACs and their second birthday, which all reminds me of the bunch of 'em down at HQ. Walking around there at noon hour is fun. They're saluting demons and they give you a great big smile with each salute. You can see them stiffen up that right arm ready to salute when they're a good fifty feet from you. It's really amusing and must be tiresome as hell to be there regularly. I hope they keep me out on field work. If not, I'm going to request a transfer. I'm no desk soldier and my record certainly shows it.

Guess I'd better hit the hay before I yawn myself right off the page.

Lots and lots of very special love to you on this Mother's Day.

Your affectionate son,
Grant H. Carpenter
(Carpy)
Remember me?

England
May 18, 1944

Dearest Mother,

I've got two letters to answer tonight. Or rather two from you, three from Judy and one from Baldy. Boy that lad is really catching hell down there. Not that he complains, but I know just how he's feeling.

Your system of saving my letters and carrying them around is absolutely crazy, but I like it. Maybe some day I'll read some of them and be reminded of a lot of good times and hard work.

The clipping about Grandfather was interesting. 92 trout is (are?) a lot of fishing. Wouldn't it be fun to go on a day trip like that now?

Do my letters have a boring sameness of late? Don't answer that question. I know the answer. In the six weeks I've been here I've been to Turner's three times and to two dances and other than that it's been work and I can't tell you anything about my work, so. Even movies are few and far between. Last night we saw "Bomber's Moon" and it smelled to high heaven.

The clippings in your May 7 letter were neat. The one about the various foods the soldiers get was darn good. I recognized a couple of quotes. You are getting awfully good at that sort of thing, Toots.

That strawberry shortcake sounded good. But I've got no complaints about food here. Our mess is absolutely the best I've eaten since joining this man's Army. I eat like a pig but I stick tight at 170 and can't get over it. I'm shooting for 175 now and if I make that I'll be happy to hold it for awhile. I wish I'd weighed 170 when I was playing football in high school. That twenty pounds would have been worth a lot.

Judy wrote me from New York and seems to be enjoying herself. She talks of joining the Red Cross for overseas work. Maybe I should tell her to go ahead. Lord only knows when I'll be home and she sounds like she needs to get out of the rut again. Mary and Kit just had another daughter and Kit just made Captain. That puts them way ahead of us. I think I'll write Kit and find out how he did it. The promotion I mean. The other is simply a system of trial and error. Lots of fun as I remember.

How was Humphrey Bogart in "Passage to Marseilles"? As good as usual? Whenever you see him, just remember that I've shaken hands with him, talked with him and had my picture taken with him. That makes me pretty damn good. I've even met his wife.

After I wrote 'Marseilles', I wasn't too sure of it so I looked it up in our World Atlas and that got me to looking at all the maps. You know, there's a lot of the little old U.S. that I haven't seen yet. In fact I've really seen only a small part of it. It seems like a small world when you run into a pal on the main street of Timbuctu but it's mighty big when you get to looking it over. I'll bet you don't even know where Timbuctu is. Sometimes it's spelled Timbuktoo and even Tombouctou but it's all the same place. I once met a girl from there.

Right now I'd like to renew my friendship with a little chicken from Williamsport. You know, I don't think she likes the English. It's a damn shame. Is it that she doesn't trust her husband, maybe? Could be.

So long now Honey Lamb Chile.

Lots 'n lots of love,
Your affectionate rat,

Carpy

May 20, 1944

Hi Toots,

It's a nice quiet Saturday night. I was listening to All Time Hit Parade and now Xavier Cugat is on. He's got a really smooth band.

There's a dance down town tonight. That's why all the guys are out. I'm just not in the mood. That's why I'm not there. Art just came in swearing. He was at the dance and looked down to discover his fly was unzipped. When he tried to zip it up he found it was broken so he had to slip out and come back and change his pants. Embarrassing moments I have known.

I'll tell you a funny one but it's got to be a secret between us. My gal Judy is slipping. She pulled a boner in her last letter that left her chin wide open. She made some crack about me leaving my English phrases over here or she'd get herself a nice 4F'er. I've been a perfect gentleman and haven't made the obvious retort, but I've alternated between being burned up as hell and laughing at myself for being burned up over it. That's even worse than waving a red flag at a bull. It isn't that I don't like 4Fs. Personally I think they're lucky, but I just don't like to be compared with them.

But a serious thought along that line: I hope she doesn't expect to get back after two-and-a-half or three years the same happy chump that left. I'm still a chump, even more so, but I've seen a lot, learned a lot, and done a moderate amount of thinking. I just want to get this war over, get out of the Army and go back to being my own man again.

Gee I seem to be in an unpleasant mood tonight. I hope it's a nice spring day tomorrow and I can get in a nice hike to cheer me up. Pre-invasion jitters I guess. I'll go to bed and sleep it off.

May 22, 1944

Sunday I lazed around camp and never did get the rest of this letter written. Today I jeeped my fanny tired again and got through work about 9:15 and tomorrow looks like a really heavy day. I was gonna go to a dance in town tonight but decided in favor of a letter and bed.

You answered some of my questions on Judy. I thought she probably called me Carp because I couldn't picture you recognizing any other name for me.

And the other thing was about Judy's being blue. I guess I just didn't realize how rough it is on the girls at home. I loved the remark of the girl who just wants to be a daughter-in-law.

Gosh I have practically nothing to report. Everything I can think of that might be interesting is a military secret.

One thing of note, I've absolutely lost all belief in that old fable of English reserve. All the English that I've had any real chance to get to know have turned out to be swell. I've been doing quite a bit of work with a pretty high up businessman and he's been swell to me. He knows me well enough now that he kids the daylights out of me and I love it. The Turners have practically adopted me. They know I'm married too, so I'm not pulling anything. I always have to brag about my Mom and my wife.

Well, Toots, I'll beat it now. Don't laugh too hard at your convented son. I always hit the extremes, don't I?

Love,

Grant

Oops

Carpy

May 30, 1944

Dearest Mother,

Is it a nice Decoration Day today? I hope so. This always used to be one of my favorite days because school was almost over and because of the parade, and you know how I love a parade. Remember the first one I was in when Warren and I, in sailor suits, pulled the Queen of Grade One in her fancy chariot?

We always used to go up to the pipe line and try out the water too, just to see if it wasn't getting almost warm enough for swimming. Lots of times it was, too. Well almost warm enough. If you dove in fast and came straight out it wasn't too much of a shock.

I am glad the corsage got to you okay. When I ordered it I wasn't at all sure it would make connections right. But I've been pretty lucky in sending stuff to you.

You and your young pals. The Boy Scout sounds like a handful. The Scouts are doing a lot here in England. Every once in a while I run into them making scrap drives and cleaning up places and sometimes just hiking or cycling. I give 'em a highball and they snap it right back at me.

Jake M. is dumb. He ought to know better than to mess with the women on a deal of that sort. And my little momma is a bad girl to get riled. She fights nastily. A local scrap of that sort does interest me. But I get bitched when they put too much effort into keeping up the morale of the war workers. Poor fellow, nothing to do at night. Just go home. S'tough war.

I think a hell of a lot of us dislike the Army as a way of living and yet I don't understand why a guy would be afraid to come into it. There's no use being afraid of getting killed because that can happen to you anywhere. And any other fear of the Army is crazy. At least you've got a couple of million other guys suffering with you and bitching too. And you can always find a good bitching session to join if your morale gets too low.

The white dress, hat, and all sounds swell. I'd sure like to come home and see it. Maybe if you'd write to Mr. Roosevelt he'd send me home. Tell him I'm a good Republican.

Sweetheart, would a few comments about your Republican party hurt your feelings? I've been reading little items here and there in the papers and about the only policy I've found yet is a policy of 'stop someone.' First they were out to 'stop Wilkie' and now there seems to be quite a movement afoot to 'stop Dewey.' Why don't they just stop talking, admit they don't know what's going on and get out. We're gonna need a hell of a lot of 'go' in the next decade and the less 'stop' the better. I've got a couple more things on my mind, but that bitch is uppermost right now. I see that the good old isolationists are getting to work again. Oh well. It takes all kinds. I guess I'm a little crazy too. I hope it's only a little.

Lots 'n lots of love,

Carpy

June 5, 1944

Dearest Mother,

Got a swell letter from you last night dated May 21. I'm glad you like being my Mother. It would be embarrassing if your mother didn't like you. I mean, you'd kinda feel like a little b------. Is it so apparent that I like you? I guess I'm not very good at dissembling.

I'll be looking for a picture of that new hat and I'll send you one of me with or without my military chapeau if I can get near enough to a photographer, but it may be a little while before I can. After all, I require a fairly good photographer if the result is to be sent thru the mails.

Judy sent me a swell letter all about her trip. Sounds like she had a good time. She didn't say anything more about the Red Cross so maybe she was just thinking out loud. I'm glad she's out of that office cause I don't like the idea of anybody threatenin' my gal. It might not be political suicide, but it's sure asking for a friendly pat on the back with my favorite sticker. When they fight with you it is political suicide.

Gee, stop telling me about the strawberry shortcake. It makes me hungry just to hear of it. I can just see one all heaped up with berries and nice rich cream pouring over it. Mmm.

Yesterday I had dinner with the Turners and had a swell time. They're just swell to your little boy. The oldest daughter was home and a Canadian fighter pilot was there so we took the three girls pub crawling in the evening. I still am not too sold on beer but I've learned to drink my share.

Diana's birthday is next month so I want two pairs of silk stockings for her if such a thing is possible. If it's out of the question, say so 'cause I don't know anything about the situation in the States. She's a little under medium height and wears a medium width, size 5 shoe. She's pretty too or did you guess that? Please.

The radio is playing a medley of Strauss waltzes. I'm for it. When Judy and I have a home of our own, I want a good record player and then I'm gonna collect all the classical stuff that I like and get to know something about it. And I include Gilbert and Sullivan in that.

There are more rabbits around here than you can shake a stick at. One is sitting right outside the window here just chewing away on the Commandant's favorite flower bush. Now something has startled him. He stood up as high as he could and then took off across country.

The news is certainly good. I keep thinking about Baldy and keeping my fingers crossed.

> Lots and lots of love to my
> favorite Mother,
>
> *Carpy*

After all the preparation, the invasion had finally begun on **June 6, 1944**. I knew it was happening, but news reports were scarce. All I could do was hope and pray that it was going well for our guys.

June 8, 1944

Dearest Mother,

By the time you get this we should have a pretty good idea of how everything is going. You probably are getting more news in the office there than we are, but I'm following the news broadcasts and papers as closely as I can, and I've got my fingers crossed.

The news from Italy is especially good. I keep wondering where Baldy is and what he's doing. I'll bet that lad is really seeing the show.

All accounts say that people at home are taking it quite calmly and with practically no celebrating or hi-jinks. Must be they're sweating it out, too.

It looks as if my present address will be fairly permanent. Dammit. Now I'll write a note to my favorite wife.

> Lots 'n lots of love,
> Your affectionate son,
>
> *Carpy*

June 20, 1944

Dearest Mother,

During the course of my wanderings about Merrie England I found myself in Bristol for a weekend sometime ago. So I hied me off to see the famous Cheddar Caves (Cheddar cheese) near there. It's a rugged little gorge in the limestone (I think) hills. Anyway it's quite a beautiful and well-developed dry cave. You walk back into the mountains a good quarter mile. There are some fair-sized rooms and a lot of nice stalactites and stalagmites standing around. The people who opened up the caves did a swell job of installing lights and they produce some remarkable effects. They also have a nice collection of fossils, flints, bronze tools and coins showing that the caves were inhabited as far back as 14,000 years ago right up to comparatively modern times. Some of the coins are Roman. I got a descriptive book of the place and I'll either mail it or bring it home with me sometime.

Judy said the circus was swell fun. She spoke especially of the beautiful horses so you two agree. I'm glad she looks after you but she's a funny one to do it. One of my strongest memories of going out with her is the way she always made me feel that I was running the date and looking after her. She's quite a gal is our Judy.

I played ball last night and managed to catch one on the tip of my finger. It didn't hurt much then but today it (the knuckle) is swelled up about twice normal size. Doesn't bother me though. Except when I go to hit somebody.

Remember a couple of months ago I told you I was living in an old manor house? Well, I'm back there again, and I guess I'll be here awhile. It's going to be awfully nice this summer and is right now. With this British double summer time, it doesn't get dark until after 11:00.

I'm wondering what sort of an answer I get to the stocking proposition. A burst of scornful laughter probably. But there must be silk stockings in the States because we read that Marlene Dietrich showed up in Africa with something like 50 pair. If they're black market I ain't interested and if they're rationed, no dice.

I'll close now and enclose lots and lots of love for the nicest mother in the world.

Carpy

After the invasion, I was sent to Liverpool and assigned to an office job.

June 22, 1944

Dearest Mother,

Gosh, Toots, if you're leading a lonely life it would require a super-woman to lead an unlonely one. Every letter I get amuses me because you are having such a good time with that apartment and you do have so many nice friends.

When you speak of Alton, you never mention his rank so I guess he must be a captain by now. Don't spare my feelings, Hon, I can take it and I do like to know how the gang is making out. You're a cagey little lass and I understood perfectly your tips on uniform.

This camp I'm at now has a couple of pet dogs, as most Army camps do, and one of them is a character. His name is "Popcorn" and his mother was a terrier but I think she was seduced by a rat because he sure looks like a bedraggled little rat. He's so homely he's cute. He knows all the bugle calls and what they mean. At reveille formation he's right out there with 'em, ki-yi-ing at any late comers. When mess call blows he makes a streak for the kitchen and when it's work call he takes off for a shady corner somewhere. Every night he sleeps on a different man's bunk. And what he thinks of officers, phooey, he's strictly an enlisted man's dog. I tried to make friends with him but he was utterly disdainful. Not impertinent (or I'd have court-martialed him) just not impressed.

> Lots of love and a hug and a kiss from
> Your affectionate son,
>
> *Carpy*

England
June 30, 1944

Dearest Mother,

Happy Birthday again, Sugar. Today being payday I sent a little present to you by radio but I couldn't put any romance in with it so I'm sending lots of love for your birthday in this letter. Have a real good time.

I know I'm a lucky guy to have such a swell girl as Judy but I wish to hell I could get home and get acquainted again. You're my Mother and even three or four thousand miles hasn't really separated us. We still know exactly what the other will say or feel or think about anything, but Judy and I are going to have to get acquainted again. And since I expect to live with the babe for another 50 or so years, I think it will behoove me to spend considerable time, energy and thought to getting oriented again with her. When I do get home.

I'm surprised (oh yeah) and glad to learn that I will be a welcome visitor at your apartment. I've already run up those steps two and three at a time in my mind. That turn half-way up is tricky.

Last night I took in a heck of a good movie. "As Thousands Cheer" with some new cute singer Kathryn Grayson and the dancer Gene Kelly. The story was just a light background for some swell songs and good comedy. Red Skelton did a drugstore skit that had me helpless from laughter and Jose Iturbi played one classical and one boogie-woogie piano selection and both of them were absolutely tops. This Grayson girl can really sing.

I think I've located Don Carpenter at last and he's quite close to me. I've tried to arrange to meet him next week but don't know whether my arrangements have clicked or not.

Did I tell you that I had a chance to see Stonehenge some time ago? In the course of my travels hither and yon I got near it so we took an hour off and looked it over. It's almost unbelievable when you remember that it's over 3000 years old. How those people moved such enormous stones over a hundred miles and then set them up is beyond me.

Well, my friends the Russians are really at it. Every time you pick up a newspaper they're 30 miles closer to Berlin. Nice guys. I hope they keep on rolling.

Have you heard these two couplets?

Girls who offer no resistance

Often lead a rich existence.

Girls with sweaters worn too tight

Often go wrong instead of right.

Gosh but it'll be nice to get back to that sweater girl of mine.

Lots 'n lots of love,

Carpy

England
July 2, 1944

Dearest Mother,

I can't say much about the robot planes and if there's a big hole here I've said too much. I've never seen one but I've talked to a lot of people who have. The English newspapers tell practically everything there is to know about them. I've wrapped up a few papers and mailed them to you. They should be especially interesting to a newspaper sob-sister like yourself.

The other evening I saw a newsreel of some action in the Pacific. One of the scenes showed shooting down a Jap plane. It's really funny to see the tremendous ack-ack those ships carry now as compared to what was thought satisfactory four years ago.

So some of the commentators irk you too. One thing I like is the calm, dispassionate way in which BBC presents the news. We never or rather seldom hear a commentator.

I guess I'm still missing a letter because you speak of having mailed the stockings and of a birthday letter to me. It'll be along in a few days I'm sure. And thanks a million for the stockings. You're a pal. I'm kinda partial to you. I'm sure they'll be swell too because it's practically an impossibility for an English girl to get a pair of decent looking stockings.

The Turners have lived in this same place for at least a couple of generations. It would be swell if you and Judy could visit. I think I understand Judy's attitude and we'll get straightened out okay when I get home. ...That sounds as if there were something to straighten, which really isn't true. Just a couple of ideas where we don't jibe. Shucks, life wouldn't be interesting if we agreed on everything.

Sometimes I gripe pretty much at you specifically when things don't suit me at home (the States I mean) as if it were your fault or you. But you always understand me and I know you will, so I go ahead and bitch and I think that you learn some things that I've learned by it. And I know that your letters have given me far and away my best picture of the States. I don't trust the movies at all. In the overall picture of this war and changing world, you're miles ahead of me. The few things I've learned are important only because I've learned them on the ground floor, so to speak.

If you haven't gotten me a birthday present yet, I have a very special and difficult request. I would like one each bottle of Scotch, Gin and Bourbon. If they cost more than you can afford the priority is 1. 2. 3. There's no hurry on them because as you get them I want you to put them far away in the closet along with that bottle of Greek brandy that Mr. Gilmore gave me the day I went in the Army. The idea being that when I do get home I want a nice little supply on hand so we can all get quietly high together. Savvy?

As for trading you in on a new model, I've been looking 'em over for a long time and I still haven't seen any I like a quarter as well as I like the Mother I've got.

Your affectionate brat,

Carpy

Had a swell letter from Essex. She got your letter and said it was a lovely letter from a very charming lady. P.S. I agree with her.

England
July 10, 1944

Dearest Mother,

Happy birthday, Toots. I've been sending you lots of love and kisses all day. I was going to start sending them when I came into the office this morning but realized in time that they would wake you up so I waited until seven o'clock your time before I sent any. It would never have done for them to arrive before you had your coffee or you'd probably have slammed the door in their faces. And it's such a long trip from England too.

I've mailed a couple of packages of English newspapers to you lately. The little sidelights and personal items all through them interest me most. And then of course there's the comic strip "Jane" in the <u>Daily Mirror</u>. The more clothes she takes off, the higher goes the morale of the Allied Forces in the E.T.O. She does all right by our morale too. Write me what you think of them, will you? I know you'll keep in mind that they're English papers written for English consumption. So many Americans over here fail to realize that fact. I could ask a lot more specific questions as to what you think of them but I know you'll give me a better comparison if you do it unprompted. After all, you are a trained newspaperchick and know in a minute about them more than I'll ever know.

Did I tell you that Busch and I have changed our billet? We're now living in a beautiful place on the edge of town. Just a nice walk from the business district. That is nice for a guy with legs like mine. It's a fairly new house and the most beautiful grounds I've seen in a long time. (Did I write all this before? It sounds familiar.) Lots of trees, shrubbery, big windows. It's nice now, but I'll bet it'll be cold next winter. I hope to hell I'm not still here.

Judy sent me a couple of beautiful dress wool shirts for my birthday and they arrived Saturday morning. Boy they are nice and they were unexpected too. You just can't buy anything like them here in England.

What do you think of the Russians? We've been making bets as to when various towns will be taken but the Russians always get there long before we figure it's possible.

I had a note from Baldy. He had spent a day in Rome. Baldy is now operations officer for his battalion. He's really seen something of this war.

I'll mail this now. Let's both of us wish that I'll be home to celebrate your next birthday. It'll be your forty-ninth, won't it?

Lots 'n lots of love,

Carpy

England
July 14, '44

Dearest Mother,

Twenty-eight months today since I last saw those good old U.S. Shores. Boy that's a long time. I seem to remember writing a year ago and hoping then that it wouldn't be another year. Well I'm still hoping the same thing. Another two months and I'll be wearing 5 hash marks for overseas service and there aren't many of those around. But I've no right to bitch. All the old gang are entitled to them too and look where the hell they are. And Gil. I just don't think about him. I don't think it's possible for a guy of his size and temperament to live two years in a Jap prison camp.

Your nice birthday letter caught up with me at last. And I know you weren't forgetting me, but you were right in not sending anything because, except for the shirts Judy sent, there wasn't a thing I needed or could use. Except maybe a little nice home grown lovin'. And thanks again for the stockings. They haven't arrived yet because mail service has been stinky but they'll get here and be darned welcome.

Last night I stopped in at the Red Cross and cut in on the dance for awhile. The band was pretty good too.

How's my beautiful bride? Gosh but I'd like to see that chick. Every night before I hit the hay I take that big picture and talk to her awhile. Busch thinks I'm crazy. Could be.

If I can get Sunday off I'm going to Turners for Sunday. I'll eat a big meal and loaf all afternoon. The life of a gentleman.

Now I've got to scram to lunch.

Lots 'n lots of love,

Carpy

England
July 26, 1944

Dearest Mother,

Everything around here has been hum-drum as hell. The bright spot in each day is the morning paper so I can see how much the Russians have advanced. How I love those lads. Purely a selfish love I'll admit. One thing I like about them is their unpredictableness. Every time I try to figure out where they'll hit next they hit some-place else. Methinks the Germans are having prediction trouble too.

I haven't been working too vigorously of late. Or maybe it's just that I've gotten my job organized a little better. But I never will be happy in this office and I'm doing my best to get out. I know you can understand why.

That date just reminded me that five years ago I finished college. Holy Mackerel how time do flee. And a few weeks later I got my first job, hired and fired in one day by the Pa. R.R. If the Army knew that they might discharge me. I hope.

I don't seem to have much to say, Toots. Just that I love you and miss you. That reminds me of the scene in the picture where the homesick soldier talked to his mother on the phone. That almost got your sentimental son. I knew just how he felt. I've never been <u>that</u> homesick but a couple of times at college I was darn near that bad.

So long now, Sweetheart.
Your affectionate son,

Carpy

HQ B.S.#2   G-4
APO #350 N.Y. N.Y.

August 1, 1944

Dearest Mother,

The answer to Judy's trying to get a job with the Office of War Information is that it wouldn't do any good to take that job now. And just to see the country wouldn't be worth the risk. It was a swell dream while it lasted. I almost had myself convinced it was worth the risk, but that was just because I wanted to see her so bad. Maybe if we're lucky I'll be home next spring. That'll only be three years. What the hell's three years to us. My God, what am I saying?

If you could just sit down and talk to Essex for awhile or spend a few afternoons or evenings at their place it would be just what you want because they're smart people and talk our language. They've known a lot of Yanks in this war too. They've learned the Yankee talk so that we can't fool 'em with our slang anymore. You'd like Mrs. Turner too because she's been so nice to your little boy. I was up there again last weekend. Hitch-hiked up Saturday afternoon and back Sunday. Saturday night they took me to a dance.

Sunday morning, believe it or not, I had breakfast in bed. I'd been kidding them about that being one of the first things I was gonna do when I got back home. So about nine o'clock they woke me up and shoved a tray in my face. Two poached eggs on toast, liver, bacon, and a cup of tea. Both the girls are planning on living in America after the war. One's engaged to an R.C.A.F. boy from Vancouver and the other is smitten with a Yank Engineer from South Carolina. He writes from France that he's going to come back and get her when it's over. She made me read one of his letters and tell her what I thought of him. He writes like a nice guy but I told her that you never could tell about these Yanks. They're a couple of nice kids and I hope they both make it to the States. Neither one of their boyfriends would be going wrong.

Diane was tickled pink with the stockings. She said it was the nicest present she got, next to a silver bracelet from her beau.

When I left Sunday, Mrs. Turner put a bag of cookies and a big piece of cake in my bag. Boy, but they were good. Busch and I feasted when I got home (back to quarters anyway).

Lots of love,

Carpy

Dear Toots

Chapter 8

France

I'd been trying to get out of that office for months. I wanted to do something toward ending the war. And sitting around an office wasn't it.   I volunteered to join a unit of paratroopers.

I didn't get my wish on that one. Instead, I was sent into France, which got me out of the office and put me to work dealing with captured materiel in Le Mans. It was my job to get the captured materiel back into the hands of the rightful owners, if possible. If that could NOT be done, I was at least to get it back into civilian hands.

When I first arrived in France, the Germans still controlled large sections of the country, but were on the run.

Later I learned that the paratroopers I had tried to join suffered very heavy losses when they dropped behind enemy lines.

France
Aug. 21, 1944

Dearest Mother,

That heading probably won't surprise you at all. The only thing about it that surprises me was that I hadn't been in France more than an hour when I ran into the old gang from the 38th Engineers. I was walking up a road from the beach to a transient camp and this sign, "HQ. 1st BN ___ Engrs" practically hit me over the head. So I immediately invited myself to supper. Those French fried potatoes, hot stew and coffee tasted a lot better than the K-rations I had awaiting me at camp.

Love,

Carpy

The first two pages of this letter are on fancy stationery printed at the top with "Der Chef des General Nabes" and the last two pages are on lined tablet paper.

September 3, 1944

Dearest Mother,

Just in case you haven't gotten that birthday present yet, I'm enclosing a money order to replace it. If you have received the radioed money, then add this to it and get yourself a nice trinket from your favorite son.

Last Sunday I had a hangover from too much to drink and today I've got one from novocaine. That front tooth of mine abscessed and this morning he pulled it and cut out the bad bone. I don't see how you stood having all those pulled at once. One at a time is all your baby (big) can stand, and at that the dentist did a nice clean quick job. I really don't feel bad at all this P.M. The abscess had just started to form and he didn't have to take out much bone and he says my troubles are over. He's going to fix me up with a nice new tooth if we ever stay in one place long enough. I think we'll be here long enough, I hope. You've noticed my new address haven't you? How do you like my captured paper?

As usually happens, Base Section HQ is very nicely located. Our quarters are swell, except for a scarcity of bathing facilities and we can always get a shower by walking four or five blocks so that's nothing to complain about. Not after some places I've been. We have a beautiful big office building and the town we're in looks nice. It hasn't been bombed or shot up hardly at all. We're restricted to our quarters after duty hours so I haven't seen much of the place but I hope that will be lifted pretty soon.

It's getting too dark to write and the lights haven't come on yet so I'll retire and say, "Good night, my love."

September 4

Gosh I feel exuberant this morning. My upper lip is stiff and you're supposed to keep it stiff anyway so that's no trouble. Now I'm at the office and as soon as I rattle off all the news that's fit to print I'll do some more work. Speaking of news, we're having a hell of a time finding out what's really cooking. The radio news we've been able to pick up has been sketchy and I haven't seen a paper in a week. I hope you're doing better. All the news I have heard has been good and the rumors are even better except sometimes they're worse. I disregard those. All in all I'm pretty happy about the whole situation. Of course, that isn't official. I'm not speaking for Eisenhower when I say that. That's purely my own personal opinion at the moment and is subject to change without notice.

That Flossie is the damnedest girl. I hope to heck she's taking better care of herself now and being careful. How she could fall and almost break the little finger of a hand that's on a broken wrist is beyond me.

I hope your vacation was super-duper.

The A.E.F. (Allied Expeditionary Forces) new sbroadcast for today just came in. It's all good. British and Canadians in Belgium and Patton's boys very near Germany. Hot Dawg.

Bye now, Toots
Lots 'n lots of love,

Carp

France
September 6, 1944

Dearest Mother,

I have two letters to answer, both written at Laporte. It makes me feel good just to read about the town and the people. I always had such swell times up there.

It's a good thing for that bear that you didn't know what he was. You might have attacked and scared the hell out of him.

I will try to get my picture taken over here somewhere. I just sent you that pencil sketch as a kinda gag. It wasn't good but you could recognize me. It made me a bit too handsome. Am I laughing! I like that "too" in there.

So you like your daughter-in-law? S'funny. I do too.

I've really been on the ball the last couple of days. Office work and reports, how I dislike it. C'est la guerre!

The dentist took the sutures out of my lip today but it's still kinda stiff and sore and my personality grin is sure shot to hell. I'm gonna have to keep grinning all the time to strengthen that muscle and get it back in proper shape. My grin is strictly a la Bogart now. Really sinister.

The towns are still off limits so I haven't been around at all but the people look well fed and certainly better clothed than the English. Which seems to indicate that it was easier to collaborate than to fight for freedom. Won't it be funny if I end up by getting to know some people here and liking the country?

Lots 'n lots of love,

Carpy

September 13, 1944

Dearest Mother,

The snaps of you are swell, Toots. I'm crazy about them. Your hairdo is neat and you sure are looking swell. That slight double chin is the cats. That outfit is quite the berries too. In the picture where you're standing, your forehead, eyes, and nose are grandfather to a tee. Notice it!

So you didn't guess France and Judy did. Just shows how much of an Army wife she's getting to be. After a while it gets to be an instinct that tells 'em where their husbands are going to be.

You've certainly been busy the last couple of weeks. I'm glad of it, too. A vacation from a job like yours is a very essential thing. Any change is a rest. And as for the Senator making passes, it just shows good sense and taste.

Baldy wrote me. He's here in France with the Army moving from the south of France. Who knows, we may meet.

I've been seeing a bit of the country. Two Civil Affairs Officers and I went on a recon trip to look at and inspect some captured materiel. We put in some good work and picked up a lot of information and managed to have some funny things happen. At one time we got about 15 km ahead of the outposts of the Army operating in that territory. The F.F.I. (French Forces of the Interior) had the country under control so we ran into no trouble at all. One of the C.A. officers is a native Frenchman who has lived in the States for the past 18 years. Naturally, every time we stopped and he started talking, a crowd gathered. Some of the towns we were in, we were the first Americans to arrive. One small city we stayed in overnight had a beautiful American-style hotel. The rooms were better than anything in Williamsport, and what a meal we had. Phoebe would have loved it. They had a celebration in this city on the afternoon we got there and we stopped to watch it. They burned a Nazi flag and made a few speeches and the band played the various Allied national anthems. When we tried to cross the square they practically mobbed us. I'll bet I shook hands with a thousand people and was kissed on both cheeks by another 500. It was marvelous but we loved it. They called us "les liberators" and we got to believing them.

In one small town we met the French movie star, Fernand Gravet and his wife. We were invited to dinner but couldn't accept because we had too much to do, but we talked with him awhile. Join the Army and meet the movie stars. That makes nine I've met since coming overseas.

We ate one meal at a guerrilla F.F.I. camp and another in a little country inn and another with a couple of French lads we met in a bar. And everywhere the food was good and the wine plentiful. And the women good to look at. Our Frenchman said that this region was famous for its pretty women. They're all small and beautifully stacked. The average height must be about five feet. A woman 5'5" is tall. One of the officers with me is a big Norwegian-extracted American about 6'3" and 220 pounds. They exclaimed over the size of us.

The women and men both dress well, better by far than England, and the women all wear cute hats. Four years of war hasn't hurt the French as much as it's hit the English, or that's the way it looks to me.

Well, Toots, I'll ramble to a stop. Lots of love from your favorite son. Kiss my cute bride for me on the 18th and wish her a very happy birthday.

Love,

Carpy

France
18 September '44

Dearest Mother,

Last night I saw a very amusing movie. Well anyway, I liked it and so did the crowd. After the movie I strolled around town for an hour and then turned in. A blacked-out city has a strange kind of fascination all its own. It's an entirely different place from its daylight self. People are shadows with voices. Sometimes they're just voices out of bigger shadows, and sometimes just a pair of high heels clicking along the walk. Those always intrigue me. Woooooo! The shielded truck lights just throw beams of light instead of the usual all pervading glare. The M.P.s direct traffic with special flashlights that are like a lighted wand. Ordinary sounds are amplified at night 'til an ordinary voice carries like a shout and the sound of a convoy is a menacing roar. –Boy am I poetic today.

I've been doing some reading lately. At night when I'm on duty here it's often pretty quiet so I get a hold of the paper-bound volumes they're printing now for the Army. My last two have been "My Antonia" by Willa Cather and "Cardigan" by Robert W. Chambers, and I enjoyed both of them thoroughly.

A couple of years ago I read a story by F. Van Wyck Mason (I think) called "Three Harbors." It was awfully good. Sometime ago I saw an ad in a magazine of two more historical novels he's written. If you could buy a copy of either of them and send it to me I'd sure like to read it.

I have the snapshots taken of you at the cabin on my desk here. They're darn nice, Toots, thanks again for sending them to me. But you forgot to send the view of you retreating.

Marg (Toots) at the Cabin in Laporte, 1944

A couple of days ago my ballot arrived from 2nd ward Montours-ville. Evidently I'm still officially a voter in that ward even though my official Army home address is Williamsport. By the way, do I owe any taxes in Montoursville for the past two years? I don't see how I could since I haven't seen the place since 1941.

The political set-up is sure puzzling me. My biggest trouble is that I can't seem to get much steamed up over who the hell is President of those United States. Frankly I think that either of the leading candidates will do an equally poor job of straightening up after the war. So it doesn't seem to matter too much.

What has been the attitude of the people at home to the statement of General Hershey that it would be a good plan to keep all the soldiers in the Army who couldn't show a definite job to go back to? Over here it's raised a lot of comment. The general one being a question: Just what in hell are we fighting for?

Lots of love,

Carpy

France   22 September 1944

Dearest Mother,

I feel in the mood to write a letter on a type-writer tonight. You won't mind if I write it to you, will yuh, huh? I was out on another little trip today. I had some business with the regional prefect. A 'region' in France corresponds to our state, but it's considerably smaller. I'm not speaking of Texas now. Anyway this chap is a young fellow. Early thirties, I believe. He speaks English well enough to enable us to understand each other what with a few hand flourishes thrown in, and we get along swell. He's without a doubt one of the keenest chaps I've met in a long time. His mind is like a good machine. It sorts out and quickly discards all bull. Unlike most Frenchmen he is very concise in his speech. Never says two words where one will do. This is the second time I've talked with him and he's impressed me more each time. From some of the Civil Affairs boys

I've picked up a bit of his history. He went in
hiding when the Germans took over and later went
to Algiers and then England. He was assigned this
job sometime last winter and has been preparing
himself for it right along. He came back to France
just before the invasion and entered the town where
he's now located. He lived quietly, absorbing the
local picture until the day the Americans arrived
and then he presented his papers and took over the
job. 'Tis a shame that more Frenchmen don't have
his push. This country would be going up instead
of down.

I've just come back from my French lesson. We
have an hour or more of it three nights a week.
Our teacher is one of the local schoolteachers. I
think maybe this time I'm going to learn enough
to get along in it. I've picked up quite a bit
each lesson so far. If I can learn enough French
to understand and make myself understood and Judy
does the same in Spanish there's no reason why we
can't get along in any part of the world.

By the way, if I come home and put on the dog
a bit, you and Judy won't let me see you winking
at each other will you? YOU'LL just let me go on
thinking I'm the big cheese won't you?

So you still don't respond to propositioning?
Well I suppose you can't teach an old, er, etc. I'm
afraid to finish that statement.

I guess it's my bedtime now, Toots, so
I'll scramez.

> Lots and lots of love from
> Your affectionate brat,
>
> *Carpy*

P.S. Honest, this letter just looks short. Count
the words. Besides, it's got a special lot of
grade A, #1 Love in it. Sweet stuff, ain't it?

France 26 Sept '44

Hello Toots,

This letter was supposed to be written Sunday but Sunday I was out on a bit of a recon trip to check on some more captured supplies. And yesterday I was in Paris. The colonel sent me in on some business and after I'd completed my job, I took a few hours and looked over the city. My first impression of Paris consists chiefly of the idea that I want to go back and really look it over. I saw a few of the tourist attractions, namely L'Arc de Triomphe, Eiffel Tower (we couldn't go up in it though), Chamber of Deputies, Tomb of Napoleon, Place de l'Opera, Cathedral of Notre Dame, and we drove by the Louvre but it was closed and anyway it would take me a month to go through there as I would like to. I walked from the Place de la Concorde which is the big square along the Seine in the center of the city out through the shopping district and up to L'Arc de Triomphe. The stores had some beautiful stuff in the windows and the mademoiselles on the streets, oo-la-la. I haven't seen so many good-looking babes since the last time I was in New York.

I even took a short ride on the subway. They call it the Metro. It's a very easy city to get around in, much simpler than London and if you get lost you just stop on a corner and some Frenchman asks in English if he can help you. An awful lot of the people speak English well enough to tell you how to get to wherever you're going. By the way, the subways are free to all servicemen.

The women are beautifully dressed, silk stockings and everything. This is the first time I've seen tall Frenchwomen. There are a lot of long-legged damsels in Paris. Was I homesick.

We came home last evening. (How do you like that, 'home?') Anyway we came back about midnight. There was a beautiful moon about half-full just setting and we were driving into it. Gee, but it was pretty.

Paris would be a nice place for a leave except that you can't buy anything to eat so they'll have to set up a transient mess before they can let the boys have passes to the city. We ate K-rations and were very happy. You can buy all you want to drink though, if you have that much money. Everything is expensive as hell.

Bye for now, Toots,
Lots 'n lots of love,

Carpy

1 October 1944

Dearest Mother,

Yesterday I got two letters from you. One of them had the latest posed picture of you. It's neat, I'm crazy about all of them and I've gotten every one so far. Today, just a few minutes ago I got a letter from Judy dated 19 Sept. That's the first one I've gotten from her since the one of Aug. 21st. It was a swell letter, too, and had three darn good photos in it. Two of her in the car and one of her sitting on the lawn at the cabin, clad in shorts and a scarf bra. Oh my aching back. My blood pressure went up to 180 and I ain't that old. She says she's not getting letters from me either and I don't understand it because I alternate between the two of you and occasionally throw in an extra one to her. I always write once a week and almost always twice. That's the schedule I try to hit.

Listen, Toots, I don't send you money for a birthday present so you can put it in the bank for me. It may be awhile before I get the rest of it straight but when I do, it's part of your present.

So, you've been robbing the cradle? I don't believe it. If he says he's over forty, I'll bet he is and besides you don't look to be much over forty yourself. If it weren't for me you could say 42 and get away with it. Why don't you? Say you were a child bride and that I was born when you were fifteen.

Lots of love,

Carp

France   18 October 44

Dearest Mother,

Today I had my picture took, but it'll probably be six weeks before you see 'em if you do. He insisted on my being very serious. They take their soldiering that way over here. Anyway I get 'em in two weeks and you'll get 'em very shortly (?) thereafter.

Last night three officers from my old gang were in town and we had a heck of a good dinner, saw a good movie, and then sat in their hotel room until 1:00 a.m. batting the breeze. We still embroider on our lies about The Rock. I also got more of the lowdown on their first month or so over here. They had some exciting times for awhile.

I wrote Judy some while ago asking her how she stood on this election and boy did I get a definite answer back. She really knows how she feels about it and no kidding. So today I broke down and voted. I'm curious to know what percentage of soldiers overseas will vote. My own belief is that even with all the effort that's been made to get them a ballot, many of them won't vote. And when I say many, I mean a greater percentage won't vote than will. I've got nothing to base that on except hearing the guys "bull" around here.

The enclosed letter is self-explanatory. It's just something I've been wondering about for awhile and I'll really appreciate a true answer. Don't let it worry you, though. I haven't changed.

G'bye now. Lots of love,

Carpy

Mother,

This note must be strictly between us. After two and a half years of this marriage by mail, Judy's and my correspondence has settled down to friendly letters between a couple of people who happen to be married. They aren't personal letters because it's been so long now that we've lost the personal touch. From where I sit, I can't see any chance of getting home in less than a year and probably more. That isn't a prognostication on the length of the war, it's just my idea based on logistics. There is so much stuff to be done and moving troops home is only a minor phase of it. So I can't see us improving our personal relationship for a pretty long time to come. Therefore I need an answer to one important question. How do you think Judy feels about her marriage now? I don't mean is she happy, I mean, do her post war plans include me? If she still thinks as I do that we've got what it takes to make a successful marriage, then all well and good. We'll just have to sweat it out. This war won't last forever. But if she's just sticking by me because it's the patriotic or so-called decent thing to do, then no soap. It'd be a lot easier on me to split up now than it would be to come home expecting to find a wife and instead find a girl waiting to divorce me. That would be hard to take.

What I'm asking for, naturally, is reassurance, but what I want more than that is a truthful opinion from you. And above all don't get any wrong ideas from this. All I want to know is how I stand. After all, it has been a long time since we last saw one another.

Carp

My friend Baldy has been mentioned in these letters. We got to be good friends after college and he stood up for me as Best Man at Judy's and my wedding.

Baldy was badly injured in one of the battles driving the Germans out of France.

France, October 21, 1944

Dearest Mother,

I got your letter of Oct. 7 yesterday. I'd already heard about Baldy from Judy. One of her letters got mixed up and came a hustling through in a hurry. I've been trying to locate him from the address, but haven't had a bit of luck so far. He's probably back in the States by now, I hope.

As is usually the case, Flossie's boy, Johnny, and I were right close together a couple of weeks before I got his address from you. Now we ain't nearly so close. But if I get a chance I'll look him up quick.

I've only had about three <u>Grits</u> in the last three months. I think it would be better if you'd cancel that subscription. I like it, but not enough to have it cluttering up the mail and possible holding up more important packages or letters.

You've probably got something on your answers to what people are going to do on V-E Day. It's swell in song and story to talk of getting lit up when the lights go up in London but it probably won't happen except in the case of a few habitual drunkards like your son who probably would get drunk anyway. It's just like the movie scenes of outfits taking off for overseas. In the movies it's a great and glorious and heart wrenching scene but really you just load on a train and take off. If you say anything it's, "So long, Honey, I'll be seeing you."

I have come to a scientific conclusion since being in France. I believe that mental telepathy is a fact. Otherwise how could these people understand the horrible French most of us talk at them? And yet they do understand. It's amazing how quickly you can get an idea across to them. But I'll never be able to really speak the language. I ain't as smart as my wife. Oh, you knew that.

Did I tell you I visited Chartres the other day and saw the famous old cathedral there? It's one of the oldest in the world I was told and I believed it.

I gotta scram now. Lots and lots of love,

Carpy

October 22, 1944

I didn't have an envelope in which to mail this last night so I'll add a little to it today. After supper, it was a good supper too, I went to a movie. It was "Home in Indiana" and was really beautiful. Beautiful girls, beautiful horses, beautiful country, and beautiful girls. The beautiful girls were a couple of newcomers whom I'd never seen before. It was the usual story but it was nice entertainment for a Saturday night in France.

Bye now. Love,

Carpy

Oct. 26, 1944

Dearest Mother,

So you've arrived at the stage where you check off six months more overseas without my even telling you. I just got the letter you wrote Sept. 15, consoling me on two-and-a-half years over here. Three dates that stick in my mind: Dec. 29, 1941, the day Judy and I left Pennsylvania. Mar. 3, 1942, The last time I saw Judy, and Mar. 14, '42, The day I sailed. Now let's add a new one -----, --, 194_. Notice I don't give it a chance to be 195_. To hell with that music.

I can't for the life of me remember giving you a lecture on the day I left for active duty. But I'm glad I did 'cause I know you needed it. You get entirely too few lectures as it is.

The idea of school kids combining school and work and working during vacations is a good one if it can be worked out. But remember how hard it was to get a job during vacations when I was in school. That Depression was rough. My biggest regret is that I didn't have some background of work before I went to college. I think I'd have gotten so much more out of college. That's one reason I'm strongly in favor of a year's military training for boys immediately after high school. It would be just the thing to straighten a guy out and teach him to make the most of his opportunities. And it would enable the country to maintain a strong reserve Army.

I've got a new job that interests me very much. It's very similar to the work I did for J&L except that I'm dealing with a lot more than just the one item. I'll be on the road a good bit and should learn plenty. Just call me T.S. from now on. And not what that usually means. This time I'm a trouble shooter.

This is just a note because I've really got to get back to work, but quick.

Lots of love,

Carpy

France
28 October '44

Dearest Mother,

It must have been quite a party if you went around all next day in the dark.

Your idea for your speech at the convention sounds like just the goods to me. They'll get exactly what they want and should learn something.

Don't worry about the sweater. You should have gotten a letter from me telling you that I have a good sweater knitted by Judy's own lily-whites. As for the books, they'll be welcome whenever they arrive.

I really don't know if France is as pretty as England. For me the answer is no. Those small green fields, stone fences, and thatched stone cottages of England made the prettiest country I've ever seen. My favorite part of England is the Cotswolds from Bristol up to Coventry. That's nice country. Beautiful hills with the neatest little villages set in the valleys. Broadway where the Barters live is like a setting for an English play.

I've driven down the Loire valley and it is beautiful but in a different way. It's bigger than England and not as big as the country at home. Some of the chateaux are lovely. Orleans is another city I've promised myself a visit to, but I haven't been able to make it yet. The thing I like best about France is the straight, wide, highways lined with poplars. The other day I drove for miles along some back roads through pine forests. That was enough to make me homesick. It was a pretty drive, too.

Now to go from the sublime to the more important. We got our bi-monthly liquor ration today. Namely a quart of Scotch and a half a bottle of Gin. The Gin I don't worry about but Scotch is more precious than gold. I have a standing offer. I'll trade my bottle for an equal amount of heart blood taken right from the heart. Two guys are seriously considering taking me up on it.

It shows all the indications of being drunk out again tonight. I never saw such a climate.

G'bye for now.
Lots 'n lots of love,

Carpy

France
31 October '44

Dearest Mother,

The letter of Oct. 12 came wandering in this morning. Most of 'em do sooner or later. So you enjoyed my trips. That's good. I did too. That's the only good thing about this Army life. At least you do see something of the world. Sometimes I think that I'll never want to travel again and then other times I figure I'll never be able to stay in one place very long again. Two months is about all I can stand of one place, then I start to fret.

You've hit on a serious problem. What to talk about when I do get home. Memory is very short and any topic of conversation that arises now reminds me of something I've done in the past two or three years. I seldom think of things before the war, except when I daydream of home. Now talking of my experiences is all well and good for a short while, but very quickly it begins to pall. Then I'm stuck because I don't remember the things that happened during the V War Bond drive or how Lycoming upped its production 100% or how the Home Guard handled the strike at the girdle plant, so conversationally I'll be a dud for the first year or so that I'm with the home crowd. Oh well, Baldy and George and I will always be able to get off in a corner and bull around.

Nov. 3, 1944

I don't know what happened to Wednesday and Thursday. I just never got back to finish this letter. Here it is Friday evening and I know what happened today. This morning I had my last wisdom tooth pulled, and I slept all afternoon to let the novo-caine wear off. But it sure is a relief to know that I don't have that to face again soon. All of the bad teeth in my head are now gone and as soon as I get one filling replaced I'll be in A-1 shape dentally. 'Tis good. The dentist did a darn good job pulling it. Didn't bother me a bit, except that I got jittery as usual, but that was just because I'm a yellow-belly about teeth. This dentist is really darn good.

I saw a heck of a good movie last night. "Conflict" with Humphrey Bogart and Alexis Smith. It was supposedly a premiere showing. I wouldn't know for sure. A very terse and thrilling mystery. A couple of times during the show if anybody had touched the back of my neck they'd have had a cleaning bill to pay.

Your letter of Oct. 17 came in yesterday. Gee Toots, you're skinny. 129 ain't enough.

I don't know enough about the logistics of the election by states, but I agree with you on the entire picture. I don't think Dewey can swing it, but I can hope.

Guess I'd better stop beatin' my gums and write a love letter to my girl.

Lots 'n lots of love,
Carpy

---

5 November '44

Dearest Mother,

It's good to know that I'm not in the doghouse. You also mentioned two letters which Judy has written but which I haven't received. In fact since I landed on the continent I've received 5 letters from Judy and 15 from you. I hope she has been writing more frequently than that.

The old rotation rumor is rearing its head again, but just rumor. If they ever put it into effect I may get back to the States some day. But it's still latrine stuff so I'm not getting any hopes up. But I can dream, can't I?

Lots of love,
Carpy

9 November 1944

Dearest Mother,

Boy, am I happy. I've had two letters from you and four from Judy in the last three days. I don't feel divorced any more. The use of red, white, and blue border envelopes is the answer to rapid delivery.

My condolences on the election, Toots. Most of your predictions were right except the fact that the Democrats still control Congress. I sure missed that bad. I'd have bet money that the Republicans would swing that. To me, that election proves what I've contended, and so have you, all along. The Republican Party is dead unless they get rid of the so-called Old Guard. They've got to start thinking instead of wishing.

Your description of Judy's clothes was swell. Do it more often will you? I asked her to send me the more intimate details so you can just cover the outer garments.

Last night I went to a dance. The liaison officer here arranges a dance for the American officers every Thurs. night. I went to the first one four or five weeks ago and didn't like it so I didn't go to any more until last night. The guys said that they were much better so I took a chance. I shoulda stood in bed. The babes can't dance. It's worse than pushing a truck, and while they do speak English, you can't carry on anything but a very simple conversation. It's too much of an effort to make small talk. The funniest thing that happened though, some gal said to me, "I suppose you like France much more than you did England." So I told her my plain, unexpurgated view on that subject. What a dumb statement that was for any person to make and it's typically French. They're a slap-happy, carefree people. I swear that they actually believe we came to liberate them and that it's just and right that we should.

I admire DeGaulle and his men so much that I wonder if they're the same race. The only hope for this country lies in men of his breed and I don't think the rest of France will back them up for fear it may cost something.

Lots of love,

Carp

13 November 1944

Dearest Mother,

I was a brat last night and only got one letter written before going to bed. But I did get a good night's sleep and you're glad about that, aren't you?

News is sure scarce this morning. I mean local news that's fit to print. No letters for the last couple days. The election is all over. Army licked N.D. 59 to 0 but you know that. Penn State beat Temple 7-6, which you probably didn't know. There is a war on in Europe as well as one in the east. You probably know that although some people still don't. —I've just been reading about some more strikes so I'm bitter.

Gosh it got much later quick. It's now almost suppertime 15 November and when I got back to the office this afternoon I found a letter from you and one from Judy both mailed Nov. 3. That 'tis all good.

I'm mad again. The <u>Stars and Stripes</u> today had two items that didn't jibe. One was casualties to date 350,000 in 35 months of war. That's a thousand every three days. The other was a notice that 34,000 workers were off work from the Superfortress factories because 1900 supervisory workers were on strike. If that strike extends the war six days, it will cost the U.S. 2000 men. Why not shoot the 1900 and send the others back to work? That would be a net saving of 100 and a gross saving of 2000 real Americans.

Honest Toots, I didn't do it deliberately. I just was going over for supper and then to a movie and then back to finish this letter but I ran into Winn and he was celebrating his birthday and I had to go on the party. We had a couple of shots of Scotch, then three glasses of champagne, then to dinner and with the dinner a big glass of vin blanc and after dinner coffee with a double shot of brandy. So I staggered home to bed. It's now the next morning.

Do I look like a hand-holding man? I don't think so, but I sure plan to be one if I can ever get within reaching distance of a certain cute little wench we both know.

Your answers to my questions about the job situation were very satisfying. What most of us want is an even break and it sounds like we may get more than that, but that sounds almost too good to be true. If I can start in again at a decent salary I know damn well I can earn it.

This cigarette situation amuses me. The <u>Stars and Stripes</u> had an article this morning giving some supposed facts and figures. It seems that they produced 16,000,000,000 packs this year and they claim to have shipped 5,000,000,000 to the military overseas. But a little figuring will show that if there were 5,000,000 troops overseas, and that's a darn nice number, that would be 1000 packs per man per year, or three packs per day, and I can personally vouch for the fact that the soldiers in the European Theater of Operations are getting one pack per day or less. All of which leads me to believe that John Q Public is taking a beating while the cigarette companies ship cigarettes to England and France to build up their smoking publics there.

I guess I'd better close this before it grows into a book.

Lots of love to you.

Carpy

---

20 November '44

Dearest Mother,

This is gonna be just a note because I got quite a bit to do this evening. I'm getting ready for an inspection trip I've got to make tomorrow and Wednesday.

The enclosed $60.00 is the first installment of 90.00 bucks which I have special instructions for you to do with. If you savvy me. I'll send the other 30.00 the first of the month. $50.00 is a Christmas present for Judy from me. If you know something special she has her heart set on, why buy it for her. If not just give her the fifty with a big kiss. $20.00 is for Pee for Christmas and the other twenty is for you to buy my presents for Bill & Edie and Bill Ader and Flossie and any other members of the family or friends that I'm still speaking to. If you need more dough, I'll send it as quick as I hear from you. I don't know if Judy is getting Grace and George and Bets and Evie something for the both of us or not but I think she is.

The painting of the town that you and Katie and Mary did sounded very good. I like painting towns, but so help me I've quit drinking so much. I've had a hangover about three days a week for the past month and I can't take it. I'm getting circles under the circles under my eyes.

That cartoon of Mauldin's was good. I'm glad people at home see those drawings. I thought they only printed them in the service papers over here. His cartoons are sharp and bitter and he portrays the real spirit of the combat infantry. It isn't so much a spirit as it is a lack of spirit. The real spirit is that one of self-preservation and of trying to preserve your buddies. I've never been in any real danger since I've been in France, but I've talked to a lot of officers and men such as Mauldin portrays. It isn't nice at the front. I don't want any of it. If I get an assignment to combat engineers I'll go because it's the only thing to do, but I'm gonna be scared as hell and I don't mean maybe. I'm hoping not to get such an assignment. I'll do 30 missions over Germany in preference to 50 days in the front lines any time.

Don't let this talk worry you. It's only how I feel, not a prelude of what I'm gonna do.

Bye now. Lots of love,
Carp

P.S.   Your last paragraph of the letter you wrote Oct. 27 got me started again. You wondered what other people think of our politics. –Don't ever let that worry you. These French are a race who take their politics seriously and there's a real difference in parties, not like it is in the States. I think the best thumbnail sketch of French politics is the one I heard when still in England. The French are never for something. They're always against something.

Bye again. Love,
Carpy

22 November 1944

Dearest Mother,

Got back from a little trip this morning and found your letter of 6 November waiting for me. It's a swell long one, but it's more than a week since the last one from Judy. I wish she'd learn your system.

Oh my gosh! Here it is Thanksgiving Day evening and I'm just getting back to finish this epistle. A bunch of piddling little jobs have kept me busy.

I'm duty officer tonight and things are nice and quiet again. A couple guys were in looking for information as to how to locate their units and somebody else wanted a thousand gallons of gas, but not one of these jobs that take half the night to do.

We had a turkey dinner this evening so as not to interfere with the day's work. It was delicious and I'm not kidding. Absolutely one of the best dinners I've had in years. All the trimmings and beautifully prepared. I'm stuffed.

Toots, I'm so damned mad I could bite nails. The last couple of days, <u>Stars & Stripes</u> has carried little notes of the spread of the telephone operator strike. My God, don't those dizzy dames know what they're doing or are they so selfish and insensible that they don't care? I'm not as mad as I am heartsick and discouraged. Three years of war, 550,000 casualties and the people of the United States permit such a state of affairs. What in hell's the use anyway? I'm not bitching at you, Mother. I'm just discouraged. How will any of us ever get home if this keeps up?

Next morning. I'm calmed down now. I guess those damn jobs are only a very, very small part of the U.S. and the majority are certainly backing us to the limit. But I have to blow off steam to you now and then; and those few can do so much damage.

Where did you get that sweet disposition she's bragging about? Aren't <u>you</u> the gal who once called me a little s.o.b. when I was flip with you? —And I do still love you so nothing really matters does it?

Did I tell you that if you don't like those pictures of me, especially the one standing up, you have my permission to burn it? I don't think much of it either. Too serious.

How do you like the news lately? That French push surprised the hell out of me. I didn't think they could do it. Twas a pleasant surprise. Here's to more and pleasanter surprises.

Bye now, Hon. All my love,
Your affectionate brat,

Carpy

29 November 1944

Dearest Mother,

I got your letter of 13 Nov. today. It had all the answers to my questions and I feel real swell after reading it. I've got some news that'll interest you too. My new address means I'll be living in Paris. By the time you get this I'll have lived there a couple of weeks and should be well acquainted with the city. I'll tell you more about it in my next letter.

A few days ago I made a pleasant discovery about this town I've been in for the past couple of months. It has one of the loveliest parks I've ever been in. I knocked off work about 4:30 and took me a walk before dinner and just stumbled into it by accident. It's about twice the size of Brandon Park and it's all up and down hill with gravel paths winding thru the trees and shrubbery, and lots of both of them. Thru one side of it there's a small brook like a little trout stream and it empties into a small lake that takes up one corner of the park. It's evidently quite old because there are lots of big maple and pine trees that are at least 75 years old. In fact there is practically every kind of tree and shrub you can name. It's really a combination botanical garden, park and zoo. Most of the animals were in their houses because it was a bit cold. But their houses and pens are made as natural as possible and very pretty. The French evidently go in for this stuff because every French city I've been in has it's 'jardin' as they call them. The one you would have liked most was the one in Leopoldville. Talk about a tropical beauty spot with strange birds, animals and plants – that was it.

By the way, don't let Judy worry about me being in Paris. I've been a good boy too long to break down now. It ain't love or anything else keeping me straight except one thing. I want a family and not a family of half-wits, therefore I don't take any chances on V.D. Maybe it ain't romantic but it's a damn practical reason and your boy Carpy is a practical guy. That's strictly between the two of us too.

Thanks for the dope Sugar. I too think that Judy and I have what it takes to make a damned good marriage. I'm gonna try.

Lots 'n lots of love,

Carpy

The Germans had looted Paris during their occupation and then commandeered over 350 warehouses in which to store their stuff. The loot ranged from warehouses full of cars to warehouses full of department store goods to one full of 10,000 new tin cans, none of which had lids.

I worked alongside an American Major and a French Liaison Officer to return the captured materiel to its rightful owners. About a month into the job, the Major was transferred, and I was left in charge of the project for the next six months.

The French were delighted and somewhat surprised at our willingness to give everything back.

3 December 1944

Dearest Mother,

I'm sitting in my room writing this and shivering like a dog. It's a swell hotel room, but no heat or hot water. I ain't bitching though. I'm lucky as the devil to be in Paris and living in a hotel. I can think of a trillion worse places. Gene, Don and I came up on the train together yesterday afternoon. We're billeted in the same hotel and eat together at another hotel near here. We're living right smack in the middle of Paris and I'm as happy as a bug in a rug. I've met some of the guys I'm to work with and they seem to be an especially congenial crew. I've been told what work I'm to do and it sounds interesting as the devil. I've done some of it already. It's more or less technical work with captured equipment. Just my meat.

You can probably guess what I did my first evening in Paris. I started at the officers' Red Cross club and just wandered around town on the subway. My idea of a good evening.

I got a swell happy letter from Judy written in New York. She seemed to be having a wonderful time and the letter just bubbled over with it.

A half hour later. –That room got too cold so I came down to the Red Cross club to finish this.

I can't get over how lucky I am to be stationed here. This is really a break. I'm gonna see every tourist sight I can and all the places I can that the tourists don't get to. This job should help me to see the place and also to see the surrounding country. I'm going to try a French theater some night next week and see how much of it I can understand.

You'll probably be getting this about Christmas time, Toots, so look for an extra measure of love and good wishes for a Merry Christmas and a very Happy New Year. And I'm not wishing you an impossibility either. I think you can have a Merry Christmas this year and a darn good new year. This war isn't going to last forever you know.

Lots 'n lots of love,
Carpy

P.S.   After I left you last night I walked down the street to a French cinema and saw an old American film, "No, No, Nanette." It was the American version with French titles and I probably enjoyed it more than the French did. The only thing that surprised me was when the usherette asked me for a tip. Seems to be the custom of the country.

7 December '44

Dearest Mother,

Nice date, isn't it? The anniversary of the blackest mark against the United States. When I think of the position we allowed ourselves to get into three years ago today, I shudder. And we didn't even know then how bad it was. I wish I were at all sure that Gil and the rest of those guys who are still living would be free next year on this date.

I have a big request. Will you try to buy me a collar holder downer? I think you could put one in an envelope without too much trouble. I had one when I left the States but somewhere in my travels it got lost. Maybe I should backtrack and look for it. That would be fun if I didn't have to take as long going back as I did coming this far.

Last night I got to shooting the bull with a chaplain at dinner so the two of us went to a special Service stage show "The Male Animal." It was darn well done and good. Both of us thoroughly enjoyed it. The cast was G.I. except two of the leading ladies, but the professional touch was present. All of them had had some legitimate experience. You can find anything in an Army the size of this one.

I'm writing this in the lounge of the hotel where I eat and in a few minutes I'm gonna head for the French cinema down the street and see another old American movie. I liked the last one so much I figure it's a good way to spend an evening and learn a little French, I hope.

Don't forget a hug and a kiss from me to my child bride via you on Christmas Day. After all, it is my wedding anniversary.

Lots 'n lots of love,

Carpy

18 Dec. 44

Dearest Mother,

My mail is starting to catch up with me again. Two days ago I got the one of Nov. 10 telling me that Flossie's boy, Johnny, is missing and today I got the one of Dec. 4 with the lecture on strikes. I still haven't written to Flossie because I don't know what to say. By now she may have definite news. As long as she doesn't have definite bad news there is a good chance of getting good news. A lot of those boys turn up in a prison camp and sometimes even back to our lines. I will write a note for her and put it in my next letter to you. If you think it will help you can give it to her. My heart aches for her. She's had too much to bear. And as for not telling me news like that, your last thought was right. I have few illusions about this war so don't try to protect me from where you are. I'm a little too close.

It was kind of a coincidence that Hosley was in to see you. I've thought of him a half dozen times in the past week. A lieutenant I'm working with reminds me so darn much of him. He would get a kick out of the Army, but he's doing a heck of a sight more important job where he is than he'd ever do here. Good farm labor is a damned scarce item.

As for your strike arguments, Toots, from the girls' point of view I guess they're justified, but from this side of the war it's hard to see any justification. You read the papers so you know what certain shortages have done to prolong this war and every strike increases shortages. To put it selfishly, the longer this war lasts, the more chance there is of my not getting back to raise those grandchildren of yours. And I most earnestly desire to get back. I'm no hero, I'm just one of a couple million G.I. Joes trying to do my job so as to help get this damned war over. I've worked about 9 hours a day every day for the past 15 days because I am doing a little piece of work that is rather urgent. But I'm not bitching, in fact I'm damned happy because I'm doing it in Paris where I'm comparatively safe, (taxis are the greatest menace), and where I sleep comfortably and eat regularly and well.

I'm sorry if I sound bitchy. You are my favorite Mother and I hope I'm your favorite son and not too big a disappointment to you. But after all, a strike is generally for more money, and when it's somebody else's money against our lives we're inclined to be selfish.

This job I've been on has been driving me ragged. Among other things it's my responsibility to see that as little is stolen as possible. But I haven't had much luck stopping the stealing. I've caught about four red-handed and fired them but I can't turn them over to the police because my office doesn't want to get mixed up in the legal end. I've fired about ten for loafing. I was even threatened by one guy but when he found out I knew what he was talking about he shut-up and apologized. That's the advantage of my size. They don't know if I'm big and tough or just big and they're reluctant to find out.

This place I'm working in still fascinates me. Every day I find another section that I haven't been in before. I'll bet I could put 10 silver dollars in plain view on the floor in 10 various parts of the building and one man couldn't find them in 10 hours of steady walking. Williamsport's biggest department store could be hidden in one corner of the place.

When I get a day off I'm going to continue my exploration of the tourist sites of Paris, but so far I haven't had much time.

I'll be thinking of you on Christmas and New Years. If my thoughts are a little confused you'll understand. It will probably be very drunk in this town.

> Good night, Sweetheart.
> Your affectionate brat,
>
> *Carpy*

---

19 Dec. '44
Paris, France

Dearest Mother,

You told about difficulties getting Christmas presents and if I haven't sent enough dough, say so quick. I don't expect you to buy my presents for me and pay for 'em too. Your system with Judy sounds good to me. I do want her to have something nice and if she can find it by shopping, let her shop.

The description of Judy was neat. I like that when you tell me exactly how she was dressed. It makes her come right into the room with me.

That literary thing must have been a lot of fun. It's a shame you didn't interview them. I know you could do it. You should have served a hitch in the Army. That would cure you of stage fright. I can stand up in front of any crowd of men now and give 'em all hell.

Who the hell in Williamsport has $80,000.00 bucks for the 6th War Loan drive? If they've made it since the last one it wasn't legal and if they've been hoarding they shouldn't have done it. —I'm just kidding, Toots, I can guess the answer. It was money that was tied up somewhere else and has just come loose. The Americans are really backing those drives and so are the sons of Americans in the Army.

You and me too on that cigarette proposition. I think it's an artificial scarcity and sure as hell ought to be straightened out. Neither soldiers or civilians are getting them.

Gotta scram now.

Lots 'n lots of love,

Carpy

---

27 Dec. 1944

Dearest Mother,

Thanks a million for doing my shopping. You're nice. And I do appreciate what a hard job it is to get nice presents.

It's swell that Baldy is home. I've only written one letter to him and then I used the first hospital address so I'd better send one to you and you can forward it for me.

Both letters had swell descriptions of my girl. I always like those. But you didn't tell me how her legs felt in silk stockings and that would interest me very much. She sent me a beauty of a Christmas card with the swellest sentiment a guy could ask for. Gosh it was nice.

I had to laugh at your saying it didn't sound like the old Baldy. I don't believe it is the old Baldy. He's done a lot and seen a lot since you last saw him. —I think you'll be a little surprised with me when I get back. I'm hoping I won't be too much of a shock to Judy.

My plans to see Paris have been interfered with by work. We call that 'Tough shit.' So I can't tell you very much about the place. I finished that special job I was on Sunday noon and had the afternoon and Christmas day off which was more than I expected. In the afternoon I went to the zoo and had a swell time roaming around the place. I'm a sucker for zoos.

Christmas morning I got up at 9:30 and woke Gene and heckled him awhile. Then I came back and washed my field coat. Boy what a job that was. I had a swell Christmas dinner and then came back and finished a letter to my child bride and then started drinking and got moderately stinking.

I got the kisses all right and I guessed right. I knew the ones with red ribbons were from you and those sexy black satin jobs were from my bride. I wonder where she learned to kiss like that. 'Tis terrific.

Your neighbors sound awfully nice. I'm glad they are and I know you're nice to be neighbors with.

I haven't written to Flossie because I just don't know what to say. There just isn't anything to be said.

I have learned a few odds and ends of French, but it's darn little. I have discovered that if they speak slowly and I listen closely I can grasp quite a bit of the conversation.

Where the devil all this War Bond money is coming from is beyond me, but it makes me feel good. I never knew that there was one million bucks in Montoursville, let alone three million.

I know you've read of the raid we had the other night. Don't ever let it worry you. When the alert sounds I find myself a good deep hole. I'm afraid of those things and not a bit ashamed to admit it.

I'll hustle this into the mail now and hope it gets home right after the first. Lots and lots of good wishes for 1945, Toots. You're my favorite mother and I guess you always will be.

Lots 'n lots of love,
Your affectionate brat,

Carp

We had the occasional air raid while in Paris. One evening as I was lying in bed in the hotel room, I heard a German bomber and somehow knew it was dropping something with my name on it. I figured if it hit near my side of the hotel, it would blow out the windows and shower me with broken glass, so I rolled out of bed and crawled underneath. On the other hand, if it was a direct hit, it didn't much matter what I did.

The bomb hit in the park, just across the street from the front of the hotel, blowing out all the windows and damaging the walls. Miraculously, none of the men who had rooms on that side were actually in their rooms when it hit, so no one was hurt.

1 January 1945
Paris, France

Hi Toots,

Happy New Year and please excuse my even worser than usual writing. I'm being as careful as I know how. The Clabes took me to their family New Year's Party last night and I didn't get in until seven this morning so I just washed up and came to work. It was a nice refined brawl. We started with champagne and cocktails and hors d'oeuvres about ten o'clock. Sang Auld Lang Syne in French and Anglaise at midnight, had a midnight supper and then drank wine, cognac, champagne, brandy and danced until daylight. At four o'clock I started to leave, but I ran into some recruits coming to the party just outside the front door and they brought me back. So I stayed for the duration.

I had to laugh to myself while we were eating supper. There were about 25 or 30 of us and only a few spoke English. I was the only American there. Everybody was chattering away in French and I mean chattering. They all talk about 15 to the dozen and the place was really a madhouse. I enjoyed myself though and managed to hold a conversation of sorts with practically everybody there. Mostly we spoke English, sometimes English and French mixed and a couple of times I resorted to pure sign language.

Interruption. It's now the next day. I had to go scrounging for some supplies. –Gene, my roommate, and I had a couple of drinks before supper and then went to a movie. "Raffles" with French subtitles. This cinema that we go to always shows an edition of "Why We Fight." That's the series of films made by the Army to educate its soldiers. I think I spoke of them in another letter and wondered if they're being shown to civilians at home. They're very interesting and should be illuminating to most people. I know I didn't know what had happened in Africa 'til I saw the movie on it. The big picture is so big that you can't grasp it until it's all over and condensed for you. One reason I like this staff work is that we do get a better view of the big picture, but only for our part of the theater.

We had a good New Year's Day dinner last evening but I couldn't do justice to it, because I was full of eggnog. The General was at home from 5 to 6 and the eggnog was tres bon. Speaking of eggnogs, we've found a bar that serves a drink made with cognac, rum, liqueur and an egg. It goes down smooth, has a good wallop and contains plenty of vitamins. That's why we drink it, for the vitamins.

Mail situation has been a little weak. I haven't had a letter from you in a week now and that always makes me unhappy. —By the way, I'm not being a brat and forgetting to thank you for my package, but I just haven't received it. That's the trouble with moving around in this Army. I've been pretty lucky though. I've gotten packages from Pee, Edie & Bill, and Judy's people. But the ones from my two best girls ain't arriv yet. They'll probably show up in April. I've known that to happen.

Gene and I are in the process of changing our billet. We've got a studio room on the top floor of an apartment house in one of the nicest sections of town. It's gonna be cold as hell until spring and then it should be wonderful. I'm gonna miss that hotel. It's been a pleasant spot in which to reside.

This will have to do for a letter until I get one to answer. It carries lots of very good wishes for a Happy New Year.

And lots and lots of love,

Carpy

8 January 1945

Dearest Mother,

We're still working pretty regular like and I'm enjoying it. However I did get Sunday off because I traded duty officer with Gene. I take next Sunday. Gene and I still haven't completed our move. We're lazy and so very comfortable in the hotel that we hate to get out. It sure would kill me to have to go back to real soldiering again. I figure this is work that's necessary and my training makes me good at it so I'll just make the best of my luck as long as it holds.

Yesterday afternoon I stopped in at the Red Cross Club and took in a tea dance. I do enjoy dancing. The French gals in this town aren't quite so heavy on their feet as they were in that last town I was stationed in. One civilian gal I was dancing with turned out to be an American who works in the embassy. Right away I started trying to figure some way to get Judy over here. That Office of War Information still sounds best to me, if she can work it. I should be here for a fair spell.

Thursday night one of the French liaison officers took me and a couple other officers to a dinner party. We had a real nice time. They were swell to us and before the evening was over we were talking French and they were talking English. Funny how wine does that to you. The strange thing is that I can't warm up to these people. They just aren't my kind. A few of the officers I've liked and really admire. Especially a couple I know that ducked out and joined DeGaulle early in the game, but most of them irritate me.

They expect the Americans to give them so much. The women are pretty, but not as pretty close up as at a distance, and they seem awfully shallow. I wonder sometimes if it's the language bar that makes me think this or if it's real. I think it's more than language.

I'm anxiously awaiting your comments on the counter-attack in Belgium and Luxembourg. You know, you can write me what you want to because all the news you get is censored. I can write something about it but I have to be careful.

I'm saving copies of the daily American paper printed here in Paris. You'll get a bunch of them one of these days.

Tonight I heard Glenn Miller's band at a G.I. Theater here in town. They were really good.

Lots 'n lots of love,

Carpy

12 January 1945

Dearest Mother,

I've got a package and a letter. The letter was mailed 29 Dec so that's the latest news I have. The Christmas package was mailed in New York (I think) and contained crackers, cheese, chicken liver spread, all sorts of good eats and caviar. That caviar got me. Was it your idea or is it part of a regular food package? Just because I'm living in Paris doesn't mean I've gone highbrow. I still enjoy the simpler things of life, like peanut butter and jam. I'm still your own little Carpy. –It's a swell package, Toots, and just what I wanted. It's impossible to get stuff like that here and I really go for my midnight snacks about 10:00 o'clock. You're an awfully nice Toots. I like you. D'yuh mind?

Don't I just know it's been three years since that Sunday night I said, "So long Toots," and Judy and Kit and I headed for Columbia. And the heck of it is that it's going to be late in '45 or '46 before I see you again. We've stood it this long, we can certainly brave out another year or so. There are too many people for whom it <u>is</u> forever.

I've been reading about the snowstorms and wishing I were home to enjoy them. We had a pretty good snowstorm here the other day. The kids were having a swell time. I was walking thru Place Vendome and some high school kid clipped me in the ear with a snowball. I pegged a few back at her but she was too good at ducking. And later in the day I passed the Tuillery Gardens and saw a battle royal between about 30 girls and 15 or 20 G.I.s. They were all having a wonderful time.

I've been seeing lots of good entertainment. Last night it was a variety show with some of the best acts I've ever seen. These French acts aren't too good at singing or playing American songs but at juggling and acrobatics they are superb. And they have some clever pantomime clowns. You don't have to understand any language to laugh at them. Two of the acrobatic teams last night had me sitting there with my chin dropped on my chest. Even seeing it was hard to believe. One couple was a pleasure just to look at. They were two of the most beautiful physical specimens I have ever seen. The girl was not only muscular but also very feminine and that is something I've never seen before.

Bye now,
Lots 'n lots of love,

Carpy

17 Jan. 1945
Paris, France

Dearest Mother,

Another swell Christmas package from you arrived yesterday. It was the one with the gloves, slippers and kit bag. It's funny about the gloves. I've been wishing for a pair like that for the past week, but I knew you couldn't send 'em in time to do any good. Then the first thing I opened was a pair of beautiful warm gloves. You're a smart girl. The slippers and kit bag will both come in mighty handy to a garritrooper like myself.

Sunday evening I went to a cocktail party and had a swell time. It's funny how much fun you can have just trying to talk to these people. A young FFI lad spent a half-hour telling me tall tales about the things they did before the invasion. And the best thing was that I understood most of what he said.

I'm always meeting Frenchmen who have been to the French African colonies and that's always a good point for a conversation. And as for the women at these parties, I just lie to 'em with my eyes and we get along swell.

Yesterday I got a letter from Judy dated Jan. 3. She enclosed a bunch of good, slightly vulgar jokes. The longer I'm married to that girl the more I know I'm a lucky guy. She's just perfect for me. –I hope she won't get too much of a shock when I get home.

What do you think of this Russian push? I'm all hepped up on it and hoping just as hard as I can hope, and watching the news like a hawk. Thank God for the Russians – which reminds me that my newest gripe is an isolationist Senator who ought to be shut up. They're letting him stretch freedom of speech to the point where his freedom of speech is costing American lives. I read a hell of a good editorial about him in today's Herald Tribune, and a good cartoon along with it.

What do you read about the food situation in this town? It won't affect the Army any but people here are starting to hurt for food. That's a rough situation and I know. I don't like to see people queuing for food when there isn't enough.

Lots and lots of love,

Carpy

Paris Is Snowy, Cold, Foodless, And Miserable

No Fuel, Potatoes or Milk, and 13° Below Freezing; Many Rail at Government

By Sonia Tomara

From the Herald Tribune Bureau
Copyright, 1945, New York Tribune Inc.

PARIS, JAN. 15. - Parisans awoke this morning to face one of their hardest days since the war started in 1939. The city was covered with snow; the temperature was 13 degrees below freezing; the city could expect no electric power all day and no cooking gas after 8:30 p. m.; there was no coal, no food on the market.

Shortage of coal as tied up almost all transportation. Potatoes have disappeared. No milk is reaching Paris. There has been no distribution of fats this month. The scarcity of flour has again produced long lines in front of the bakeries.

It is a common comment here today that this is like the winter of 1940-'41, when the cold was bitter and the only food for three weeks was rutabagas and beets usually fed to hogs. There is intense critisim of the government, which is blamed with not having forseen the cold or the food shortage, and with not having taken measures against both.

De Gaulle Foresaw Trouble

As a matter of fact, the government did see trouble coming. More than once General Charles de Gaulle said that even harder times were in store and that no improvement could be expected before spring. He said his ministers tried to get shipping from the Allies, but war needs came before France's civilian requirements. Now the cold has arrived, and with it public grumbling.

Ice has blocked the canals along which coal is usually shipped to Paris, as well as the streams of the Auvergne which normally generate power for the city. As a result, the city goes without electric light until 5 p. m., and even factories cannot work in the daytime.

The coal shortage has forced the government to stop all passenger traffic except in Paris suburbs. Trains have been full of Parisians going to Brittany or other rich provences in search of food. The number of trucks which can bring food into the city has also been curtailed by shortage of spare parts and tires.

Even milk for children is now impossible to find. A few days ago butter could be bought fairly easily on the black market for $6.50 pound. Today it has disappeared.

Paul Ramadier, Minister of Food, is trying desperately to supply the city with meat and vegetables. But potatoes have vanished from the market since restrictions were lifted from their sale. During the fall, vegetables were plentyful—leeks, carrots, cabbage, radishes today were hard to find.

Crowds gathered today in Toulouse, protesting against the shortage of food. In Paris the prople are still quiet, particularly because they are so cold; but if the bread supply fails the situation will be grave.

To try to counter criticism of the government, both the semi-official "LeMonde" and the "Paris Presse," for example, quoted General De Gaulle's warning of new difficulties in his Jan. 1 message and added: "These difficulties have come. Frenchmen will accept them because it is their duty to do so and because they are courageous. But General De Gaulle must explain the situation himself to the people and inform them of the remedies he intends to take in order that confidence in the government's action may be restored."

The fact is that too many Frenchmen have forgotten the winter of 1940 and remember only the better winters under occupation. Some have already begun to say that things were better under occupation.

One of my men reported back to me that he'd found a cave full of German loot. I drove out with him to see it and was stunned at the enormity of the place. We were told that the cave had been used for growing mushrooms before the war. It consisted of many, very large rooms into which the loot had been organized. One room would be full of artwork, one of wine or other booze, and room after room was filled with food.

Because of the grim food situation in Paris, I organized a truck convoy and we hauled the food into the city to feed the Parisiennes. There was enough in the cave to feed the city for about ten days.

19 Jan. 1945

Dearest Mother,

Your reaction to the pictures was funny. Judy frankly stated she didn't like 'em cause they weren't smiling, and you said you liked 'em even if they were unflattering and I agree with both of you. They do look like me so you can like 'em 'cause you're my Mother and Judy can dislike 'em because she's entitled to a glamourized version of her husband.

I liked your comment on the news. They do tend to overplay it, both good and bad.

And then they bitch at the home front for getting too optimistic or else too low. –I think the average guy reads it all with a grain of salt.

This cleaning of your apartment sounds like an endless process to me. You're always cleaning and cleaning and cleaning. That's the one very noticeable difference between American homes and European homes. The average English home isn't too good and the French are worse and it isn't just wartime conditions either. You know I don't like a home so clean that it isn't livable, but these people keep their homes livable as hell. Kinda like Gil and I used to keep our room at Triangle Fraternity. Remember?

I think we agree on the union question. They are a very necessary thing, but they aren't controlled in the States and they must be controlled. What the hell! Even our government has a system of checks and controls but these unions don't even answer to themselves and that's not right.

This question of drafting labor still puzzles me. I really don't think it would be necessary if they would cut out this mollycoddling of people on the point of bad news. And yet some news must be kept quiet. For instance if the Japanese had known just how bad the situation was after Pearl Harbor they would undoubtedly have continued their attack on Hawaii and I think it's generally agreed that they would have taken it. And so that news had to be suppressed even though it would have done wonders if the home front had known the truth. I know it would have changed my attitude if I'd really known the truth.

They have been releasing casualty figures as fast as they can. I saw the dope on the Bulge casualties about a week ago.

And speaking of news, I'm just hanging on the reports of the Russian drive. I keep praying that they will keep on rolling.

Gene is my roommate. He's a big blonde happy-go-lucky kid. He's been in the Army almost five years now and was just 23 this month. –And he seems to be the same age as myself. He's sure seen and done a lot for a kid that age. I was certainly a little dumbbunny at 23, only I didn't know. –I probably still am and don't know it.

Lots 'n lots of love,

Carpy

22 Jan. 1945

Dearest Mother,

The January 5 letter with the other collar clip came in yesterday so I'm well equipped. Eclipped is a better quip. —Must be I drank too much coffee this morning.

Speaking of the news, and who isn't, the Russian drive is certainly a beauty and I can hope like hell, but still in the back of my mind is the lurking suspicion that it's still going to take a hard fight to get to Berlin. If the Russians do go straight on to Berlin as they say they will, it'll certainly be a blow to American pride. We won't hear many guys talking about how the Americans won the war. We're doing our share and can be justly proud of it, but so can a couple dozen other Allied countries.

What a cosmopolitan family we've developed into in the past few years. Pee has become a Westerner, Judy toured the West, I've looked over Africa and Europe, Bill & Edie are South American Yankees and you've traveled all over by paper. You got gypped. Only I'm awful glad you're there at home kinda keeping your hands on the reins.

I've been reading about more and more snow there at home and have been just as envious. You know I always was a sucker for a good snowstorm. But I can understand why you don't like it. It was certainly smart of you to pick such a well-located apartment.

We've had quite heavy snows for Paris lately and I get a kick out of the way these people take them. Any and all of them will indulge in a snow battle at the drop of a snowflake and the soldiers are just as willing. It's as much as your life is worth to walk down Rue de la Paix or over to Boulevard Haussman.

My old trouble is coming back. I'm getting itchy feet. I've been here seven weeks and I'm willing to move on.

Lots 'n lots of love,

Carpy

29 January 1945

Dearest Mother,

One evening last week, Gene and I went to see "For Whom the Bell Tolls." I'd seen it before in London but it was the first time he'd seen it and we both sat through it enthralled. I wonder why that didn't get an Oscar. It's the best casting I've ever seen and beautifully acted. And Ingrid, Oh Ingrid! Okay, so I'm fickle, but the only reason I like her is because she's got a beautiful mouth and eyes just like my wife. And you know how beautiful she is. Nice personality, too. I like her.

How come I always get interrupted when I write to you? I don't know. Anyway in the interim a letter from you to me arrived. It was mailed Dec. 16. In the same mail I got one from Judy mailed Jan. 19. One of those letters loafed coming over. It was a nice newsy letter.

It also contained some very true information on the fact that the strikers get all the publicity when actually they're such a small group. The people at home are doing a very tremendous job and doing it well. Judging them by the strikes is like judging the entire Army by the AWOLs. There is only one thing to be said for the Army on the AWOLs. When they catch 'em they hit 'em. One week's AWOL will net a first timer the loss of whatever rank he holds and six months pay and a two timer will catch a Dishonorable Discharge and two to five years hard labor.

The production records don't amaze me as does the way the shekels roll in on these bond sales. Where is it all coming from? Just think what that country could do if it really felt it was working and fighting for its life as the Russians did. That would really be something. I hope to hell it never happens.

That party with the Authors must have been a heck of a lot of fun. I'd particularly liked to have talked to Ogden Nash and Dorothy Parker. I'll bet they're not nearly as witty to talk to as a lot of people who don't have their talent for writing. As you say, they're just human.

Bye now. Lots and lots of love,
Carpy

1 February 1945

Dearest Mother,

One month of 1945 rolled back already. It's a funny thing to say, but time certainly hasn't been hanging very heavily on my hands for the past year. I never saw a year go quite so fast. It must be because of all the moving around I've been doing and being busy and being in on so many important happenings. At least I haven't had time to sit back and feel sorry for myself. Not often, anyway.

The news of the Russian advance is still good this morning. I keep hoping that the Germans will wise up and quit and yet I wonder if they won't resist until the day the Yanks and the Reds shake hands.

I'd like to have heard the speech on Russia. If we really do think alike it'll certainly help toward promoting a better world. That's one reason I'm so partial to the blinking Limeys. I know we think alike.

This language bar is the biggest single detrimental factor toward world peace in my mind. You automatically distrust a guy you can't understand and you're inclined to trust one you can understand.

I finally got a letter from Baldy with a new address and answered it immediately. He says he's going to get married in March or April. I'd sure like to be there, but I'm afraid Uncle Sammy has other plans for me.

You know how prone I am to make snap judgments of people. I made one the other night. I met this cute girl at a party and spent most of the evening shooting the bull with her. She evidently comes from a good family because she's been all over Europe, especially the winter resorts. She likes skiing and skating as much as I do. She's married and her husband is a prisoner of war in Germany. They're in worse shape than Judy and I. They were married four months and he has been a prisoner since 1939. I decided she was decorative and a good conversationalist, but not much use as a citizen of France, part of the upper crust that was responsible for the bad situation in France before the war. Then the Liaison Officer who took me to the party explained that she is a doctor of law and a practicing lawyer in Paris specializing in handling cases for poor people. So I gave her a mental apology.

Lots 'n lots of love,

Carpy

10 Feb. 1945

Dear Toots,

I'm burned up. I'm furious. If I can ever lay my hands on the son of a bitch who is responsible for this V-mail racket I'll wring his damned neck. Those things aren't a bit faster and they're worthless when they do get here. We live for and by the letters from home and those bits of paper haven't the slightest connection with home. They're just a dirty stinking trick whereby some filthy racketeers are making a fortune at the expense of defenseless G.I.s thousands of miles from home. Boy, I'm hot. That racket is one that really burns me.

Sorry, Sugar, I just hadda blow off steam when I read that you'd fallen for their latest advertising gag. –I use them only when I'm too rushed to really write or don't have any paper, but at no other time. You do the same please.

I just got your 28 Jan. letter and that's what roused me. Incidentally, I haven't gotten any of the V-mails which you mentioned writing before you wrote this letter.

I got another food packet from you this afternoon, but I won't open it 'til tonight. Thanks a million, Toots. You're a pal.

I also got a letter from Judy with two pictures of Kit's family. Those kids of his are certainly good looking. Man I wish I had a couple. I'll be an old man before my kids are in school at this rate.

The news hasn't been spectacular lately but it's certainly all in our favor. If I'm lucky, I may be home by next Christmas. It's a pleasant thought.

Lots and lots of love,

Carpy

Among the captured materiel I had to deal with was an entire warehouse full of cars. A number of the cars were a particular brand of luxury car. I found the local dealer for that brand and went to see him to enlist his aid in tracking down the owners. He seemed astonished that we were trying to give the cars back to his former clients, one of whom was the King of Spain. Anyway, the dealer was so pleased he kept pressing me to accept some rather generous rewards. I had a helluva time convincing him that I didn't want anything for doing this. This was just part of my job and I was determined to avoid any accusations of impropriety. I finally got through to him that, after the war, I wanted to go HOME, not to Leavenworth due to a court martial.

15 Feb. 1945

Hi Toots,

Well, I think I'll be able to write Flossie now. Honest I've started a letter to her three times and never been able to do it.

The article on Annabelle from where she's stationed was swell. Her letter sounded just like mine must have when I first headed out. All enthused over everything and getting a big bang out of seeing the world. I guess I'm still that-a-way only I'm getting homesick. I want to either go home or move on to some other place.

The stories about food and coal in Paris are undoubtedly true. Thank God I'm with the American Army. We get our rations as always. It's a funny situation, not funny really, just thoroughly confused. The black market is so strong that I wonder if they'll ever break it. For four years it was the patriotic thing to do. Now suddenly it isn't and yet the nation is so small that it is impossible to live without buying on the black market. Whenever I go out to dinner, I know that most of the food I'm eating was bought on the market. Maybe I should refuse to go and yet they ask me and certainly seem to want me to visit them so I can hardly refuse without being rude as hell. You can live in Paris if you have money. Otherwise you just exist and are lucky if you don't starve.

I didn't even know it was Valentine's Day yesterday until some-body mentioned it in the bar last evening. I'm a heel. But I love both Mrs. Carpenters and want them to be my Valentines. How about you?

Sunday night Gene and Little John and I went out and did the town. Boy was I plastered. It was a farewell party for Gene. He left Monday night at midnight for the States. His father is very ill. Cancer of the lung, I believe. I sure felt sorry for him going home that way. I'm gonna miss him too. That's the trouble with the Army. You just make friends and then you lose them. It's T.S.

Bye now.
Lots 'n lots of love,

Carpy

18 February 1945

Dearest Mother,

It's Sunday afternoon in Paris and Sunday morning at home so you probably won't be writing to me until I'm in bed tonight, but it's nice to know that every Sunday my favorite Maw parks herself at her desk and writes me all the news that's fit, and some that isn't.

I had a good night's sleep last night because I went to a cocktail party and then to dinner and then home to bed. The party was for the French and American officers who worked together on the captured materiel. I was really traveling with the brass. We had a couple of Generals and so many Colonels there that I could hardly count 'em. And much, much champagne. I had four or five glasses and it didn't faze me. Which reminds me, you asked me to tell you when to start worrying about my drinking. Okay, I will. But don't start worrying yet. I still refuse more than fifty percent of the drinks offered me and the boys know that when I say "No" I mean it. –I got mad one night when they kept pestering me so now I have no trouble. But I do enjoy a few drinks before dinner, not every night, but three or four nights a week and I seem to succeed in getting high about once a week except that I miss a week occasionally. –How is my post war cellar building up that you promised to save for me? Every once in a while my mouth waters for that bottle of 7-star Greek brandy Gilmore gave me the day I left for the Army.

What do you think of the Pacific news? By the time you get this you'll probably know the answer, but I'm baffled by this raid on Tokyo. I can't see what they're aiming at. But it's good to know that we're powerful enough to do it.

My opinion of MacArthur has gone up plenty. He's evidently a damn shrewd tactician. That Bataan and Corregidor stunt looks like a risk that is paying dividends.

> Bye now.
> Lots and lots of love,
> *Carpy*

25 February 1945
Paris, France

Dearest Mother,

It sounded like an awful nice Sunday when Flossie visited you. That's a nice thing about that apartment. It's handy for you and handy for your Montoursville friends too.

Is it almost two or three years now that you've been away from the town? I know it's three full years that I haven't seen the place.

This has been another nice, peaceful Sunday. I slept late, ate a good dinner and then went on a tour of the Latin Quarter with this Swiss-French boy I've met. His name is Jean-Jacques and he is in the International Y.M.C.A. Services, which is the gang that checks up on treatment of P.O.W.s. He's quite a student of languages. His English is perfect and his French too, naturally, but he also speaks German, quite a bit of Chinese and a smattering of Japanese. He showed me all the places he used to hang out when he was a student here before the war. We also went to the Pantheon where lots of famous Frenchmen are buried and, although it's forbidden, we sneaked up into the very top of the tower and had a wonderful view of Paris. It's the highest building on the left bank, except the Eiffel Tower. We ended up our tour out in Montparnasse and then took the subway back to the hotel for supper.

I'm in the writing room at the hotel and across from me is a replica of "Winged Victory" the same size and same degree of dustiness as the one at home. Whatever happened to her? Did one of the boys take her or do you still have her?

Thanks for the razor blades. I'll last another couple months now.

This is an awfully dumb letter, Toots. I honestly haven't done a damn thing but work and sleep for the past week. I've had this nasty cold that I've been trying to break up, so I haven't even seen a movie. Maybe next week I can do better. Anyway, you're still my favorite Mother.

Lots 'n lots of love,

Carpy

This is a typewritten letter on a half sheet of nice quality writing paper, which was apparently left behind by the Germans as it is imprinted at the top with "Kommandostab, Abt. 1 c, Paris, Den".

4 March 1945

Dearest Mother,

Something new in the way of writing paper. I kinda like this stuff. It looks good.

I keep thinking you and Judy are due for a shock when I finally do get home. The difference in looks between 24 and 28 is liable to be considerable, and I hope I make it while I'm still 28. It's funny how the guys in the States want to get over here, and all we want to do is get home. But such is war. C'est la Guerre.

I saw another good Variety show Tuesday night. The Special Service has certainly dug up a wealth of talent in this town. Or maybe it's just that I'm a vaudeville fan at heart. Thursday I heard and saw Glenn Miller's band again. His drummer, Ray MacKinley is running the band now, and he's plenty good. As long as they have a good man like Mac fronting the outfit and Eddie Gray arranging for them they can't miss.

Okay, if you insist I'll try and stick around to see what Paris is really like in the Spring. But I ain't promising, you know how this Army is.

So Judy's wearing stockings again. She is a lucky girl.

I'm still working like a slave. This job has been really keeping my nose to the grindstone for the past few weeks, but I love it. I even have to come in on Sundays now and spend a couple of hours cleaning out my "in" basket and lining up work for the next week. Tomorrow I got one of these hot priority jobs where the brass tells you to do something practically impossible and doesn't say how. It's gonna be fun, but I may get shot before I finish it. For some reason the Chiefs of Services, usually colonels, don't like to comply with orders issued by a lieutenant.

The news is certainly good enough. But it sure looks like it's gonna be a fight until the Russians and the Allied Expeditionary Forces are shaking hands in the middle of Germany. And I was a guy who firmly believed that the Germans would quit when the fighting got on their own soil. What a prognosticator I am.

The home news that irked me even more than the strikes was the announcement that Swooner Sinatra's work is essential. Oh brother! That's all! We've had it! It wasn't so bad when they just said he wasn't man enough for the Army. But this.

It's about time for me to scram now.

Lots 'n lots 'n lots of love,

Carpy

---

11 March 1945

Dearest Mother,

I've got your letter of 25 Feb. to answer and since I'm duty officer today I hope I have plenty of time to answer it. Sometimes this duty officer job is a snap and sometimes it's a pain in the neck. I'm not only on duty in my section today but I'm on for the Headquarters tonight so I ought to be pretty sleepy tomorrow.

The commentator was absolutely right. Neither England nor France has had to make any midnight curfew ruling. The rationing is so darned strict here that such a ruling wouldn't make a whit of difference. England has always had an eleven o'clock closing of all bars and you should have known that from your reading, and in France there is no coal to heat such things as theaters, clubs, civilians or anything except the Army and essential industry. That commentator was certainly working overtime for Goebbels.

This gal Ernestine sounds like she's playing with 'the buzz saw.' Don't injure her permanently, please, but go ahead and tame her down a bit. I think she needs it.

I had a swell letter from Judy. She'd had the Ford out for the first time in months and seemed to enjoy it. She was worrying about a flood and since I've been reading about the river being up I'm wondering what happened to you-all, but not worrying because you told me not to worry.

She told me all about her date with Baldy. It sounds as if Baldy is getting along pretty darn good. I sure hope so.

Judy hasn't given up hope that I'll be coming home soon, but I don't expect it. Not until the war in Europe is over and only if I'm lucky then. They'll need young officers with my experience out in the Pacific. It's rough but it's true.

My nightlife last week was rather slight. This job is keeping my nose to the grindstone but I love it. However I'm really fagged at the end of the day. I've lost a little weight, but I'm in pretty good shape and feel swell.

Lots and lots of love just for
you, Toots,

Carp

---

13 March 1945

Dearest Mother,

I'm busy as a little bee this afternoon, as you can plainly see. Honest, I am, only right now I'm waiting for my liaison officer to come in so we can go out and argue with a Frenchman. He should be in any minute now so this may get interrupted.

My duty officer job Sunday night turned out to be quite easy. Except for answering a lot of foolish questions, it was a snap. Only I didn't get much sleep. I stretched out on a couch in one of the offices about one thirty and proceeded to have one of the worst nightmares I've ever had in my life. I think the coffee and doughnuts I had at eleven plus the uncomfortable sleeping position did it. I dreamed I had a nervous breakdown and was going crazy and the hell of it was I was half-awake and half-asleep. I knew where I was and what I was doing and I swear it took me half an hour to shake it off and get back to normal. Man I was wringing wet when I finally got straightened out. I sure hope I don't do that again.

Well, I got interrupted and it's now the next day and I've completed three years overseas. My secretary sewed my six Hershey bars on this morning and I've been wearing them proudly. That's quite an armful of stripes.

Last night Elroy and Hoff from the old gang were in town and we took in the variety show. This morning Hoff took off for the States. He's the last of five brothers: two were killed in the Pacific, one in the States, and one in Luxembourg so they're assigning him to permanent duty in the States. He's been over two-and-one-half years so he's no rookie.

When I think back to three years ago and remember my feelings then, my first sea voyage, the thrill I got in going all over that boat and learning my way around from stem to stern, and the excitement of the submarine alert we had right outside the harbor. Those were the days when submarines were thicker than fish on that eastern seaboard. It's been so long now that I'm actually beginning to forget things that happened that first year. But probably when I get home and start telling you about things my memory will come back.

Judy sent me a copy of <u>Look</u> magazine with her picture in it and enclosed in it was the greeting from <u>Gazette and Bulletin</u> with a beautiful picture looking upstream from Blair's dam. I have it on the wall beside my desk and it makes me homesick every time I look at it. Gosh, but that's pretty country.

Now I'd better get back to work or they may fire me, I hope.

Lots and lots and lots of love,

Carpy

At long last, I was promoted to Captain.

19 March 1945

Dearest Mother,

The mail has been treating me right. Saturday I got the letter you mailed Monday and today I got the one you mailed the Monday before. Also I got a package of grub from Judy so I'll have a feast with the drinking we're gonna do tonight. O'Brien and I are throwing a little party for the G-4 gang to celebrate our change in address. I think it'll be drunk out tonight.

Now for the news. Thursday Alton walked into the office. He just stood here and grinned at me for about half a minute 'til I swallowed my surprise enough to say his name. He looks swell. This combat life seems to agree with him. He had a 72-hour pass so we had Friday evening together. Took in the Special Service Variety show and then went back to his hotel and imbibed Scotch and shot the bull until about 2:30. Gee, but it was wonderful to talk to him. I don't know when I've had such a grand evening.

This is just a note, Toots, 'cause I gotta go host the boys now. I'll write lots of news soon.

Lots 'n lots of love,

Captain Carp

25 March 1945
Paris

Dearest Mother,

I think Staunton is the nice chap who came into the engineering section after I left the mill. I met him once. Lambert is an old pal of mine. He and I went on a half dozen trips together including the one to North Carolina. He's one of the best damn rope splicers in the United States. He's really an artist. –The way Pete greeted you sounded swell to me. Down deep in my heart I still have a yearning to go back and work for him. All other plans are alternate in case Pete doesn't need me.

Things must be rough in the States when a telegraph girl gets agape over my picture. All I gotta say is I wish I were there to see it.

The news this morning is certainly good. The Airborne and the 9th are across the Rhine. But I think that finding the Ludendorff Bridge still intact was about the best piece of luck in a long time. And it stayed up long enough to give us a really solid bridgehead down there.

The package of food came thru swell. Thanks an awful lot, Toots. We have midnight snacks in somebody's room every couple of nights. I've been cadging up to date but I'll do my share now. I'm glad you sent two boxes of tea 'cause I'll give one to my Irish landlady. She'll like that a lot' cause tea is a forgotten item in Paris. Even the black market doesn't sell it.

Now I've got to do a little work so I'll have things lined up for tomorrow.

G'bye Toots,
Lots 'n lots of love,

Carpy

April 2, 1945

Dearest Mother,

The letter Judy wrote me from New York was just bubbling over with good spirit. Gee, but it does her good to go down there. She seemed to be a little worried over Baldy and Edith, that they weren't happy enough about the whole thing. I hope it's just honeymoon bashfulness.

This past week has been hectic. Lankford has been in town and we've been out every night. Monday we went to hear Glenn Miller's band. Tuesday we went to the movies and then to the Red Cross dance. Wednesday I had dinner with two of the guys I work with from another headquarters and we sat around and shot the bull all evening. Thursday we had dinner with BB, another of the old gang and we drank and batted the breeze all night. Friday we went to see the Casino de Paris. Saturday we went to the Folies Bergere and then to the Bel Tabarin Cabaret. Last night was peaceful. We just quietly sat around and got drunk. It's funny but it took me four months in Paris to get started making the rounds and then I hit most of the high spots in two days. I just needed a good excuse and Lankford being here was it. Next week I'm gonna try and get some sleep.

The French had a big show this morning. Gen. DeGaulle presented the regimental colors to all the units that have been reactivated and then they had a big parade. But it was a quiet crowd. None of the furor and hubbub that I expected.

The Folies is quite a show. It isn't a strip tease like our burlesque. It's more like an ordinary musical show and they just frankly don't wear anything more than a bespangled gee string. The girl who is the leading lady, so to speak, is about the most gorgeous thing I've ever seen. She would put the proverbial brick house to shame, she's even better built. The settings and lighting are the thing. They are magnificent. They look like settings for Hollywood shows.

The Bel Tabarin is quite a cabaret. There must have been a thousand people in there, about three-fourths of the men are soldiers from practically every Allied nation. Their floorshow is quite something too. The Casino was the poorest of the lot.

Now speaking of other topics, the news is certainly good. The poor old <u>Stars and Stripes</u> is so excited it doesn't know what to print. I'm excited too, but I'm just waiting and watching the papers and disregarding any latrine rumors I happen to pick up.

Lots and lots of love,

Carpy

10 April 1945

Dearest Mother,

Judy told me all about New York including her dates. I think it was swell that she could have the chance. This three years has been a damned rough deal for her. –I still hold to the Pennsylvania Dutch theory that the only person who may approve or disapprove of my wife's conduct is me. And I approve. I've got a damned sight more confidence in Judy than I have in me, and I still don't owe any apologies.

My bride is a lovely child isn't she? Gosh how I like to read about her. –Don't you two get an idealized version of your son and husband too well in mind. Remember I'm a homely rat and this war hasn't improved me any and I have a flash temper and I'm bossy as hell and stubborn and sometimes just a bastard. –No offense Toots, a legal bastard but still a bastard! –I got to thinking how pretty she is and what a shock I'm gonna be and that's what started this forecast.

Thanks an awful lot for the food. You are doing right well by me. I even have enough razor blades for awhile. Five or six months to be exact.

Gee, Toots, if you're gonna have a love affair be careful. Remember, life begins at forty. –How about the time I chaperoned you? I'd like to go now. I think Judy and I would be wonderful chaperones.

The news is good and best of all to me is the sober way everybody is taking it on both sides of the ocean. I think the United States is growing up. This isn't a game any more, the tickets are too expensive. –The picture of "Wilson" made a strong impression on me. God help us if we turn isolationist again. I'm afraid this is our last chance. If we can't establish a good hard peace this time we won't have another chance.

Guess I'll quit philosophizing and hit the hay.

Lots of love, Toots

Carpy

13 April 1945

Dearest Mother,

The news this morning ((of President Roosevelt's death)) was certainly shocking... It just didn't seem possible that I'd learn something like that by reading the headlines of a paper over somebody's shoulder. For a minute I couldn't believe it and I still don't want to.

It's even more of a blow to the people outside the U.S. The Americans will get along, but to a lot of people in little countries all over the world, F.D.R. represented their hope of a real peace.

If I remember my history correctly this is once again proof that our ancestors were smart people. Didn't the original plan for electing presidents call for the man who got the most votes to be president and the man who got second to be vice president?

I imagine that Mr. Truman is a worried man today. He's inherited a terrific responsibility. If he succeeds, the credit will go to Roosevelt for starting things right and if he fails the blame will fall on him for failing to carry thru.

The French all ask us who Truman is and what will happen now. And I can't answer either question.

I'm anxious to hear your comments. It's funny when you consider that I voted against him twice and still had such confidence in him. I think that history will call him a great American. We've taken a beating in the past six months with both Wilkie and Roosevelt gone.

The war news is still good if not better than good. The papers here keep implying that it's all over but the shouting but I'm still waiting for SHAEF (Supreme Headquarters Allied Expeditionary Forces) to decide when it's over. I think a lot of guys may get killed before the shouting.

Lots 'n lots of love, Toots,

Carpy

17 April 1945

Dearest Mother,

I've got two good letters to answer today. Of course the one you wrote the day Flossie was there was just a note but you're forgiven. In fact you're such a good correspondent I couldn't complain if you just plain forgot me occasionally. But you won't. Now I know how Grandfather was elected to the House of Representatives. Weren't you on the election board in those days? Gosh you're dishonest. I'm glad I don't take after you. I'm as honest as the day is long. But you know that.

I hope Mrs. Davis is okay by now. I didn't know twins were any worse than just having one. Maybe Judy and I better not try catching up that way. But it sure would be nice to have twin daughters. Just twice as nice as one.

Your sketch of Judy was beautiful. I recognized her immediately as soon as I read the letter. –Where are those patches of gold embroidery on the front of Judy's black dress?? Judy's just modest. She's a darn good cook too. All the women in my family are. Which just proves how smart I am.

It's certainly been wonderful weather here for the past week or so. I get out of this office as much as I can and that still isn't enough.

Sunday evening I went out to the house of Capt. Douzon, he's the brother of the lawyer girl I met last winter. It was the first time I'd seen them for about a month so we sat around and shot the bull all evening. After I left I got to thinking about what a nice time I'd had and it dawned on me that only the lawyer spoke English and French. The Captain's wife speaks a very little English and the Captain speaks none and I speak lousy French and yet we all jabbered away and understood each other quite well. It's fun and it's funny. If we got stuck we'd have the lawyer translate, but she didn't have to very much.

Remember that once, when I first landed here and was talking about how much I disliked the French, I said that probably as I got to know more of them I'd come to like them just as I did the English. Now I've got to admit that since I've been working here with a liaison officer every day and meeting Frenchmen and working with them I have met a lot of darn nice guys. Of course we still run into meatheads all the time but Marchin and I outmaneuver them and usually get the results we want. I don't get mad as quickly as I did at first. I think it's been good training for me.

Lots 'n lots of love,

Carpy

24 April 1945

Dearest Mother,

I'm crazy about the pictures of you taken along the Laporte road. You don't even look your 40 years. My secretary won't believe you're my mother. The suit is really good-looking and I like that way of doing your hair very much. 'Tis tres chic. How do you do it? I'm right proud of my reporting Mama.

I've put the note of Johnny's grave in my wallet and if I ever get a chance to go near there I'll try to find the spot.

The news is still pretty good, pretty damn good, but I don't think it's finished yet. I made a little wager about a month ago and picked a date near my birthday. I hope I'm not being too optimistic.

I'm enjoying life here just as much as ever. Sometimes I feel a little guilty, but then I salve my conscience by remembering Africa. And I am doing an important job and doing it well, so I think.

Gee, Toots, your love life is sure doing all right. And the descriptions all sound like good guys. I'm right pleased. —Of course six kids is quite a drawback to a widower. You'd never be sure he wanted a wife or a nursemaid.

Lankford was in town Friday and we did a bit of drinking and then went to a Red Cross dance. It was American night and all the girls were either nurses, Croix Rouge, or embassy. It was a lot of fun with much cutting in and lots of laughs and kidding. You can't equal American girls anywhere in the world. They're the tops.

I've moved into my billet out at Montparnasse and am quite happily located. I gave my landlady one of the boxes of tea and Sunday morning she brought me tea and toast in bed. That's the English influence. She's really a nice woman and I think it will be very pleasant staying there. However it's certainly not as convenient as that hotel.

Now it's lunchtime and I've got to hurry or I'll be late. —Mighty good office I got. Everybody's working like hell but me. That's what you call efficiency.

Lots 'n lots of love,

Carpy

29 April 1945

Hi Toots,

This is Paris calling in the American Service. Today we have a program of news, fun, and information brought to you by courtesy of the Army Service Forces in the E.T.O. Your announcer for this program will be Grant "Playboy" Carpenter, a long-standing member of our staff.

Now that that's over folks, do you remember who used to call whom a couple of five-cent playboys? Which reminds me, where is cousin Bud now-a-days? I haven't heard of him in about a year. I wonder if he's managed to tame Kitty down a bit.

So Pee hadda be slapped down a bit? She bitched at me a bit in a letter the other day, but I gotta admit, I've neglected her a little. –I think your philosophizing is pretty true. You gotta love someone a little more than you love yourself or life doesn't mean much.

This boy Irv seems to be making your life very interesting. More power to both of you. Be good and have a good time.

The Time magazine that came out the week after Roosevelt's death had a lot of good stuff in it. Its picture of the future and Truman is quite promising. They base most of their ideas on the fact that he knows how to get along with Congress. Could be.

This town has really been happy for the past couple of weeks. The released prisoners of war are coming back by the trainload after five years and maybe you think they aren't getting a happy reception. And to top it off these peace rumors are floating around. –It keeps everybody excited and happy anyway.

Our in-laws are nice people, aren't they? But shucks, they'd have to be, to have such a nice girl as my Judy. –Give her a kiss for me the next time you see her, will yuh? I'd like to do it myself but this long distance stuff is no soap.

One thing about magazines and papers at home that tickles me is the way they keep harping on whether the returning soldiers will or will not be difficult to adjust. They're sure having fun with the question. –I can't decide whether I'm gonna be a homicidal maniac or an introvert of the first order. Anyway you figure it, I'm sure gonna be weird. I'm gonna run around drinking milkshakes and making passes at Judy at inopportune moments. And eating shrimp cocktails and hamburger sandwiches. And telling fabulous lies about my experiences in the wilds of many foreign countries. Oh boy, it's gonna be fun.

Lots 'n lots of love,

Carpy

By now the Allied Forces were finding and liberating Concentration Camps. The news – and the pictures – coming out of those camps was stomach turning. It was hard to grasp the inhumanity behind the treatment of the people in those camps.

2 May 1945

Dearest Mother,

Today finishes my fourth year in the Army. Four years ago today I drove to Ft. Belvoir to stay overnight with Gil and report in the next morning. Three years ago tonight I got thoroughly plastered for the first time in my life. Tonight I'll probably stay sober.

The news is certainly good. Mussolini killed and Shickelgruber reported dead. Now if they'll only drop a bomb on that Son of a B---- H-------- in Tokyo, things will really look up.

I don't know if I'm any bitterer over the atrocities than I was before but I still don't like them worth a good God damn and I don't even consider the possibility of there being such a thing as a good German. All the good ones are dead and the rest should be. Okay, I'll shut up now.

So Irv's writing love letters, hmmm, sounds serious. –I've almost forgotten how to write a love letter.

Last night I saw an awfully good comedy. It was a U.S.O. production of Noel Coward's "Blithe Spirit." Just my kind of humor. I sat there and howled.

Night before I saw "National Velvet." I read the book a couple of years ago and thoroughly enjoyed it and thought the picture was darn good too. The little girl who had the lead was a typically nice little English girl.

Lots 'n lots of love,

Your affectionate son,

Carpy

7 May 1945

Hi Snickery Snee,

Didn't the sound of guns to the right and left of him go snickery snee in "Ballad of the East & West?" Sometimes that brain of yours is just like a bolt snicking open and shut, especially when I try to put something over on you. —Wonder if that's one of the reasons I like you so. I don't know what brought up that train of thought. I guess I was just daydreaming of the good old days.

Not much news from this end of the line. The French papers have announced unconditional surrender but SHAEF (Supreme Headquarters Allied Expeditionary Forces) hasn't so we're still sweating out V-E Day.

I told Judy what my situation is. And briefly, it's this. If I'm lucky, I'll see you all this fall. So far in this war, I've been quite lucky except for that one little factor. I don't seem to be able to get home. And I wanna.

This is a note, Toots, but I got none to answer and my think box is tired. But I love you very dearly and you and Judy can compare letters and read the newspapers to find out what I'm supposed to be doing over here.

Lots 'n lots of love,

Carp

9 May 1945

Dearest Mother,

It still doesn't seem quite real to me. This city went quietly mad last night and not so quietly either. Gee, but it was pretty with the lights on all over the place. I walked around the gardens and thru the Concorde for awhile but about 10:30 I pooped out and went home to bed. The crowd was just going strong about then. I'll swear that three of Paris' four million population were swirling around the Concorde and along the Champs. They were still celebrating at four this morning and it kinda looks as if they'll be out again tonight. Today and tomorrow are holidays in France and crowds are thronging the streets even now.

At 2:30 yesterday afternoon we met at the Trocadero and had a short ceremony and heard the President's speech.

Your letter of the 30th of April arrived today, and was welcomed with open arms. —I always greet 'em that way.

Your story about the pint-sized pink wool sweater was swell and those clothes mean an awful lot to the people here. I remember last winter when some were given to the kids from Montmartre. They thought they were brand new 'cause they'd never had any clothes that good before. It's a sight to behold the way these street urchins run around in the raggedest hand-me-downs. There are an awful lot of awfully poor people in Europe. It's almost pathetic the way they think of the United States. At home we dream of a Utopia but over here they dream of America. Even the British, as proud as they are of Britain and of being British want to visit "The States" and see for themselves.

I'm all thrilled over the way Bill Ader has gotten along in the Scouts and I want to see him go on up. I think a couple of weeks at Camp Kline would be a help. They have all the facilities there to teach him things he needs to know to get his merit badges. I'd sure like to see him do it. Will you find out if he's interested and if it's okay for me to foot the bill for two weeks? I think twenty-five bucks would do it. Will you arrange it and I'll send the necessary francs? I can't quite realize that he's bigger than you are. But I guess it's true because three-and-a-half years is a lot of growing time.

Five letters from Irv in one week? Oh boy, Toots, you're doing all right. Only worry I've got is what he'll think when he meets your slightly indecent son and daughter.

Gosh Sugar, I just realized that it's Mother's Day on Sunday. I'll be thinking of you real good and hard and sending lots of love and kisses your way, Toots.

Bye now.
Lots 'n lots of love,

Carpy

13 May 1945

Hello "Love in Bloom,"

Got your letter of the 3rd today all about the swell weekend. I like this guy Irv, he sounds like a good Joe and you sound like you're having a good time. Only he's definitely not a wolf. Maybe he's a fox. That's a wolf who sends flowers, in case your education has been neglected.

Looks as if your prediction on V-E Day was a heck of a site closer than mine. Now what about Japan?

I hope they haven't been bothering you. Those rocket-propelled kisses I've been sending all day for Mother's Day. I got a couple aimed wrong at first and some babe in Australia is gonna be surprised as hell about 9:00 o'clock this evening, but I think the rest were right on the beam. You might give a couple of the extras to Judy. She ain't no mother but I got hopes.

Did I ever tell you how glad I am that you're my Mother? I didn't! Well, remind me of it sometime and I'll tell you, 'cause I am, very, too. Next Mother's Day I'll try to stop by and give you my kisses person-ally. I'd promise to do that if it wasn't for the way the Army keeps interfering with my private life.

Speaking of the Army and just in case you and Judy read the papers, I've got 91 points. 48 months in the Army, 38 months overseas and 5 points for my Battle Star. I've got another battle star that isn't on my record, that's the African job and I guess all of us in the 38th are getting screwed out of that. But I got more than the limit anyway so if I were an enlisted man I'd be getting out of the Army. As it is, I don't know, but don't expect anything. If I just get Statesward I'll be tres happy.

Hmmm, it's getting dark. Five minutes of ten so maybe I had better turn on the lights.

I'm swinging into this new job of mine and it has the earmuffs of a stinkeroo. It'll keep me busy anywho.

Always I send lots and lots of love, Toots, but today it's an espe-cially happy brand because you're my Mother.

Your 'baby,'

Carp

2 June 1945

Dearest Mother,

I got your swell letter of 27 May tonight, with the clipping about Ascension Island and also the latest report on Irv. I like the way you talk of him. He sounds like a hell of a nice guy and he likes my Mother just the way she deserves to be liked. And here's a piece of advice (free, too), don't let age worry you one little bit. I will personally vouch for the fact that you ain't a day over 35 and you gotta stretch to make that. At least most times you don't act it. We're a young family. I'm sure at least 90% of the time that I never should have been allowed to wear long pants. And every once in awhile I embarrass my subordinates by acting plain crazy. We enjoy life too much to worry about age. Gosh look at Grandfather, he never aged until those last few months.

Grandfather Charles Lose & 11-year-old Carp, 1928

That dope on The Rock is interesting. I just can't imagine fresh lettuce or tomatoes or cucumbers there. They must do it with mirrors. That's something I'll never forget, how good the first lettuce we got tasted. It was the summer of '43 in Dakar and we ate it like it was candy. Man, but that did fill a diet need.

The enclosed money order is fifty bucks for your birthday and $25.00 for two weeks at Camp Kline for Bill Ader. If it's more than that let me know. Buy yourself something nice and foolish for your birthday and then tell me what you bought so I can gloat over it. I like to buy presents for you. You're so far ahead of me on the game.

This job is still keeping me hopping. I'm running the project and building it as we go. About the middle of next week I'll have a company of P.O.W.s working for me. I have them part of the day now to build their own stockade. They're good workers if you keep on them, and I do. I think that's my racket, foreman on a big job will be just my meat.

I've been at my favorite hobby this evening. We have a hundred-yard rifle range here and I shot up about a hundred rounds of carbine ammo tonight. That's a nice little gun. Not as accurate as my twenty-two but it sure pushes a lot of 'em out quick and all of them would keep a guy ducking, if the first one didn't get him. I got 15 hits in a six-inch circle at 100 yards in 30 seconds. That's better than I can do with a pistol. Fifteen hits in the side of a barn at 20 yards in 20 minutes would be a good pistol score for me. You always could beat me at that.

Always lots 'n lots of love,
Carpy

My project was to build a camp just outside of Paris. Its purpose was to organize units of men to be redeployed to the war in the Pacific.

16 June 1945

Dearest Mother,

Gee, I've sure got a chewing coming to me. For slipping on my letter writing the way I have the past month. The enclosed clipping explains a little of it. Anyway I'm Camp Commandant of Camp P.A. and have been since it was organized, so the job of ironing out a million and one small details has fallen to me. At first I didn't like it, but then I got interested and it's turned out to be a good job. It isn't at all hard but it is long hours. I have a half dozen good American non-comms and a hundred German prisoners to do the work around camp, i.e. policing up, putting in latrines, building what facilities I can, and in general helping the troops with their housekeeping and processing. Most evenings it's eight or nine before I quit and then I read a few minutes and hit the hay. A couple nights a week I go to town to keep from getting in a rut. It's no excuse for not writing but it is the reason. There's nothing wrong with me that six months in the States won't cure. I'm homesick as hell, but my health is excellent.

I've gotten five "Grits" in the past two weeks, all late ones. Dated just before and just after V-E Day. The casualty lists were sure mounting up and a lot of 'em guys I knew.

It is good to read now of prisoners released instead of guys missing in action.

Bill Ader and his mother each wrote me an awfully nice letter. Those letters certainly more than repaid the cost of a couple of weeks at camp for Bill. Shucks the pleasure I got out of the idea put me in Bill's debt. He's a swell kid. And his letters show that he's certainly grown-up in the last three-and-a-half years. I know I won't recognize him.

The dope on the food situation helped a lot. I've seen too much of this starvation diet here in France and it frightens me. The black market is more at fault than an actual lack of food, so I have no mercy for black marketers on purchases. The diet you described certainly won't starve anyone, and that's good.

I like your political plan. Lycoming County could certainly use a new Republican Committee and you ought to have a hand in it.

Lots 'n lots of love,

Carp

Newspaper clipping enclosed about Carp's current job.

Service Units' Processing Fast

Service force units have been prepared for shipment to the Pacific in the record time of seven days, Brig. Gen. Pleas B. Rogers, CG of the Seine Section, announced yesterday, revealing the operation of a special redeployment camp near Villacoublay Airfield.

The camp, know as "PA" (Processing Area), has been established to help smaller, high-priority units of company size or less leave the Paris area in 30 to 45 days less than the normal time required to process men and equipment.

Brainchild of two Seine Section officers, Col. Henry Ahalt, G 2-3 officer, of Blacksburg, Va., and Col. Loren W. Potter, G-4 officer, of Lacelede, Mo., the processing area was developed in March when it became obvious that certain smaller service units would have to be moved quickly.

19 June 1945

Dearest Mother,

My crew talked me into pulling CQ while they go to chow so if the phone doesn't ring you'll get a letter from me. They're a good bunch of boys. They work like hell and can play just as hard.

I'm p----- off. The French have been holding parades and celebrations for their victorious armies. Every time you turn around the

Champs Elysees is blocked to all traffic and that sure complicates movement in Paris. Especially from the point of view of a guy who's got a job of redeploying troops thru the G-- D--- place. They don't even seem to realize what a joke it is, the only nation in the war that has been defeated by both sides and they're celebrating the victory.

I could sympathize with the French if they'd make some effort to straighten themselves out and get rid of the black market. But they just shrug their shoulders and say it can't be done. There are a few good Frenchmen who really think and worry about the future of France, but most of them think everybody's gonna help them and they don't have to do anything themselves.

For so many years now they've made a fetish of personal freedom and now it's degenerated to the point where they all believe only in personal freedom and fail to realize that it also entails the little duty of seeing to it that your own personal freedom doesn't harm someone else.

Well, enough of this bitching. Did I tell you that I saw a <u>Life</u> magazine the other day with a couple of good pictures of Ascension? The place has sure changed.

Every day I'm dreaming more and more of home. Today is a hot dusty one like I'd like to be spending immersed in the Loyalsock Creek about up to here. If you get what I mean.

I got a kick out of today's <u>Stars and Gripes</u>. They had an article about some preacher in the States criticizing Patton's cursing. Quote, "Damn it, it's no fun to say to the men you love – go out and die – but by God they did it". I'm a guardhouse lawyer. I say the minister spoke treason. Patton's speech says that we did it "by God" and that implies that God was and is on our side. The minister says that that's cursing, so he implies that God is against us. That's God-damned little faith to have in your country's battles.

Shucks I ran off the page. That's what happens when I get long-winded.

Lots and lots of love,

Carp

22 June 1945

Dearest Mother,

I got your letter of the 13th yesterday. Be sure and tell me all about what you get with my birthday present for you. Your idea of a bond for my birthday is swell. I'm well stocked up with food. To top it off, as Camp Commandant, I can hit any of the messes in camp anytime I want to, just to inspect and sample their food. 'Tis a good deal.

I'm glad your shoulder is well, even if I haven't gotten the letter yet telling me it was bad.

May I correct your spelling? —In reminiscing you should have said you were 'whaling' me in the woodshed and I was doing the 'wailing.'

It's been a long time since I've had the pleasure of correcting you. You're getting too damn smart with this newspaper work.

Yes, I agree that it was smart of you to get me instead of Al or Lukie, but for this — about finding me under a cabbage leaf. I think you better go to Judy and get her to straighten you out on that. 'Tis time you knew such things.

This afternoon I took a stroll thru the woods back of camp to see what the situation was. We've had trouble with girls from town following guys to camp here and shacking up with them in the woods. I didn't rout out any chicks but I did run across something that interested me. Remember me telling you about seeing Stonehenge in England? Well I ran onto a very similar formation here, but on a much smaller scale.

Don't misunderstand me. I didn't discover this. There is a well-defined path right by it and signs of people visiting there but it isn't well known like Stonehenge. The circle itself is probably 35 feet across. The stones look to be very old and are quite pitted and uneven except for the center stone and the big stones, which are of some smooth, hard variety.

The woods are also filled with unexploded bombs that nobody has had time to defuse and remove. I found a French kid with a hammer and chisel trying to remove the time fuse from a 500-lb cluster bomb. He wanted the watch mechanism. I chased his fanny to hell out of there quick.

It's an interesting life running a camp like this.

Give my beautous bride a heck of a big hug and kiss when you see her.

Lots 'n lots of love,

Carp

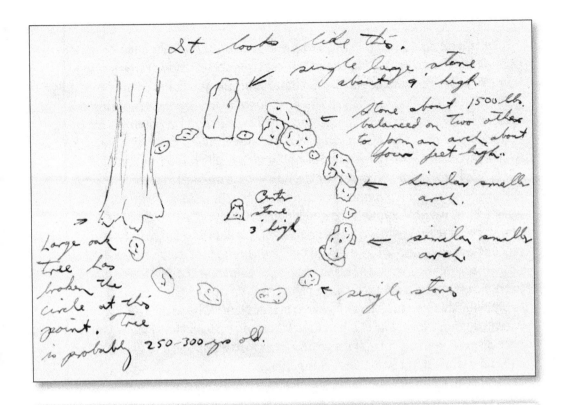

It looks like this.

← single large stone about 9' high.

← stone about 1500 lb. balanced on two others to form an arch about four feet high.

← similar smaller arch.

Outer stone 3' high

← similar smaller arch.

← single stone

Large oak tree has broken the circle at this point. Tree is probably 250-300 yrs old.

---

25 June 1945

Dearest Mother,

I got your letter of the 19th today with the booklet on Montoursville. The kid in two of the pictures looks like I picture Bill Ader only I think maybe Bill's bigger than that now. That booklet was a nice idea, even if Louise did take the pictures. –I was sure lucky there, wasn't I? Nice stuff, but only a passing fancy.

I got a swell letter from Sautelle Barter day before yesterday. She says Essex's husband is back from the Middle East but didn't mention any of the rest of the family. She remembered my birthday and timed it just right. –I got a cute card from Evie today too so I'm right proud of myself.

You said in your letter that I must be a man now. I sure hope so. I was 24 when I last saw you and I'm 28 now. That's a pretty good gap. S'funny though. I don't feel as old now as I thought I would four years ago.

My only trouble now is homesickness. Boy, I got it, but bad. I knew it would be this way as soon as the war was finished here, but I didn't know it would be so bad. I don't want to set the world on fire. I just wanna go home.

I'm gonna do some plain speaking and trust your intelligence to understand me. Now that I think there is a pretty good chance of my getting home this year I want to warn you that when I do get home I'm undoubtedly going to neglect you for maybe the first month or maybe more. I don't mean that I'm not coming to see you, but I mean that I'm gonna have to concentrate on Judy. You are my Mother and that's a fact you're stuck with irrevocably. This three-and-a-half years really hasn't separated us a bit. We know each other perfectly, but with Judy and me it's different. We're gonna be pretty damn strange to each other. And it's important as hell that we get acquainted quickly and rightly. It's too early to make plans, but if it looks to me like a good idea, I'm liable to take Judy and pull out of Williamsport the day after I get home just to give us a chance to get acquainted by ourselves. That's just an idea. I don't make plans without sizing up a situation and that can't be done from here. I'm just explaining this because I want you to understand whatever I do, it isn't because I don't love you, it's because I love you so well that I know you won't ever divorce me, but if I make a wrong start with Judy she may decide to call it off, and I don't want that happening.

Now you better write me and tell me you understand me and I'm still your favorite brat.

Lots 'n lots of love, Toots,

Carpy

---

2 July 1945

Dearest Mother,

I got your birthday letter today and also the one you wrote the Thursday before. I've already apologized for that gap in my writing. But a week was my longest miss so it's partly the mailman's fault. I know just how you feel. You don't worry, you wonder.

Bill Ader spoke of going out for football this fall. I sure hope to get a chance to see him play.

The new ensemble sounds like a million bucks at the very least. – You got a real system. One boyfriend (me) buys you dresses so you can knock the other guys' eyes out. Gold diggers, every one of you. I'll bet you'd ditch me quick if a richer boyfriend comes along. Women – pish! Women – tush! Women – I love 'em! Well anyway, a couple of 'em.

So you're still a sissy about drinking? I must confess I am not. But I have found that no matter how much I drink, I get just so happy and slightly fuzzy around the edges. It seems to reduce my field of vision to about a 30 degree arc straight in front of me but I can walk (not absolutely straight, but pretty good) and I always know just where I am, what I'm doing, and what everybody else is doing. I think I have inherited the old man's ability to carry my liquor. Only good thing I have inherited from him; well almost. I got a grin that comes in handy with the pretty girls. But, I digress.

That two weeks vacation sounds wonderful, Toots. I'm all for it. And I want long letters telling me about it.

The idea of my coming home is just as fixed in my mind as it is in yours but actually I haven't the slightest idea when it will be. I keep hoping for the fall but remember I ain't no General. It would sure help if we knew an approximate date, but the Army doesn't work that way. So you keep hoping (but not dreaming) and I'll keep hoping and dreaming a bit and one of these days I'll be seeing you.

Friday night I ran into Higgins again. He's now stationed in Paris in communications at Naval HQ. We shot the breeze for an hour, about where everybody was and what they were doing. He had just gotten his copy of the book of pictures of Montoursville and we hashed that over thoroughly. It sure is fun to just talk about the town with another guy who knows it as we do.

I had just been to the theater to see a "Jeep Show Revue". The Jeep shows are small teams of Army entertainers who traveled with and in the Armies and put on entertainment wherever and whenever they could. They were military personnel gathered from the Army for the shows. Cpl. Mickey Rooney and Cpl. Bobby Breen were in the revue. It was a big show made up from six or eight Jeep shows. Rooney is even funnier in person than on the screen. He's just a bundle of nervous energy. Doc Zangara and I went together and Doc commented that he bet Mickey had a high blood pressure. The rest of the acts were just as good as Mickey and the show had us howling all the time.

Guess I'd better stop or they may not let me mail this.

The birthday messages and kisses were swell.

Lots 'n lots of love,

Carpy

13 July 1945

Dearest Mother,

I have your letter of 5 July with the answers to a couple of my problems. As we say in French, "Vous etre tres gentil," and I'll bet you know what that means. Anyway it's a swell letter.

I was nursing an ice cold Coca-Cola, so cold it was half frozen and I couldn't concentrate until I got the last bit of that Coke out of the bottle. Thanks for the tip on drinking. It's funny to think of Judy worrying about me drinking. When we first started dating she could drink me under the table. How things have changed.

Unless my G-2 is misinformed, the mother-in-law who went to New York to meet her son is out of luck. All personnel leaving the continent are warned that no civilians are permitted to meet the boats and they will leave the boat and go direct to redeployment camps around the port before they will be permitted to see anyone. So-o-oh! Anyway she sounds like the kind of a mother-in-law I'm glad I don't have. Gracie is my idea of a good one and she's by proxy.

So the old tree is down. Gosh it's just like losing an old friend. I wonder how many times I've played hide and seek under that tree. Damn near every summer for about 10 years.

I think Jean has a good idea there. The college deal under the GI bill of rights. By the regulations of that I can now have five years of college. I think I'll just go educational, finish my M.E. and then get another degree in C.E. and maybe another in Metallurgy. All good subjects that relate to my work.

Did you get my love and kisses on your birthday? I hope it was the nicest 49th one you've had. Next year we'll try to make it even better.

I got interrupted. The Doc and I got to talking about wounds and stuff and he was explaining some of the things they've learned and developed on surgical practice over here. He's certainly had a lot of practice. His section handled 900 surgical cases in one month, that's himself, a couple of nurses, and a couple of ward boys. That must have been a pretty busy time.

Lots 'n lots of love,

Carpy

20 July 1945

Dearest Mother,

I just finished a letter of thanks to Bill Ader for his birthday box to me. He's a nice kid.

Now I have your letter on your birthday. You were having a hectic time, but it sounded nice. What with parties at Laporte and Irv in town, even your letter sounded rushed. —I ain't bitching, I'm commenting.

That gal Judy certainly has her hands full with work. Shucks I think it'll be a relief to her just to have one husband to look after – and maybe a half-dozen kids. I'll bet she was a cute little girl. I'd like to have known her then. Her Mother must have been a swell woman to have two such kids.

You sound kinda mixed up on your own birthday presents but happy about the whole thing. Tell me all about everything.

Stop worrying about me when I forget to write and don't you dare give me the absent treatment. There's nothing wrong with me that 60 days at home won't cure, but I am homesick. I'm riding a see-saw high for awhile and then I hit the dumps. When I'm down I can't make myself write and when I get up I take off for town like a big a-- bird and raise hell so I don't have time to write. Only once a week and sometimes oftener I stay home and catch up on my correspondence. But always I love you and think of you and home and my bride and everything. So don't worry about me, please.

I've sure been lucky with the women in my life. Two of the world's best.

I love you, Toots,

Carp

26 July 1945

Dearest Toots,

Ever since you first told me about the Davis' twins and how Mrs. D is doing, I've been worrying about her. Something like that just doesn't seem fair. I don't see how Davis goes on with his job. I'd be just blowing my top and no good for anything. —We are lucky. Our troubles are small compared to something like that.

This job of mine has that one drawback. It's a little difficult for some-body coming to Paris to get in touch with me now. But it has other advantages. Paris is sweltering, but out here in the country it's quite nice.

Us and our swearing. It's a good thing Judy never tried to tame me down. —But then she's practically a perfect wife anywho.

I agree with you on Russia, but I do have one question. I wish she'd defi-nitely side in against Japan – that would settle any question in my mind.

As for the U.S. being cordially hated the answer is no. At least I haven't seen any evidence of it. All I've seen has pointed the other way. I think that back in the '30s when we were riding isolationism so strongly, it might have been true.

As for its being our world, that may be true, but the sad thing is that we don't want it. I'm afraid that the same feeling will be prevalent after this war that was so noticeable after the last. The feeling that created isolationists. We're so damned tired of foreign countries that we'll want to forget all about them. I hope I've got brains enough not to let me get that way, but I don't know. I'm pretty tired.

Gee I'm sorry to hear that Ed Sr. is in such bad shape. The guy who said War is a young man's game wasn't kidding. I've seen too many of these old reserve officers blow up in one of two ways. They either work themselves half to death as Ed seems to have done or else they just let the work slide down on the junior officers until they themselves aren't capable of carrying on with their jobs. The only thing that keeps a lot of them in the Army is that they figure they've already invested 5 or 6 years and another like number will make 'em eligible for retirement. Don't ever let me keep my reserve commission a minute longer than the law requires. I'm gonna be a manufacturer in the next one.

Now I'd better end this broadcast. Gee, I'm a bull------- aren't I? Oh, well, I come by it naturally. My Uncles, I mean.

Lots of love,

Carpy

30 July 1945

Dearest Mother,

This military life is getting me down. The stuff we call chicken s--- is getting so thick around here a guy can't operate. Since V-E Day it's been building up and building up. I don't know whether it'd be better to be in a Repple Depot ((Replacement Depot)) somewhere sweating out the points or trying to operate here. I better not blow my top anymore or I may get a court-martial and they'd do it too. Which might not be a bad idea. As an enlisted man I'd have enough points to get out of the Army. But enough of this.

That airplane crashing into the Empire State building was certainly a freak and unhappy accident.

I've been reading over your 19 July letter again and the questions about Russia. You say that the two countries are, at heart, more alike than any other two countries. I think when you said that, you were considering England and U.S. the same country, as I do. It's my wish that the Aussies, New Zealanders, Canadians, Britains and Yanks could get together in some form of united government. I guess it's just a dream, but I think it'd be a damn good thing for this world of ours. It'd be a little rough on England's native colonies because real quick they'd be bickering among themselves and starving to death.

I guess I told you we started our own mess here about a week ago. It's certainly an improvement on where we've been eating. Yesterday dinner we had fried chicken that was delicious. These Germans are good cooks.

How are you and the boyfriend getting along? It must be serious because you haven't been reporting – or else you're getting bored.

What did you think of England's elections? I was surprised and unhappy 'til the thought occurred to me that a landslide like that certainly shows what the people want so it's only right that they get it.

I haven't been doing anything interesting so this is a kinda dumb letter. I'm sorry.

Maybe I'll do better next time. Anywho, you're still my favorite Mother. Arencha glad?

Love,

Carp

3 August 1945

Hi Toots,

It's really illegal for a guy to feel as good as I do this early in the morning after a night like last night. Don, Maj. Brown and I got together and imbibed a few and then went to the Red Cross Club and saw the floorshow. (Believe it or not it's a restaurant where they serve coffee and donuts and have floorshows, usually USO.) It must have been a good show because everybody enjoyed it.

I came in from camp early to see the Colonel, but he had taken off on an inspection trip so I screwed off too and went to see the Air Corps exposition under the Eiffel Tower and afterward I went up in the Tower to the second level, about halfway. That's as far as they let people go now-a-days. It gives you a swell view of Paris. Not quite as good as the top would, but still plenty nice.

Yes, I got a Varga calendar and it's adorning my room; and I also got a swell little painting of Pee's shack and surroundings. If she's able to be about after that operation she's lucky. That's an operation I dread even the idea of.

The slight application of kerosene to this letter is a fly spray. It's Sunday evening now. I was trying to nap this afternoon and the flies made me so mad I drenched my room with the damn spray.

I got your July 26 letter when I stopped in the office this morning. Right now, you should be enjoying a sunny Sunday afternoon at the lake. Are you?

That sounded like an awfully nice crazy time in Kelly's bar. He must be a darn nice boyfriend.

Don't ever stop telling me about the fun you've had. Shucks, Toots, I've had fun everywhere I've been over here. Even in Paris. Did I say even? —And some of the most fun I've had lately was a book by Bennett Cerf called "Try and Stop Me." It's a book of anecdotes of well-known people, mostly wisecracks and the facts that occasioned them. I could hardly put it down it's so good.

Now it's getting to be my bedtime so I better retire. Have a nice vacation, Toots.

Lots 'n lots of love,
Carpy

10 August 1945

Dearest Mother,

You're the perfect newspaper woman. Go on a vacation right at the time world events are making the greatest head-lines in a long time of great headlines. I'm ashamed. Ain't you got no nose for news? Couldn't you smell this coming? —If that atomic bomb is half what they say it is, it's still some-thing. In fact I've decided that war as an institution is some-thing I'm through with as soon as we finish this one. I'm just plain scared.

I have a confession to make. It begins to look as if my fall prediction was too optimistic. The way things are breaking here I can't see me getting home before the first of the year, which after all isn't too far away. My luck with this man's Army has been consistently bad or maybe it's good. I'm still alive. But bad as far as the ordinary good breaks go, like being stationed near home awhile or getting leaves and stuff. But I can take it and one of these days it'll be over. I get bitched off, but on the whole I don't worry too much.

We had a nasty accident here the other day. —Remember I told you the woods back of camp were full of unexploded bombs. They're okay if you leave 'em alone, but yesterday two French kids got smart and were throwing the little one-pound babies at a couple of 1000 pounders and the 1000 pounder let loose. We found out how it happened from a third little fellow who got scared and hid behind a tree. It just knocked him on his can, but the other two practically disappeared. I can't understand why they were doing it because the oldest was 17 and that's old enough to have better sense. —Now I got the ordnance out here moving the nearer ones farther into the woods. I think I'll go in town while they're working. Don't worry, Toots, they aren't close enough to kill me, but they scare hell outta me when they let loose and I don't like that.

There are lots of things in England that need improvement including the school system and the housing. Maybe this new government will do something. I think they probably will, but as for that election being a repudiation of the capitalistic system that's for the birds. That's the system that won this war (i.e.

the production end of it) and the English are too conservative even on their left side to really take up communism or socialism. At least that's my opinion – and I know you'll value it. But don't quote me.

I hope you're having a swell vacation, and getting the dope for this dope. Give my love to my bride if you see her, the brat.

Lots of love,

Carp

16 August 1945

Dearest Mother,

This is your 91 point, hungover son as you've undoubtedly guessed, also spelled gassed. Tuesday night when we celebrated V-day, we stayed quite sober so last night we made up for it. Twas a very pleasant evening. About 11:00 o'clock I headed for the latrine. I never did get there and it took me 45 minutes to find my way back.

P.S. Don't tell your d-in-law.

Tuesday night we went to a show and came out right into the middle of an impromptu victory parade so we joined it for awhile. When we got tired of that we (Bart was with me) went up to Montmartre and went nightclubbing. We ended up at the Paradise, drinking champagne and dancing with the show girls. We left at 4:00 and walked halfway across Paris to my billet and got in at 5:00. It was a very good night. The thing that I noticed most was that all the celebrating in Paris was done by the Allied soldiers. It didn't mean anything to the French.

The <u>Stars and Stripes</u> said this morning the priority for going home would be given to officers with arduous combat duty or long overseas service so my hopes are up again. Maybe I will make it home this fall. I hope. –I don't mean that as it sounds. The paragraph I'm quoting referred only to officers. High point men will continue to be sent home as quick as possible.

Love,

Carp

17 Aug. 1945

Dearest Mother,

I got your first letter from Laporte yesterday dated the 7th of Aug. It sounds like a swell vacation.

The slacks outfit sounds weird, but it must be a bit of the all right. I'm glad they're a present from me.

My mind has sure gone to pot in the last two days. All I can think of is coming home and as yet I have no solid information to base my dreams on, so I'm just hoping to make it by Christmas. The <u>Stars & Stripes</u> print so much b--- s--- you don't know what to believe. But I'm dreaming.

If I'm lucky I'll be getting out in the spring. Only five years of my life wasted in the Army because we weren't prepared for this war. At least I didn't pay with my life as so many thousands have. I've sure been lucky there, but what I've learned isn't going to make me very friendly toward our isolationist pals. I can't for the life of me under-stand the opposition to peacetime training. It looks to me like our only hope because I'm convinced we can't get a volunteer Army the size we need. Too many guys feel like me, that we've done our part but it won't hurt these kids coming up to do a year, especially if it'll save 'em five later on. –I guess I'm strictly a war-mongering militarist and always have been. Shame on me.

Maybe I'd better quit bulling and mail this. Bye now.

Lots 'n lots of love,

Carpy

27 August 1945

Dearest Mother,

As for me coming home, I'll repeat what I told Judy. The ASR ('Adjusted Service Rating' points) for officers in this section is down to 95. When it comes down to 90 I'll apply for return to the States, and the Colonel will okay it. So, barring Army snafu, I hope to make it home in October. There is nothing in the least definite on that. The Army is neither fair nor consistent so anything can go wrong, but I can dream, can't I?

Where did you get the idea that being a madam would be new and different? After all, it is the oldest profession – or did you just mean new and diff for you?

I can just picture George giving Evie away at her wedding. I'll bet he really was sweating. That was nice of the kids, but then they're nice kids, especially mine. I know you think I'm good enough for her, but sometimes I wonder. She's really an awfully nice child, isn't she? Pretty too.

You take the prize as a newspaper reporter. You take a vacation while history is made. It's sure good that you like to write nice stories about people and stuff. Nice stuff, no murders. But don't worry, I love you and I like the stuff you report too.

Sometimes I think I have the wackiest crew in the world here at this camp. Darn near every morning in the week somebody has a terrific hangover. We got quite a shock this morning. We counted noses this morning and found Lt. Bartlett, S/Sgt Cooper, Cpl. Looney, PFC Taylor and me all in camp, all up for breakfast and all sober. It was unnerving.

Just think of the thrill I have coming to me. I still have to meet Irv. Maybe soon I hope. Honest, Sugar, I'm just kidding. But I really do want to meet him. I promise not to chaperone you as I used to.

Lots 'n lots of love,

Carpy

1 September 1945

Dearest Mother,

I got your letter 22 Aug with all the dope on your post war plans. I sure hope they work out the way you want. <u>Grit</u> Company seems to me to have some pretty nice people, judging from your letters, even if you don't get along with old man D. And even there you've got lots of support from your co-workers.

Don't even mention fresh corn to me. The very idea of it is almost too tantalizing to stand. Sweet, luscious, yellow bantam on the cob. Oh my aching back. I hope you ate lots for me.

You're bitched at <u>Grit</u> and I'm so p----- off with the Army and our beloved crack-pot Congressmen that I don't know what to do. From Ike on down they're all publicizing how quickly everybody is gonna get home and yet today there is absolutely no authority for a guy who's been thru the mill as long as I have to even request return to the States. My trouble is that you haven't enough grandchildren. ((One point was earned for every month in the service, another point for each month overseas, five points for each combat decoration and 12 points for each child under the age of 18.)) –I could bitch like this for pages.

The Army occasionally makes a blunder and does somebody a good turn. One of my medics has been over here since December '41. He's married to a nurse who is also in the E.T.O. Both have been transferred to a unit that is going home and by sheer accident it's the same unit. So unless some high brass finds out about it and snafus the deal they'll go home on the same boat. Such cases are few and far between in this man's Army I assure you.

My camp is being invaded by a large body of transients Monday and we're getting ready to take care of them. What a mess. More darn work than I like to do. Setting up a mess for 1000 men. Phooey.

Guess I'd better go back to work.

Lots of love,

Carp

5 September 1945

Dearest Mother,

Got your letter of 26 Aug. yesterday with the clippings of Evie's wedding. They are certainly a good-looking couple. And I'm glad to hear that the matron of honor was the best-looking gal there. Only how my child-bride can be a matron of honor is beyond me.

I don't know why Judy isn't hearing from me because I write at least once a week and usually about 3 times every two weeks. 'Je ne comprende pas.'

You've got me worried about fathers now. With all these bad examples in our family, I don't see how I stand a chance of being any good.

So Irv's lost his gal already. Independent cuss, aren't you? But I'll admit you've got a right to be.

I'm glad you're reading all that crap they're printing in the newspaper, but for the luv a Pete, don't believe it. Every crack-pot Congressman who wants a little publicity comes up with a new idea for getting them out. The paper this morning quotes a Sen. Pepper who favors a short occupation of Germany. My God! What a fool's para-dise he lives in to have a memory that short. And all these jokers who want to stop the draft now. God dammit our friends and neighbors were willing enough to take three and four years out of our lives to win this war and the lives of half a million or more to boot, but they're afraid to ask one-and-a-half or two years from the kids coming up to win the peace?

God damn but I get hot when I see these jerks trying already to throw away a victory it took us four years of "sweat and tears and blood" to win. I guess our only prayer is that the Russians and British aren't as criminally stupid as some of the Americans are trying to be.

I'm a hotheaded s.o.b. aren't I? Nothing personal. The b stands for bastard (male type).

The enclosed money orders are my Christmas fund. Will you save it for me? Please. By the way, did I tell you not to send me any Christmas presents? Well, don't. I want 'em at home or not at all.

Lots 'n lots of love,

Carpy

11 September 1945

Dearest Mother,

You didn't say that Judy is getting a divorce so I'm hoping she isn't, but I still haven't gotten a letter since 10 August which was 32 days ago. And yet your letters have been coming thru regularly. —I hope it's the mail. One of my boys hasn't heard from his wife for 43 days. S'bad.

I still think it'll be October. Along toward the end of the month. Bart took off yesterday. He might even make it this month. I keep wondering if it's really true that I'm going home at last.

My transient camp deal started at last and we've been busier than a couple of blackbirds. Everything seems to be shaping up okay. The boys running my mess are darn good and the 'prisoner cooks' they have are good too. That's half the battle in a transient mess. Getting good meals into their bellies.

I've been a good boy for the last couple days. That hangover I had last week was too rough. But I sure did feel good while acquiring it.

Lots 'n lots of love,

Carpy

I'll be seeing you.

17 September 1945

Dearest Mother,

Got a letter from you, one from Judy, and one from Pee today. All airmailed on the 10th of September. Judy's letter was the best I've had from her in a long time. She was kidding me just as she used to do. It had a picture of the gang at Evie's wedding. Boy I'd sure like to have been in that picture.

Evie's Wedding
L to R - Judy's Aunt Bets, George, Grace, Evie, Bob, & Judy

You're really doing okay, Toots. 100% increase in pay in less than five years. That retirement scheme of babysitting your grandchildren sounds pretty good to me. Of course you realize that 20 years from now when you're, um, 65, my oldest daughter, pardon me, your eldest granddaughter, will be tending babies for other doting parents to go to the movies. But we might let you keep an eye on little Susie, our youngest. She and Bobby are a handful.

My favorite song now is "Gonna Take a Sentimental Journey." The A.G. told me today that I'll be relieved from HQ Seine Section on the 26th or 27th of September. I'll probably ship out from 10 to 14 days later and reach the States 10 to 14 days after that so I should be telephoning you between the 18th and 25th of October. I hope, I hope, I hope. Oh boy, I do hope.

I'm still getting my stuff packed and excess turned in in readiness for my departure. Talk about an excited boy. That's me. All I can think about is coming home. Now I'll go to bed and dream of it.

Lots of love,

Carpy

25 September 1945

Dearest Mother,

For the past week I've been packing, throwing away, and re-packing my junk. Now I'm about ready to leave. Thursday morning I start the first leg of my journey and for me the worst leg. I'm sure gonna hate hitting a Repple Depot after all this time in the Army. Phooey. And they say I'll be there at least seven and probably 10 or 12 days. This may be my last letter until I see you. It depends on the situation there. Of course if they snafu me, all bets are off. —Capt. Putnam, a guy I've worked with, was pulled off a boat at LaHavre and sent up to Germany because they needed an officer with his Spec number for A. of O. He has 113 points too. So anything can happen.

Gosh, I hadn't realized how much property I signed for in the four months I've been running this camp until I started accounting for it and turning it over to O'Malley. All week I've been discovering pieces of equipment I'd entirely forgotten. I think I'm cleared at last. I sure hope so.

Tonight I'm having open house for the gang that's worked with me here.

Don't worry if you don't hear from me.

Lots 'n lots of love,

Carpy

Phoebe Starr Lose
Tucson, Arizona

3 October 1945

Dearest Aunt Pee,

That's a fresh way to address a favorite Aunt, isn't it? But I know you won't mind because I'm feeling awfully good today. I'm heading home at last. A week ago I reported to this reinforcement depot and they put me in charge of a packet of troops heading for Indian-town Gap. I've got a couple hundred men and about 20 officers, and I get rid of them as soon as we hit the "Gap." With luck I'll be there about the 25th. Day after tomorrow we get on board 40 and 8s for Antwerp where we catch our ship. I hope it's a fast train. Now that I'm really heading home I'm in such a dither I hardly know what to do. The responsibility of this packet is really a break because it takes my mind off home while I'm working.

I'm a month behind in answering your letter because I've been busy as hell for the past six weeks. For two months of the summer we had only routine work at my Processing Camp. Then just about the time I got orders to turn all property and the command of the camp over to another officer, they started throwing in groups of four and five hundred casual troops and they're a real headache when you have to supply 'em with food, bunks, showers and everything you can to keep 'em happy. But we got the job done and I got cleared okay.

I've written Judy to meet me at the Hotel Hershey if possible and we'll spend a few days together before going home. A few days at home and then I want to take a month or six weeks to go to Florida and see Uncle Jimmy. Of course those plans are subject to what the Army decides it wants done. I have 99 points so I'm hoping to be discharged.

My plans for the future are vague as hell, naturally. I've got to get home and see what J & L is offering before I can make any plans.

So, so long from the E.T.O. I'll be seeing you.

Love,

Carpy

They sent me by train up to Belgium and put me in charge of keeping 400 guys together and out of trouble long enough to put us on a freighter bound for the States. The crossing took about a week and a half. We sailed up the Hudson River, past West Point and landed at the deployment camp on October 21, 1945—three years, seven months and seven days after I'd left the States.

From there they put us on a train to Hershey, Pennsylvania. After I settled my 400 troops into the Indiantown Gap discharge camp near Hershey, shortly before 5:00, I was relieved of duty. I left camp and met Judy at the Hershey Hotel. After our first embrace, she reached into her purse, pulled out a bank passbook and handed it to me. I asked her what it was and she told me it was my money. I'd been sending money home to support her the whole time I was away. But she had put it all in the bank and had worked to support herself. As we continued to talk, I found out she was expecting me to divorce her. Not a chance!

I explained to her that since I'd only had four days leave the entire time I'd been away, that the Army owed me, and I intended to use that accumulated leave to take her on an extended second honeymoon so we could get reacquainted. She made me the happiest man in the world when she agreed.

I reported back to camp by 8:00 the next morning. By 4:00 I was put on permanent leave from active duty in the Reserves. I went back to the hotel to meet up with Judy again and was delighted to find Marg there as well. We all climbed into the old Ford and headed straight for Williamsport that evening.

Gets French Award

AWARDED the croix de guerre by the French government for his liaison work with the French army in the liberation of Paris during the Second World War was Capt. Grant H. Carpenter, above, of 1100 Broad Street, Montoursville. He is the son of the late Mrs. Margaret Lose Carpenter. Capt. Carpenter spent 42 months overseas with the engineers, and received his award for supervising administrative details in the distribution of foodstuffs and other war material in captured warehouses.

DÉCISION N° 154

Le Ministre de la Guerre **A. DIETHELM**

cite

à l'ordre de *la Division*

Le Capitaine *Grant H. Carpenter*
Hq Seine Section

" pour services exceptionnels rendus au cours des opérations
de la libération de la **FRANCE** »

Cette citation comporte l'attribution
de la Croix de Guerre avec étoile d'*argent*

Fait à PARIS, le 25 Octobre 1945

Signé : DIETHELM

Pour ampliation :
Le Chef de Bataillon LEMOINE

Chef de la Section Décorations

Afterword

One of the hit songs of the day started with the words,

"Kiss me once, and kiss me twice, and kiss me once again,
    It's been a long, long time."

With their "three years, seven months, and seven days" separation, they considered it 'their song.'

After a visit with Judy's Aunt Grace and Uncle George, they loaded up the '41 Ford and heading south on their delayed honeymoon.

They stopped along the way to visit Mary, Kit and the kids in North Carolina. From there it was on to Daytona Beach, Florida where they stayed for a week – "bumming around and camping on the beach" - before meandering up to New York.

When they finally got back home in December, they moved in with Grace and George, until they could find a place of their own. (Housing was tight with all those men returning to the States.)

On January 2, 1946, Carp returned to work at Jones & Laughlin Wire Rope Plant in Muncy, PA, where he continued to work until his retirement in 1977.

With the money Judy had saved while Carp was overseas, they were able to find and buy their first house together, in Montoursville.

In short order, they got started on that family they both wanted. Marg was excited about the prospect of becoming a grandmother.

However, in August of 1946, after a dinner double-date, Marg and her three friends went back to her apartment because Marg wasn't feeling well. As Marg walked toward her bed to sit down, she fell, half on the bed. Her friends, hearing the commotion, came in to check on her. They swung her legs up onto the bed and called for a doctor. She was dead of a massive stroke before he arrived.

Carp and Judy were both heartbroken.

Four months later, Carp and Judy were blessed with their first child, the "handful, Bobby" whom Carp had predicted in his letter of September 17, 1945.

Two years later they had their first daughter. The plan to name her Judith Ann changed when someone asked how "Little Judy" was doing. Judy realized instantly she didn't want to go through life as "Big Judy" and named her Peggy, instead. With the addition of two more children, they outgrew their first house and built a home big enough for four rambunctious kids.

Carp remained friends with his and his mother's friend Flossie. Flossie's son, Johnny Weaver, did not make it home from the war.

Carp's friend, Baldy got married and started a family of his own. But Baldy's health was not good, apparently from complications pertaining to his injuries. He died before his first child, a son, was born.

Carp's fraternity brother, Gil, survived his years as a Japanese P.O.W., returned to the states and married the girl who was waiting for him.

Carp's half-brother, Don Carpenter, worked as a mechanic on jet engines after the war, until one of them blew up, killing him instantly.

Judy's sister Evie also had a lifetime marriage to her war-time sweetheart, Bob Leach. Bob retired from the Navy with 20 years of service, after which they settled with their four children in the Philadelphia area.

Aunt Phoebe, of necessity due to her breathing problems, stayed out in Arizona the rest of her life, passing away in 1962.

On his 91st birthday, Carp continued to maintain that he was the luckiest man ever. Several months later, after celebrating Judy's 90th birthday with a family reunion in September, Carp passed away on October 8, 2008. Judy joined him June 3, 2011.

Timeline of World War II

1939

August 23 . . . . . . Germany and the Soviet Union sign the Nazi-Soviet
 Non-Aggression Pact
September 1 . . . . Germany invades Poland, starting World War II
September 3 . . . . Britain and France declare war on Germany
 Battle of the Atlantic begins

1940

May 10 . . . . Germany invades France, Belgium, and the Netherlands.
May 20 . . . . Auschwitz is established
May 26 . . . . Evacuation begins of Allied troops from Dunkirk, France
June 10 . . . . Italy declares war on France and Great Britain
June 22 . . . . France surrenders to Germany
July 10 . . . . Battle of Britain begins
September 16 . . . The United States begins its first peacetime draft

1941

March 11 . . . . U.S. President Franklin D. Roosevelt signs the Lend-Lease bill
May 24 . . . . The British ship Hood is sunk by Germany's Bismarck
May 27 . . . . The Bismarck is sunk
June 22 . . . . Germany invades the Soviet Union (Operation Barbarossa)
August 9 . . . . Atlantic Conference begins
September 8 . . . . Siege of Leningrad begins
December 7 . . . . The Japanese launch a sneak attack on Pearl Harbor, Hawaii
December 11 . . . . Germany and Italy declare war on the United States; then the
 United States declares war on Germany and Italy

1942

January 20 . . . . . The Wannsee Conference
February 19 . . . . Roosevelt issues Executive Order 9066, which allows the
 internment of Japanese Americans
April 18 . . . . The Doolittle Raid on Japan
June 3 . . . . The Battle of Midway begins
July 1 . . . . First Battle of El Alamein begins
July 6 . . . . Anne Frank and her family go into hiding
August 2 . . . . Guadalcanal Campaign begins
August 21 . . . . . . Battle of Stalingrad begins
October 23 . . . . . Second Battle of El Alamein begins
November 8 . . . . The Allies invade North Africa (Operation Torch)

1943

January 14...... Casablanca Conference begins
February 2 ..... The Germans lose the battle at Stalingrad, Soviet Union
April 19....... The Warsaw Ghetto Uprising begins
July 5 .... Battle of Kursk begins
July 25 .... Mussolini resigns
September 3 .... Italy surrenders
November 28 ... Tehran Conference begins

1944

January 27...... Siege of Leningrad ends
June 6 .... D-Day
June 19......... Battle of the Philippine Sea
July 20 .... Assassination attempt against Hitler fails
August 4 .... Anne Frank and her family are discovered and arrested
August 25 ...... The Allies liberate Paris
October 23 ..... Battle of Leyte Gulf begins
December 16.... Battle of the Bulge begins

1945

February 4 ..... Yalta Conference begins
February 13 .... Allies begin bombing Dresden
February 19 .... Battle of Iwo Jima begins
April 1 .... Battle of Okinawa
April 12........ Franklin D. Roosevelt dies
April 16........ Battle of Berlin begins
April 28........ Mussolini is hanged by Italian partisans
April 30........ Adolf Hitler commits suicide
May 7.......... Germany signs an unconditional surrender
July 17 .... Potsdam Conference begins
August 6 .... The United States drops the first atomic bomb on
                 Hiroshima, Japan
August 9 .... The United States drops a second atomic bomb on
                 Nagasaki, Japan
September 2 .... Surrender of Imperial Japan

Index of Photographs and Articles

T

V

W

CPSIA information can be obtained
at www.ICGtesting.com
Printed in the USA
FSHW022355180521
81611FS